TOO EARLY, TOO LATE,
now what?

DAVID L. HAWK

Too Early, Too Late, now what?
Copyright © 2022 by David L. Hawk

All rights reserved. No part of this book may be reproduced or transmitted in any form or by any means, electronic or mechanical, including photocopying, recording, or by any information storage and retrieval system without express written permission from the author, except in the case of brief quotations embodied in critical reviews and certain other noncommercial uses permitted by copyright law.

Printed in the United States of America.

Brilliant Books Literary
137 Forest Park Lane Thomasville
North Carolina 27360 USA

Table of Contents

2019 A Foreword on Then and Now vii
2019-Environmental Deterioration, Evolving xiii
2019-The Researcher, Questioning xvii
Acknowledgments: Family, Friends, Colleagues xxi
Preface xxv
Conclusions, 2019 xxxv

1979 - THE DISSERTATION THESIS

CHAPTER 1: RELATIONS 1

1.1 Human Nature 3
1.2 Deterioration, resulting from Humans wanting to be Artificial 10
1.3 Entropy and Man's Future: Ignore, Deny or Defy 18
1.4 Deterioration, Beyond the Entropic 22
1.5 In Search of the Artificial 30
1.6 Can Humans Access the 4th Dimension? 39
1.7 To Manage the Human Project in Five Dimensions 41

CHAPTER 2: REGULATIONS 46

2.1 Humans Regulating Humans 46
2.2 Perceptual Environments leading to the Conceptual 57
2.3 Attempts at Regulating Humans 62
2.4 Regulation Options: A) To manage the bad or B) To seek the good .. 65

CHAPTER 3: CHANGELESSNESS AND CHANGE 67

3.1 Changelessness, a Human Preference, against Natural Change 69
3.2 A Prognosis for Human Deterioration 82
3.3 The Problem Area 85

CHAPTER 4: REGULATION OF RELATIONS AND CHANGE 92

4.1 Regulation of Relationships 94
4.2 Type I: Regulation of Man to Nature (Technology's Domain) 100
4.3 Type II: Regulation of Man to the Man-Made (Technique Domain) 101
4.4 Type III: Regulation of Man to Man (The Social Domain) 102
4.5 Type IV: Regulation of Man to Self (Psychological Doman) 104
4.6 Rethinking Regulation, To Encourage Business as Unusual 109

CHAPTER 5: INTRODUCTION TO THE THEORY 114

5.1 Complexity and its Regulation 114
5.2 Formal and Informal Problem Solving 117
5.3 Definitions 123
5.4 Postulates 130
5.5 Hypotheses 130
5.6 Evaluation 141
5.7 Contextual Comparison of Regulation Modes 146
5.8 Comparisons of Municipal Treatment of Sewage 149
5.9 Industrial Pollution Sources 150

CHAPTER 6: RESEARCHING ENVIRONMENTAL PROTECTION REGULATION 152

6.1 The Research Project 154
6.2 Research Method 160
6.3 Data Collection and Major Participants 163
6.4 The Research Domain 166
6.5 The Research Sponsor 170

CHAPTER 7: THE RESEARCH REPORT 171

7.1 Summary of the Research 174
7.2 Conclusions from the Report 187
7.3 Evidence from the Research: Specific Cases 195
7.4 Issues that can be Generalized 207

CHAPTER 8: REGULATION AS INTEGRATIVE 215

8.1 Integration and Disintegration Processes 216
8.2 Dialectical Concepts 219
8.3 Integration as a Dialectical Concept 224
8.4 Adaptation 230
8.5 Social Regulation Towards Integration 239

CHAPTER 9: TOWARDS BUSINESS AS UNUSUAL 244

9.1 A New Idea(l) of Regulation 244
9.2 Legalism 246
9.3 Anarchism 252
9.4 Seeking a Better Way Forward 255
9.5 Summary – Appreciative or Legalistic Mode 272
9.6 Conclusions 280
References 283

2019 A Foreward on Then and Now

Then was 1979. Now is 2019. In what follows much comes from then, with a touch from now, and a concern for those who must occupy tomorrow. Normally, with a forty-year gap in an endeavor, the back-then serves as a baseline. Success can thus be measured in managing the initial concern. From this we can propose measures for improving success. Such will not be found herein.

There has been no success in applying findings of very concerned company and government people forty years ago. They saw an urgent need to control environmental deterioration resulting from human activities. They helped recommend a new model for regulation. The situation was fluid, not fixed, and in need of ideas for business as unusual in both private and public organizations. Back then it was shown how deterioration was expanding and efforts to regulate and limit such were turning bad into worse.

The situation of environmental deterioration can no longer be addressed via expanded research, invention of new technologies or in modifications in meeting humans needs and wants in adjustments to the current neo-classical economic model. We have moved beyond those somewhat understood traditional responses. We now face the consequences of greatly expanded environmental deterioration. It is now culminating in very dire phenomena such as the one only briefly mentioned in the 1977 study called *climate change*. The best information now suggests humans must move from their business as usual responses to meeting the very real human bio-needs while completely rethinking the holographic domain of human psycho-wants.

Humans need to find responses of a different logical type. The tradition of reductionistic, analytically managed processes in search of cause-effect conclusions, that we have long been so proud of as human science and development are not helpful when dealing with systems. Our relying on such to distinguish humans from nature probably needs to be left behind. For example, turning to tougher legislation applied by sterner governance based on causal logic will lead to little success. Such seems to move success further away, as the study documented forty years ago. Therein deterioration grew as one of the effects of punishment via threats. It seems timely to turn away from that stream of business as usual, and not emphasize its value. Elsewhere, there are signs of optimism, such as in reintroducing longer-term values. Via Consequential Management replacing MBA style management humans could change the industrial to address long-term deterioration by rethinking the numerous decision points arising from short-term economic valuations.

A human future awaits a serious concern for living systems on our planet, not its further degradation. We need to find a way to better judge the seeming need for relying on 2-dimensional regulations, as based on 1-dimensional thoughts and ideologies arising from pointless wants for individual power. We need, urgently, to look for differences that can make a difference. While aspects of what follows can be said to be complex, we might keep in mind how accusing something of "being complicated" has long been the best excuse for retaining business as usual. We need to urgently seek business as unusual.

The research discussed herein originating fifty years ago. It came from obvious signs of environmental deterioration beginning to have consequential impacts for humans. The actions of humans leading to deterioration had been undertaken in the name of improving human lifestyles. The research showed that humans were not very concerned about the consequences of this choice. They did not want to leave economic development based on the eternal Faustian Bargain, and its shadow known as the Faustian Tragedy. The logical conclusion of this kind of bargaining with the human future was central to the work of Nicholas Georgescu-Roegen as best represented in his 1971 thesis that current economic models are entropic aids, and end in additional deterioration.

A modified thesis then emerged after several years of research begun in 1975 at the Stockholm School of Economics. It found there to be no viable way to fix neo-classical economics, nor improve traditional governance to slow deterioration of the natural environment. We, my friend Gunnar Hedlund and I, then proposed a move to "business as unusual" based on developing a non-Faustian economics model. Attempts were made to test this in economic and social development, all in line with expanded appreciation of life's context – nature. The model was to show examples of rejecting human subservient to the ideal of the artificial. To date, the success in this effort has been minimal. Gunnar's 1996 death from a chemically initiated brain tumor was then treated with radiation to fix the problem. After his death the surgeon published a paper on how radiation fixed the cancer problem. Unfortunately, it "fixed" the patient as well. The world of the artificial and its expansion continued.

The central issue forty years ago was with the deterioration consequences from an economic model that made dollars, but little sense. The model politically justified a model of production and consumption activities, one that made even less sense to life's continuance then its economic end. The model focused on expansion of the idea of industrialization production and then product use; all presuming eventual regulation of its harmful to life consequences.

The study began with concern for industrialized consequences to nature in light of a nineteen-sixties acceptance that environmental deterioration was the price of life. Those in the study were looking for more effective ways of regulation, to manage the undesirable from producing the desired. Economists in the study argued that the contemporary model would adjust to resolve the problem. A group now known as "ecological economists" argued for going much further with regulation via price manipulations.

A friend and mentor, Nicholas Georgescu-Roegen, argued against that title, pointing out ecology would consume economics. I agreed with him, yet ecological economy greatly expanded in the next thirty years. So too has environmental deterioration. Perhaps something deeper is at work; something that relates to nature, each other and us? Just now I'm much less optimistic about finding a way out from the prognosis of our decline. Ecological economics seems more like another pacifier, in the same class as the pattern of purposeful recycling. We take our trash to the curb. It goes away from our view. It is not seen again, except in trash dumbs or floating in the oceans. We seem to invest little in experimenting with radical recipes of business as unusual, a location where schools and enterprises need to go.

Late in the study, with the deep collaboration of major Petrochemical leaders, the notion that a phenomenon called climate change was emerging emerged. This would take humans far faster and further towards a fateful end then the deterioration effects known in prior science. It seemed to pose as a determinant of the human fate. Climate change would be the consequence of continuation of business as usual. Since that time, evidence for the effects of climate change consequences has greatly expanded. The obvious question becomes: how far have we come in developing innovative alternatives to business as usual in four decades? What should business as unusual have come to look like? How can we encourage more of it, but what is it? Business as usual and the consequences from it seen in production and consumption, then deterioration, is clear, then seen as clearly a threat.

It is important to step back and remind ourselves that we have long had an underlying dilemma behind our ideal of human prosperity. Any projection of industrial consequences from economic thinking, via business as usual, seems bleak. Research from forty years ago suggested that the consequences were sufficiently dire and that usual ideas of problem regulation were becoming insufficient. Since then, that fear has become reality. A new model of regulation is now needed or a new definition of social civilization. The argument about shortfalls in regulation of environmental deterioration is informative to our current challenge. If nothing else, it seems to serve as a benchmark of man-nature relations, to see what progress has been made in appreciating that relation, or not. Comparing the conversations from "now" to the research "then" allows some understanding the conditions of life, and their prospects.

More now sense the human situation as becoming dire. Some progress has been made to improve understanding the situation, but not in improving it. If worsening, do we at least understand why and what needs to be done? For four decades did we at least come to learn the role of humans in being problematic, and what they need to change? Can we respond to "what now?"

That seventies study found that tradition regulation was not working, and possibly could never work. It did find small signs of hope in non-hierarchical management of the network form. With some humor this came to be known in the project as a "more anarchistic"[1] version of "human regulation." It somehow operated to bring out more innovative, more non-rational, repairs to a situation via what came to be a negotiated order. It was far more interesting and much more successful then reliance of the false success in the rationality of legal order methods. Thus, it seems important that we review ideas from the research of 1975-1977 to better regulate environmental deterioration.

The strength of negotiated order was seen in the appreciation it required. The weakness of the legal order was seen in the hollow threats it depended upon but could seldom deliver. Now that social organizations are shifting to a network form of management, via internet, IT and AI, it seems timely to shift this model to how humans relate to nature, and each other. Why do we not do so? We still concentrate on seeking more effective means of threating via tougher legal orders.

Much of this book was submitted to the Systems Sciences Program, Wharton School of Business, University of Pennsylvania as a dissertation. Back then, it was controversial. It is presented again to see if the controversy continues. Most university-based scientists saw it as speculation on the hopeless. They argued that there were economic measures to quickly correct the problem of deterioration, if indeed there was a problem. Some went deeper to point out that if the environment deteriorated to the extent projected, beyond economics, then society could shift to tougher and more threatening regulations via collective political will. Now, as the deterioration situation arrives, political leaders mostly go into hiding beneath it.

The 1979 work showed how more and tougher legislation would not solve problems of deterioration. They were systemic and not to be understood in analysis. Perhaps there is now hope for change as there

---

[1] This was of the Kropotkin, i.e., Socratic and Lao Tzu, form of anarchism as self-governance of human-generated problems that mattered most. These tended to be too much a part of being human to be handled via legal order from legal analysis leading to targeted threaten.

is greater appreciation of the systemic over the analytic and more evidence of the urgency for change. Against this is the considerable evidence that the reasons for hopelessness are omnipresent. Many humans still portray nature as irrelevant to their life, or its enemy. The disrespect for nature and others is now more clearly seen as disrespect of self, and dilemmas of the selfish.

The research attitude shortcoming in relating to self was found to stand in the way of human concern for what was called environmental deterioration. In 1979 the concern was seen to be beyond the capability of environmental protection regulation. In 2019 the concern is seen to be beyond management capabilities of science, technology and industry.

Mentioning concern for climate change from environmental deterioration in 1979 often halted a conversation. Back then the Head of the US EPA, Douglas Costle, sent me a letter with all copies of my reports he could locate writing: "We have no further use of these reports, your research, or you. I will ensure no government funding ever supports your further research."

Today, the subject often starts conversations but usually turns to much acrimony on all sides of the concern. Some, mostly scientists, fear there will be no human future on the planet. Others, mostly consultants to business, become angry at any call for radical changes to business as usual due to projected disasters. The second group quote from many sources, including the Bible, to argue why nature is a resource to be used at human will. Some argue how business as usual practices, with masculine leadership, are sacrosanct to human life. Others become very angry about any arguments of moving to business as unusual. They see it as a door to anarchy, with anarchy defined as a bad as the French and Americans so defined it. This differs from the rest of the world, including the Greeks that defined the idea. As such, concepts of how humans relate to each other, and themselves, seals the problem for how they relate to nature. Our hope in 2019 is that some of the world's leading businesspeople[2] are already operating well into the world of business as unusual.

---

[2] These would include the leaders of such firms as IKEA, China State Construction, and a few IT companies.

2019-Environmental Deterioration, Evolving

In 1979, the dean of the Wharton School was upset with the project described herein. He did not see environmental deterioration as a concern for business. He thought students should concentrate on learning business as usual before going off and speculating on Hawk's "business as unusual." He also became concerned about research into issues like anarchy, which Hawk had called self-governance in organizations of the "network form." Reviewers of the time did note that environmental deterioration did seem to be better addressed via expanded innovation encouraged in the network form. This dean's appraisal was not his fault. He was speaking for his Wharton business leadership council of mostly Americans. They were firmly in and from business as usual. They seemed determined to protect that legacy.

1979 business leadership closely aligned itself with the Catholic tradition of management control and responsibility via fixed hierarchies. For them, the emergence of Information Technology was mostly more of the same, of science fiction humor, that could eventually help them firm up the hierarchy of control. Within the research, as described later into environmental deterioration from factor operations, hierarchies were valuable, but mostly for cataloguing the bad, not for encouraging ventures of the good. With a Herbert Simon hierarchy, workers would go home after commenting, "It's not my problem." Within an Eric Trist type autonomous workgroup, the more likely response was "We need to fix this, any ideas?"

Many in the study expressed concern about the meaning of life beyond the fight of man versus nature. They asked if there were approaches to life that could avoid the war against nature they were involved in, and that resulting in environmental deterioration? Perhaps humans cannot manage such change? In attempting to bring humility to being human, Stephen Hawking points out:

> *"The human race is just a chemical scum on a moderate-sized planet, orbiting around a very average star in the outer suburb of one among a hundred billion galaxies. And that I can't believe the whole universe exists for our benefit. That would be like saying that you would disappear if I closed my eyes."* [3]

The dominant purpose herein is to redevelop the idea of regulation in a way that can enhance the opportunities for the desirable potentials of mankind to emerge, not threaten what is seen as undesirable. Current modes of social regulation predominantly attempt to restrict the undesirable characteristics of mankind. Several modes of social regulation are outlined and investigated in this dissertation with respect to their ability to control complex societal problem issues.

The focus for the dissertation is environmental deterioration. The environment is conceptually analyzed in terms of man's relations to nature, the man-made environment, other men and himself, (no disrespect is intended towards women as the term men is used as an abbreviation of mankind in general). This conceptual scheme is narrowed down with an empirical research focus on the specific domain of attempts to regulate pollution from industrial production facilities.

As there is a final report from the research project which this dissertation is based on, the empirical evidence is only outlined in this document. The research report is titled "Environmental Protection: Analytical Solutions in Search of Synthetic Problems," 1977. The report is available from the Institute of International Business at the Stockholm School of Economics, Stockholm, Sweden. The author is the same as of this dissertation.

The dissertation is the conceptual realization of a thesis derived from the research data. The reporting pointed to difficulties in the

---

[3] Hawking, Stephen, *"Reality on the Rocks"* TV series (AP), aired, March 6, 2016.

current operation of environmental protection. This dissertation places those difficulties within a context. Many of the difficulties relate to the extensive use of the mode of regulation I shall call Legalism, which is inappropriate for describing complexity. An alternative mode of regulation is formulated and proposed within the dissertation which offers a more desirable response to complexity. The alternative mode I have called Appreciation.

This document can stand alone conceptually, but if you need the empirical basis you need to look into the three original research reports done at the Institute of International Business, Stockholm, Sweden. It chronicles economic motivations leading to industrialization practices that end in deterioration of the environment, the environment humans depend on. Each practice is seen to have strong economic argumentation, when see in bi-polar studies. Business as unusual would instead make use of the "both plus more" attitude and model of synthesis. In business as usual evidence is used to ensure facts showing how one side is right, usually the side that pays for the study. With business as unusual, the management function looks beyond the hoped-for results and includes the longer-term consequences as part of the price. The process begins in can it be true, then is it true for me, then what can we do about it? Humans seem unready to avoid the consequences of their values in actions that will deteriorate.

Clearly, human activities on earth have led to deterioration of its environment in terms of loss of biodiversity, pollution, depletion of natural resources, massive landscape conversion to artificial uses, defaunation, and a warming climate.[4] Business as usual practices will soon lead to no business between humans and nature. What is most difficult to appreciate about all this is that as the consequences of some actions become clearer, we humans seem to expand them and emphasize doing the wrong things more efficiently, not exploring what innovation of the alternative can achieve. "It's Too Late," is used in a special way in this book. This point will be examined in more detail later, but somehow human hope springs from feeling a threat is so omnipresent as to define hopelessness in its too late. Once its perceived to be too late in a human setting leadership goes into

---

[4] E. Stokstad, *Science* 364, p. 517-518, 2019.

hiding, or falls back, thus giving the opportunity to experiment with business as unusual.

Can someone instead prepare to write a different book, one that picks of the pieces of the past that are not linked to deterioration, and that allows for a tunnel of hope out of this mess and towards a new future? In theory it could all have been different, yet why was in not different? The "United Nations' Intergovernmental Science-Policy Platform on Biodiversity and Ecosystem" panel report concluded that about 10% of the 8.7 million living organisms will soon go extinct due to activities set up to serve humans.[5] From that scary beginning, the rate of demise is to expand.

---

[5] J. Tollefson, *Nature* 569, p. 171, 2019.

2019-The Researcher, Questioning

I have seen little change in the attitude of human predominance over all things since I was working in the family garden on the family farm at the age of four. I could not understand why humans needed to be so artificial while opposed to the natural. Back then, I remember asking why is it this way? My family thought I was funny.

- Later, when I was thirteen, I was banned from attendance in my local church for related questions.
- When I was fifteen, I was elected president of my 4H chapter. My first act was to close it. I argued that the members treated their animals very badly and should not hide that behavior under the shadow of 4H.
- When I was seventeen, I became president of my local Future Farmers of America Chapter. I had campaigned to halt a high school program set up to make the world a better place. The program assigned points to students who brought in bags of animal and bird parts, including heads, to school on Monday mornings. School employees would then inspect such and assign points. This had been set up to help extinguish the local pests and varmints. Such was thought to help in a better way of life. On closer inspection the Monday morning evidence revealed how the occasional cat or dog could be defined as a pest while some argued that such can be pesky as well. Administration halted the program but only for a bit, and with anger towards any who appeared to disrespect their authority in having and managing such a program. As punishment, I was not allowed admission to college preparatory math or English during high school.

- When I was eighteen, I was given the Isaac Walton award for writing an article in the local newspaper that kept local government from removing a large bird-filled tree from a stream. Government officials had argued how life would be improved and safer for humans if the storm water ran away faster.
- Ten years later, as an architect, I had the responsibility for doing an Environmental Impact Statement Review for a proposed ten-thousand-person housing development in Florida. After the review process, with Federal and State approval, I recommended a design which proposed the retention of swamps and minimal human impacts to the nature on the site. When I presented the approval document to the developer, he threw it and the proposed design into his trash can. His expression was: "Now we can get to work." He thus returned to his ideas of business as usual, clearing and leveling the property.
- Two years later I entered the Wharton School PhD program in systems sciences. The work described here was carried out and written up while in that program. I avoided science steeped in cause-effect charting from analytical thinking after segmenting, reducing and redacting problems. Consistent with systems sciences, the work herein looks at problems in terms of relationships, in a context, not effects from causes, where the causes are to be regulated and governed without appreciation of context.

Regardless of news reports I see little change in human thinking and behavior since I was four. Perhaps there is now greater anger at many things, including the environment and each other. The research discussed herein includes that as a major departure from business as usual.

After the concern for environmental deterioration seen herein was presented to faculty of the Wharton School, it was found acceptable a year later by seven professors at the University. Five ended up being drawn from schools outside of business. Seven questions were raised by that group during its review. They reveal much about the research topic, and its context then and now.

1) Why would a student in the Wharton Business School attempt research into the prognosis of human continuance relative to growing environmental deterioration from economic activities? I responded at the time that it appeared as a good doorway into problems in business and humans that mattered.
2) Why would business school faculty advisors allow such? My advisors — Russell Ackoff, Hasan Ozbekhan, and Eric Trist – strongly supported what I believed I should work on. All three were unusual humans. Based on their stature in the university the concern against my work was dropped.
3) Why did the research need to be moved to Sweden, and not be based in the USA? I asked the committee to reference any similar research projects they could find based in US institutions. They found none on the subject as framed, with such enthusiastic governmental and corporate involvement, especially not at US business schools.
4) Why did the review committee of 1978 need to be expanded from three to five professors from several departments, and then again expanded to seven? I was only told it was because of the range of disciplines involved in the study.
5) Why did it then take one year of review to gain approval of the evidence for the thesis? The normal review is a few weeks. Meeting notes seen afterwards showed committee concern that humans were the cause of human, then environmental troubles. They felt speculation on things like climate change should be dropped. It was kept.
6) Why did Wharton's Dean refuse to sign off on the approved document? He commented: "I do not see what environmental deterioration has to do with business." I responded to him agreeing with his statement. He clearly did not see the connection.

7) Why did only one of the four approved volumes get sent to the University of Pennsylvania Library archives, and none were ever forwarded to the University of Michigan PhD Abstracts?

These questions were then addressed twenty years later in a European Conference held to discuss environmental concerns. After an additional twenty years many say the area of study is obviously worthwhile, yet the answers await discovery. Some say the answers are obvious, but there is disagreement about the nature of obvious. A few now say the only question that now confronts humans is to decide on: Which scientist, representing which discipline, will write the most humanly significant book ever written, to be titled: *"On the End of Species"*.

Such a memorable obituary on humankind will thus serve as a bookend in home libraries where the other end of the shelf will begin with books on optimism for industrialization beginning with the 1859 book "On the Origin of Species." In between can be a collection of scientific literature presenting the human optimism in the dreams of reason realized via industrialization. These can cover the historical expansion of technological and scientific knowledge, and advances in going further with the dreams of the artificial.

All of this will outline the misguided faith in what might best be called humanism. Armed with human arrogance and steeped in human ignorance, the 150-year history of this optimism chronicles the demise of the human condition. It ends in the deterioration of the necessary conditions for life as systems of living order. It is in the order of suicide. Herein, I am mostly trying to communicate with myself. If you can gain anything from the echoes, I will be less sad.

Acknowledgments: Family, Friends, Colleagues

I give my deepest thanks to the following for making what lies herein possible:

- <u>My family, former students and friends</u>: They come from and live in many countries, and have attended many schools, yet hold a common concern for the ethics of life. It is said that there are about ten thousand names on my course rosters from thirty years.[6] Even as dean I taught a full array of courses, as that was the reason for the university, or so I thought back then. I'm still in contact with about a thousand of those former students. Via emails and phone calls they keep teaching me much from their negotiations with life. I feel sad that two of them recently lost their fight With the consequences of chemicalization of life: a) Garry Gordon Rasmussen, and b) Vajislav Ristic, two very close friends and forever great minds, like the thousands of other students that hope to know life. My vision has long been restricted to one eye thus I am eternally grateful to my three daughters for the care they take in helping with the contents found herein. So sorry to leave a not so good planet in their care.
- My brave mentors at the Wharton School, the program in Systems Sciences: <u>Professors Russell Ackoff, Hasan Ozbekhan</u>

---

[6] I can't say, as New Jersey Institute of Technology's leadership removed the rosters, six boxes of my library books, the 1970s data behind this book, and a daughter's stuffed animal from my office saying it was their property? Yes, deterioration runs deep in the human condition.

and Eric Trist. Eric, a founder of London's Tavistock Institute, carried out many studies of humans finding themselves in the workplace. He updated the 20,000-year-old "hunting party" with the "autonomous work group," as then used by Toyota, Volvo, et.al. His 1965 hypothesis with Fred Emery, on environmental typologies and turbulent future environments, proved prophetic to opening the climate change research. Russell Ackoff brought great skill in quantitative methods, then qualitative ideals, to use in discussing mess management, as seen in this research. He argued that the original three volumes from the research study should be my dissertation, as it was a clear example of why Wharton needed the Systems Sciences programs. He felt this book was not crucial. Hasan Ozbekhan, a director from Rand Corporation and initial Chair of the Club of Rome, then became a Wharton Professor, and my good friend. He was very important to framing the study on which this book is based. At the end he recommended I take it easy and learn more about belly dancing. He argued that in each person there is a book, and if the person is lucky the book comes out before death. If his friends are unlucky, the book comes out again, and again, and again….

- Gunnar Hedlund: My best friend in life. He and another friend, Lars Otterbeck, created the Institute of International Business at the Stockholm School of Economics in 1976. I joined the Stockholm School in 1975 to work with them in setting up the Institute by launching it with this project. The topic was unacceptable in normal business education but Gunnar and his Board, containing leaders of Swedish business, thought it was crucial to study. Climate Change might well provide the context for all business of the future with an emphasis on international business. I was very pleased to work with them until Gunnar's death in 1996.
- Göran Persson: Director of the Foundation for Strategic Environmental Research (MISTRA). There later was a Swedish Prime Minister of the same name. He made use of the research that the first Goran made possible with his support without

reservations. His ethical core was unquestionable. He ran meetings by simply being present. I didn't know the second Goran very well but assumed he was also a good person.

- <u>James F. Black</u>, Senior Scientist for Exxon Research. He was essential in the early parts of the research, then, in fall 1977 he presented his own findings to industry representatives. His lecture was on "Potential Catastrophic Impact from Burning Fossil Fuels." This became the first evidence in the study of what he titled "climate change from human activities."

- <u>Nicholas Georgescu-Roegen</u>. A great friend and eager supporter of my projects in research and teaching. Author of 1971 "The Entropy Law and the Economic Process" his thinking provided part of the intellectual basis of the research found herein. Known as the father of Ecological Economics, he turned down membership on its Board saying: "Ecological Economics? Someday your economics will be consumed by the ecological." We drafted a paper together called "Second Law Economics." Its humor was unpublishable. Each year he sent me his favorite unpublished paper of the year, as a Christmas present. Each year he was nominated for the Nobel Prize in Economics, by economists in Asia and Europe. Via the most adamant opposition to his ideas from North American economists he was always dropped. His passion was having breakfast with my wife Barbro, without my talking crap. Miss him, much.

- <u>Richard Garwin</u>: Co-designer of the hydrogen bomb with Teller, and the subject of the book *True Genius*. He was very helpful to this work on human difficulties, as created by humans. Ending the species via environmental deterioration was an alternative to nuclear war. Once started, both will irreversibly change the environment life depends on. He was instrumental in helping me stage conferences at my university and in New York City. They were to discuss human potential, for both good and evil.

- <u>Yongda Yu</u>: Professor of Public Policy, Tsinghua University, head of China's Leadership Center. Professor Yu, a very good and kind friend, helped me much with many things scientific, cultural and humanistic. We found his book on *New Theories of International Economics* important to business as unusual; i.e., the future. He did not speak English; I did not speak Mandarin. We could travel together without problem. The greatest teacher of great students, or so his students still show me.

- <u>Ning Yuan</u>: President of China Construction America. A good friend that is the essence of an exciting leader in initiating and managing business as unusual. He leads a very innovative company but his workers, in the tradition of Lao Tzu, believe they did it themselves. It is a great reward to be near him. CCA workers reconfirm this to be true on many construction sites, in many parts of the world. Our discussions over dinners and lunches were very helpful to many things I was trying to do. I thank him.

- <u>Tsien Hsue-shen</u>: Chinese born scientist who pioneered the American space age, then returned to China to make similar accomplishments, while initiating economic development in the sixties and seventies. His Great Wall Trading Company was important to China's scientific and economic development. He helped my students a great deal in the nineties by organizing trips for them to leading Chinese companies. Prior to his 2009 death he made very helpful comments on the science behind the subject reported herein. A systems science researcher as well, a new think tank is being established between China and AAAS (American Association for Advancement of Science). I adore the writing of his step daughter, Zaihong shen, in "Feng Shui," 2001, as well as Zaihong.

- In addition, I deeply respect and thank the many governmental agency directors and company directors that approved the study, then took a direct role in it. They were instrumental to what we learned. I was very impressed with their attitudes, and enthusiasm to always learn more, as well as their ability to appreciate and implement business as unusual.

Preface

We see several forces in serious conflict. Humans are at the center. We choose to fight with nature, each other and ourselves. Perhaps resolution of these human inspired conflicts awaits the results of the arguments we have with ourselves, when alone. The first conflict is seen in industrialization and the natural environment. The conflict begins in deterioration, then gains strength and breadth to disrupt then destroy systems of life, of which humans are intrinsically connected. Humans, in general feel something is wrong but can't see it because years of education and social training have brought them to believe in the great barrier of humanistic thinking – analysis. They can only see cause effect relations in real time of three dimensions, not conceive of the consequences playing out in the fourth dimension. They do see where it begins in one dimensional thinking of my point, or your point, but no connection, and, ultimately, no point. All this is fixed in two dimensions for human laws and legally drawn legislation. This worsens a fateful situation by pretending to fix in time that which naturally changes and as it becomes troubled it changes more erratically thus bringing about fate more rapidly.

More simply put we have engineers creating a dilemma between life and death via industrialization, followed by lawyers fixing that dilemma in the concrete specifics of two-dimensional actions. Living systems need more than the shortcomings of these two role types. We can begin with a new idea of what ought to be; i.e., an articulation of the normative that repositions humans and nature into a both plus more, then move on to the more and allow it to manage the third dimension in terms of knowledge of the fourth. From this vision we must reorient the education of engineers than lawyers to be consistent with a world of both plus more, not cause-effect inscribed in two dimensions based on one dimensional thinking that eventually becomes pointless.

Much hope for humans is now vested in Artificial Intelligence (AI) rising to compensate for seeming lack of natural intelligence (NI). What was learned in the research behind this book is we perceive problems threatening our future then look for solutions that will solve the problems without disturbing the business as usual that supports our status quo. Technological solutions seem to offer "fixes" that seemingly do not change the context; i.e., insure changelessness.

As with conceptions of environmental protection, environmentalism, recycling and sustainability, the change in human activities will be insufficient to an appreciation essential to understand life in and with the natural. In the 1970s some of us defined an environmentalist as someone who bought their summer home last year. Recycling mostly allows business as usual in industrial production and rabid consumption to continue unabated, since the normal costs to the environment can simply be "recycled." This is a problem even if the environmental costs of collection and remanufacturing are ignored or given a discount for hearts in the right place. More questionable in the recycling process are the entropy cost build into the initial product designs and uses. Recycling of mistakes does little to eliminate the mistakes that underlie the mistakes. As scientists of the status of Einstein and Hawking long ago pointed out, the Second Law of Thermodynamics is sacrosanct in our universe. Soda cans are no more recyclable than are humans.

Two challenges have come to define the human future. These will become clarified as humans perceive a need to change how they define conditions of life. The current perception is an artifact of 19th Century Newtonian-inspired industrialization, designed as a mechanical system that can eliminate or at least compensate for natures' irregularities. The industrial is managed with principles consistent with the industrial paradigm and its mechanization, and operates in opposition to the vagaries of the larger environment. The results have been somewhat impressive. The longer-term consequences of these results seem to be great, perhaps greater than life can afford.

There is growing need to rethink the industrial and its impact on the larger environment. The consequences of its operations are becoming significant. A rethink can begin in the seemingly trivial practices imbedded in human resource management, as taught in business schools and practiced in their graduates. An example could be the Maslow 1943 Harvard business school human resource management theory for worker and societal motivation.[7] Beginning there can shine a new light on industrial processes and their role in deteriorating the relations between humans and the nature upon which they rely. Let us begin with a small look at this means of managing humans as resources for the industrial.

From research into humans as resources for industrialization, Maslow came up with a relatively perverse management form titled "hierarchy of human needs." It was to help mangers motivate lower humans to move up through a hierarchy of accomplishments. Such was needed to induce natural beings to spend life in un-natural settings. Human resource management thus becomes party to a larger environmental deterioration problem, working in the service to manipulating natural beings to function in industrialization settings. The environmental deterioration challenge is much wider than smoke from a coal-fired power plant. It involves much of what we define as civilization.

Going deeper into this seeming triviality, we see how Maslow's hierarchy becomes used to encouraged humans to work ever-harder to access goods to meet their bio-physical needs. Then, the problem expands as humans strive to expanded possession of the results of industrial production. This process is organized towards the top of Maslow's hierarchy. Workers come to believe if they work harder, they will access increased power and/or wealth and become "self-actualized."[8] Herein lies the basis for humans expanding the problems

---

[7] "A Theory of Human Motivation," *Psychology Review*, Abraham Maslow, Harvard, 1943.

[8] There is much irony in this theory of organization. In it, hard work will propel you from grounded needs to ephemeral wants, and may allow access to the ultimate, self-actualization. In fact, those most referenced to have become self-actualized in the species were those who ignored or actively rejected fulfillment of ephemeral wants thereby finding higher priorities for life in nature.

of industrialization from meeting limited human needs to the grasping for human wants.

There were obvious problems in this model. Must strategic deceit be used to get natural beings to occupy un-natural settings for much of their lives? Why place an idea like self-actualization atop a hierarchy in that they rightfully are irrelevant to each other? Does this not further the problems in the ongoing war of humans against nature, via the industrial? To date the accumulated wealth gained from progress up the hierarchy is seldom connected to self-actualization; it's mostly used to insulate those who can't find self-actualization and are bothered by it. As such, the idea of self-actualization has been translated in ideas about the mission of life being the acquisition of ever more "stuff;" as produced via industrialization. The result is an ever-expanding industrial basis to serve society's needs and wants.

The research outlined herein calls for a drastic rethink of industrialization, a mechanical process that is now at the core of the development and management of the human project; a project that faces consequential catastrophe. Posterity will be responsible for leading humans through the changing conditions of the two challenges. Some leadership participating in the research behind this work see an ominous need for change, but they were in a distinct minority.

The first challenge comes from many human activities being seen to *deteriorate* nature and the natural environment essential to a biosystemic natural order. Central in this is the production and use of Petro-chemicals seen as essential to human activities even as they eliminate other species, and habitats. From the same homocentric attitude comes the destruction of air and water cleansing natural environments composed of trees, soils, oceans, lakes, ground waters and atmospheric conditions. Emerging knowledge warns humans of conditions of change via human activities at the earth's surface. These release CO_2 into the atmosphere thereby warming the atmosphere. The dire conditions created by this emerged from the work of a scientist in the study near its close in the fall of 1977.

Most of the problems raised herein, and with humans in general are relational. This is why we must shift from vision based on and in analysis of parts, separated from context. We need a systems vision and approach to see relations, not parts pulled out and messed with, which create a larger mess when they are put back in their system; a system that had since moved on. Thus, relations and relationships are crucial to see, appreciate and manage. In this respect we look at relations between humans and nature, between humans and the built environments they surround themselves to protect the artificial from the natural, and between humans and other humans. All this stems from the most crucial of relations, the most difficult to repair and/or manage: the relation to our self. The following diagram begins to outline the problem and the promise for change to business as unusual.

The challenge for humans is that their activities result in deterioration of the environmental conditions essential to their life and life on the planet. This poses a challenge to life as science defines it. As we learn more via science, we find less basis for optimism for continuation of that life which is presumed to be developed from science and technology.

Research shows a continual deterioration in the conditions of the natural environment due to human activities. Meanwhile, humans believe they are the crowning achievement of a cosmic trek called the human project. As such, humans continue to use, ignore or degrade all species and systems of life; systems that are lesser in the hierarchy of life, as humans define it. This provides us with the ideology that we should *desecrate* nature, which becomes the logic for allowing and/or motivating deterioration of the natural.

Desecration is an idea of a religious tone that serves short-term humanistic needs, and then, unfortunate human wants. Humans believing there are technological solutions to all harmful consequences from their ill-considered actions in meeting their needs illustrates the importance of humanistic ideas. The unfortunate process is justified in combining Adam Smith economics with Darwinian conceptions of competitive advantage, both of which sponsor a particular dream of human evolution. This leads to the ideas behind business as usual between humans and the sponsorship of a kind of *industrialization* to supply that business and the distribution of its goods and services.

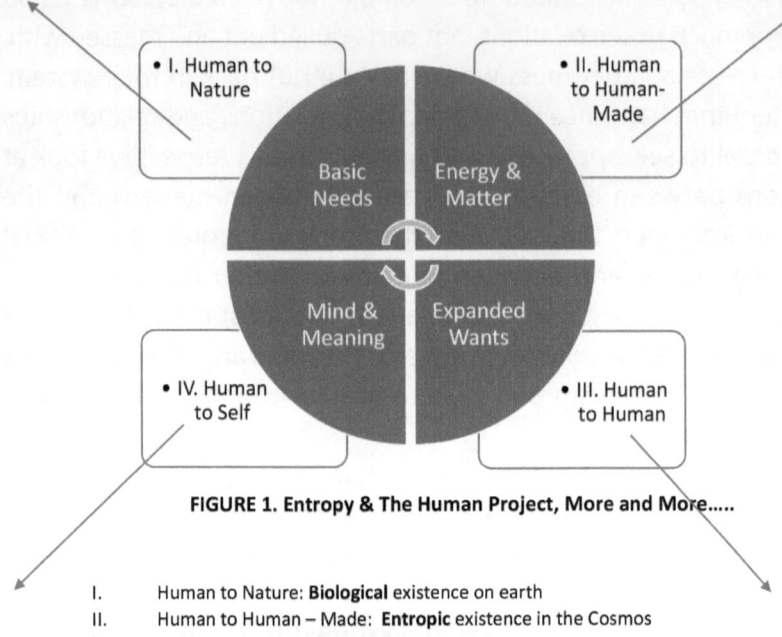

FIGURE 1. Entropy & The Human Project, More and More.....

I. Human to Nature: **Biological** existence on earth
II. Human to Human – Made: **Entropic** existence in the Cosmos
III. Human to Human: **Social-political** activities
IV. Human to Self: **Meaning of life** introspection (mentally fu_ked up)

Ideas in one domain profoundly affect the other domains. The systemic emphasizes context, the analytic obscures connectivity in context. Domain I is of the systemic while Domain II is derived from the analytic. Domain I provides the human context, Domain II provides the dilemma addressed by environmental protection efforts. The Economics of Doman II increases entropic speed.

Behind industrialization, and its desecration of nature, stands a) religious scriptures, b) economic theories, and c) legalistic weaknesses. Values of what we call humanism define the value of all three while ensuring continuous deterioration of nature. These issues emerged from the research interviews as rationales for why change would be difficult, maybe impossible?

a) Justification for activities of humans that deteriorate are seen in religious texts. They emphasize the lowly role of nature relative to humans aspirations: *"Be fruitful and multiply, and fill the earth, and subdue it; and rule over the fish of the sea and over the birds of the sky and over every living thing that moves on the earth."*[9] Most religions teach humans to aspire to and work under this belief.

b) Economic ideologies presume the value of an unfettered growth of production, distribution and consumption. As worshippers of *The Economist* teachings firmly believe, increased productivity is the ultimate measure of a business enterprise, where deterioration consequences are expected, are usually insignificant, and can be managed via price, if ever needing to be managed. Few economists of the western tradition agree with Nicholas Georgescu-Roegen, that economic acts are entropy-aiding.

c) The role of legal process is seen as outside the pathways of ethics and truth, while forcefully directing humans to abide by laws with a questionable foundation. For example, the traditional legal process requires paper, much paper. Thousands of trees are destroyed to provide two-dimensional platforms ordering obedience to one-dimensional ideas. Questions about the illogic of "humans protecting the environment from humans" are ignored within that dimension. There are problems with humans being human.

Stepping back, to see the environment more holistically and systemically, shows the danger of using segmented, analytic efforts to manage a larger, holistic phenomenon, such as the environment. It seems to add to its deterioration. Analyzing a systemic problem, to find its cause, generally expands it. We need to understand this, and appreciate the resulting dilemma, then find innovative ways out from it. As such, this is the second challenge herein. The difficulties become more complex as we find examples of effects preceding causes, as seen in early cybernetics. As such, nature can be more interesting than the science that attempts to know her.

Behind this second challenge, research reveals a deep human belief in future hope in what is being called the artificial. Defined via its abstraction from the natural it is lauded in books under the heading of "sciences of the artificial." Through it humans see a

---
[9] *The Bible*, Genesis, 1:26-30

doorway to a better future, while its results to date are mostly seen to add to deterioration of the environment. The values behind the prominence of the artificial are due for a questioning. This will require an appreciation of what and how humans do what they do, especially under the flag of industrialization. In addition to the natural deterioration from nature's 2nd Law Entropic process[10] we add man-made processes of industrialization.

From this challenge to change we encounter a second challenge – it arises from serious concern for if, when and how humans can respond to the first challenge, that of deterioration of the natural environment. Just now this is an economic discussion. Is there are way to effectively regulate the current definition of economic systems, or are there new ideas about the economics of nature?

Both challenges can be hard to visualize but are dire and growing. Interview data illustrated how urgency is masked by humanly creating complexities from false dichotomies. This leads to double binds and Catch 22s that form polarized debates about relations between man and nature, man and man, and man and self. One such debate stems from a dichotomy in a war between man and nature, where the two are in fact interdependent. This begins in the desecration of nature that leads to its deterioration. The internal war that sponsors the external war with nature is seen in immortality projects created to fight against the mortality intrinsic to the nature of life. Results of a study on which this is based show why and how societal approaches to regulation of individual human acts will not resolve either challenge; perhaps it is responsible for much that has come to be wrong between humans and their environments. With some urgency we need to move the human mentality towards authority via differences that make a beneficial difference.

The first challenge is to get humans to see that what they have done and are doing is a problem. The second challenge is how to deal with what was noticed, should it be noted before it's too late. The following illustrates the pervasiveness of the challenges in business as usual. It describes how a serious effort to rethink the costs of "business

---

[10] Nicholas Georgescu-Roegen, *"The Entropy Law and Economic Progress,"* Harvard Press, 1971.

as usual" to the natural environment by human activities, was derailed in practices of real-time accounting for the sake of ever shorter-term profitability. Humans have long had a problem with their environment.

Many humans argue that they will always find ways to avoid a fateful conclusion, based on more extensive analysis, except of course for the systemic aspects of their own death, and/or enjoining a religious apocalypse, and, of course, the cosmic entropic conclusion. None-the-less, humans like to think of themselves as separate from nature, and even above nature. They find ways to ignore all evidence that they are linked to or even dependent upon nature. A group of humans argue that their actions cannot have unfortunate consequences. When evidence of the unfortunate meets their reality, they turn to investing recourses in order to obscure copiability. Why is it this way?

Via a business-as-usual attitude. change is defined in the manner that would suit the dwellers in the "Plato's Cave," as depicted in "The Allegory of the Cave." Families, schools, companies, governments and other social institutions support the bias towards retention of business as usual at all costs. Just now the costs seem to be significantly growing.

Two hundred years of industrialization via science implies that humans can solve all problems, even those that result from technological solutions to non-technology problems. Regardless, the human project moves forward from a deep belief that humans will solve any and all problems. Thus, we arrive at the religion of humanism – a creed that humans have an ever-expanding power to control their reality while eliminating any and all challenges from it. Reexamination of humanism and its attitude towards the natural environment may be essential to finding beneficial change. Are humans capable of such self-reflection? Science shows us that change is a key definer of nature. Can humans ever accept change?

The social bonding forces of cultures and their traditions bind social organizations, but the price they pay is to consistently resist change. Attitudes want to be fixed and practices follow the values that structure attitudes. The common expression about this within a business is "Around here we do it this way. If you are uncomfortable with this perhaps you should look elsewhere." Diversity is seldom seen as an asset. As was often mentioned in the research interviews, as the reason for continuance of business as usual, "We do it this way because we always did it this way." Humanism helps to avoid seeing emerging problems to humans and their conditions of life. This was most clearly seen in the efforts of those trained in law schools in the US. Evidence of the end state of the written law can now be seen in the way the seemingly most intelligent lawyers compose their words to end as regulations. Contemporary environmental laws rely on ever longer paragraphs, sentences and words.[11] It's as if these individuals' sense that the system they were educated to work in is not working, thus they mask the problem by using 125 plus word sentences. It's as if they don't know how to begin a statement and wish to avoid ending it.

Humanists counter change by arguing how change is always taking place, thus it is a constant, thus it can be ignored. In this way change is strangely defined as permanence. Relative to climate change the humanist ideology mistakenly argues that weather (which is not climate change) is always changing, thus it's a constant and climate change doesn't matter. For them, what then is the problem? From interviews in the study behind this work it seemed that the more ominous a change facing humans, the more openly they would ignore it. Their creed was that its best to simply ignore change, as it will change away anyway and thus be gone. Except for the subject matter at hand, this seemed funny.

---

[11] This will be discussed later but it was common to see laws of hundreds of pages and sentences of 125 plus words where the authors seem to not know how to enter and why to exit a sentence. Many participants in the research on which this is based saw this as a lawyer joke in the reverse sense; where the joke was on those relying on the legal system to solve systemic problems.

Conclusions, 2019

- After forty years the effects, then the causes of environmental deterioration, are being seen in science turned upside down, inside out, as it examines its history in building the industrialized environment of the artificial against the natural, that provided the world with the consequences known as deterioration of the natural.
- Who will win in the war with nature? No one and nothing. Winning is a human construct. Entropy continues despite who and what humans are. Are humans a small problem restricted to planet earth? Can humans be anything more than a problem?
- Where will humans go? Most likely, they will continue into the deeper and darker with much that is artificial to light the way into the unhappy darkness. It is as if humans are returning to from where they escaped; back into Plato's Allegory of the Cave. Why do many humans prefer the changelessness advised by Parmenides and Confucius, and Plato, and avoid the ideas about a better chance in the change of Socrates and Lao Tzu, and then Heraclitus? Why do most humans not know of those who set the stage for unaided rationality, industrialization, then deterioration?
- Cultural institutions and social organizations must shift to explicit questioning of business as usual in a human search for beneficially innovative business as unusual. Schools with their youth very interested in a future public good can be leaders in this. Most teachers are ready for such, if they could set the rules that encourages the innovative to replace the tried and truly wrong.
- Learn to be nice to each other and nature, we are all in this together.

- Redesign your life and the infrastructure that connects. Fewer airplane trips, more public transit, especially high-speed rail to connect the various parts of our earth. A conference was held in 1991 on this; "Conditions of Success: Grand Hotel, Stockholm."
- As was said at the end of the newscasts that mattered in America, by a newscaster that cared about his mission: "Good Night, and Good Luck." (A movie about him.)

1979 - THE DISSERTATION THESIS

CHAPTER 1

Relations

The history of human relations to nature is interesting. Humans were and are biologically linked to nature. They depend on the well-being of an environment they share with nature for conditions of life. While some humans seem aware of this, many ignore or openly reject it during their lives. The evidence for this is seen everywhere in their choices about life and manner of living. As such, there should be a deep concern for the human future. There is not. A recent attempt to modify the human attitude towards nature came in environmental protection regulation. Sadly, the mostly legal then governance activities have signified a continuation of the traditional attitude towards nature. A few problems were resolved but those could have been addressed in more efficient and effective ways. The topic herein moves beyond ideas of the natural environment needing human protection. Interest herein is centered on the longer-term consequences of nature's relations back to humans, more than humans arrogantly attempting to protect nature from human activities planned to continue.

Some human history is written in terms of relations to nature although more concentrates of human to human history. That which involved nature seldom mentioned humans causing environment deterioration. This changed with humanly directed scientific discovery, especially our accessing the science of erasing humans via nuclear war, or development of chemicals dangerous to life. Thirty years later, we see danger signs from more widespread problems in the long-term consequences of industrialized pollution becoming near-term hazards to life. Just now there is new research posing that the consequences could end up changing planetary conditions, the conditions essential to life. Just now this is introduced as "climate change." Thus, the relations to nature are growing much more serious than mutual creation of life or the accommodating the hostility to nature in her irreversible processes of entropic death.

To organize their opposition to nature humans developed what we will call the "human project." Its mission was and is to gain control over natural processes then nature or replace her with the artificial. Underlying this project humans wish to find meaning in the limits to human life. One means is to work to create neg-entropy in defiance of natural entropy. Via their passion for this project humans work to develop ways to avoid, ignore, denounce and/or destroy what nurtures them.

Why do humans praise the artificial and de-link themselves from nature and the natural systems of life? It seems rejecting nature is essential to growing up, much like teenagers rejecting their home and family in order to go off and development meaning of self, via selfishness. Such human logic has long been responded to in religious dogmas and business school texts. Is it assumed to be important to human development to do such? Perhaps it's only a distraction to avoid seeing ethical shortcomings of humans involved in conflict and destruction? Or, it's a way to put entropic death outside a passion for life.

Clearly, many humans have a negative attitude towards nature. This attitude begins in the religion of environmental desecration and moves into environmental deterioration. Perhaps it is a self-imposed suicide of the species via explicit destruction of its essential context? Clearly there is some form of a self-destructive process underway as evidenced by environmental deterioration from human activities. The process has grown from background noise to a noticeable and then noteworthy threat. How much further must it expand before it can mobilize humans to upgrade the mythology of human purpose and its artificial meanings?

Just now, in 1979, we seem to be approaching a crucial moment in history. We face some fateful choices about life and human activities to support or deny that life on the planet. There are early signs of a need to create a new myth around which to organize the human project.

Hope lies mostly with the young. The work presented herein is mostly for them, as they will carry the cost of the elder's errors in judgement and practices.

1.1 Human Nature

The following is about a war. We need to gain a clearer sense of who or what we humans are, and what we strive to become, or at least do. We want to win but not sure against who or what. We often are at work against other humans but underlying this we seem at war against the natural, including the nature in ourselves. In so doing we praise the artificial.

Humans have negotiated with nature for most of their existence. Intimate collaborations over creation of life, hostility about the march to death, and general misunderstands of what nature is have sustained an interesting one-sided discourse. Humans arise from nature while remaining biologically thus remain dependent on her and of course her well-being until their death. None-the-less humans generally act with much arrogance and little appreciation for nature, and what she represents in the universe.

In this, it seems appreciation is key to beneficial change. As used here, appreciative systems come from the social sciences work by Sir Geoffrey Vickers. He outlined the importance of this missing attitude in his 1965 "The Art of Judgement" book. He then elaborated in more detail on why we need to learn appreciation in his 1970 book: "Freedom in a Rocking Boat: Changing Values in an Unstable Society." Appreciation, as Vickers presented it, was key to his framework for how to change what we value, then now to upgrade values via a wider appreciation of context. He argued how we make decisions from values while modifying the decisions but not the values dictating them.

Systemic appreciation can lead towards self-management. It can point to the need for self-limiting, self-reversing and openness to redefinition. This opens the door to upgrading via allowing for fluid and open processes. Vickers's appreciative systems seem ideal to encourage human nature to come to appreciates the nature of nature.

> "Learning what to want is the most radical, the most painful and the most creative art of life." (Freedom in a Rocking Boat, 1970, from the introduction). [12]

This underlines the need to transform the process of humans working to meet their needs then coming to expand that work into processes of expanding into seemingly unrestricted wants. This is primarily done via discovery and development of industrialization and the areas of science set up to feed it. This has allowed a shifting from direct human experience with nature to building and expanding on the world of the artificial. This encourages humans in failing to appreciate nature and initiate activities such as leveling parts of a forest to build a housing development that removes much nature and then brings deterioration to the remaining nature. To obscure this process, humans invent mythologies around the importance of "human projects." These projects, such as an expansive one called industrialization, seeks meaning for humans by transforming the "is of the natural" into the "human idea of what ought to be." The current stage of this human project has been called "post-industrialization." It is clearly even more industrial then post but more significant herein is how it lacks appreciation of nature at an even more expansive level. It illustrates a muddled dichotomy in human thinking. It espouses actions to protect the natural environment from human actions but therein introduced a self-reinforcing contradiction in values with no obvious escape.

This industrialization human project has introduced a more extensive de-appreciation any former signs of appreciation of nature. It did this via an enthusiastic denouncing, ignoring, avoiding and/or destroying sign of nature. It's an unhappy situation for systems nurtured by nature. The question then becomes why do humans want to de-link themselves from nature and the systems of life that define nature? Is moving out from nature a good thing, like teenage humans moving out from home, parents and background. In many religious

---

[12] Vickers, Geoffrey, <u>Freedom in a Rocking Boat</u>, Penguin Books: Middlesex, England, 1970.

dogmas and business school texts there is an image of nature as an economic resource that should be used in support of human ends.

Why is our attitude towards nature so uncaring or negative? Our attitude goes from environment as something to overpower, to something to desecrate. In both activities we work to deteriorate nature via our relations with it. Thus, we carry out destruction of the context of life. While being part of life we thus carry out a self-destructive process. While acting to increase environmental deterioration via our activities we endanger ourselves. The consequences are now noticeable. Soon they will become devastating.

Is it possible for humans to create a new mythology from a new human purpose? Can we come to appreciate nature as fundamental to life? We are just now approaching the moment in human history, when such choices matter. There are signs of recognizing a need for a new myth to guide human development. The following work is mostly for the youth, as they will carry the cost of the elder's manifest errors in judgement and practice.

Herein I disregard the excuse of human's incompetence and thus their need for forgiveness. The human attitude towards nature and the supporting actions are clearly derogatory and now sufficiently dangerous to the context of life to require urgent change. What can be done, how should humans change, where should change begin? Let's begin with the dominant problem solver of modern society, regulation. This has become the general means to respond to evidence of a societal wrong being done. From bi-polar beliefs and/or analytically filtered evidence regulation is drawn up by those with limited beliefs, no science and analytic filtration as acquired in law schools. This is done in the cause of creating social regulation against the cause of the effect. Western society is quite proud of the results of this for organizing and improving society. It has been attempted for about a decade in use to slow and then reverse environmental deterioration processes. The evidence for what this brought society comes from the research project mentioned above.

Regulation efforts are seen in the factories, refineries and company headquarters that assisted with the research behind this writing. The evidence shows regulation to have missed the contextual issues, usually done very late, and often turned counterproductive? My responses come from evidence in a two-year research study of various national systems of regulating environmental protection. Some who helped with the study believe it may now be too late although it may appear as too early. These included those in industry who knew most about the role of industrial by-products and how they don't, as in the minds of some legally educated politicians in the United States, simply disappear if a law is passed to dispense with their potential for harm to life. In addition, there were government officials with calm insight into the pending problem for living systems in continuation of business as usual and believed we cannot long afford factions arguing over how much pollution is tolerable. One member from industry, an American, argued that current industrial practices will lead to fundamental change in our planet's climate. Two regulators, one each from Canada and Sweden, went deeper to argue that we in essence are dependent on a support system that will soon encounter planetary deterioration at an unresolvable scale. At that point solutions like pollution catchment, limits on population growth, halting destruction of natural terrain will seem small to irrelevant. No regulators trained in the law ever voiced such a concern in the project.

Humans have come to occupy a parallel world that they have created mostly from and in two-dimensions. It is commonly called known as the world of the artificial. In it we occupy an artificially constructed habitat that we define as superior to living in nature. We often go so far as believe the artificial is superior to living "with" nature. Where from does this human want arise? Is it genetic or acquired via mental constructs? Why do humans feel they want to or even need to be distant from nature?

Perhaps the ideology arises from the mentality of myths. If so, this will be difficult to address in that myths are often the unquestioned untruths of societies. Humans deeply feel they need to be in charge of their place in the world, a feeling that easily becomes a passion for being in charge of the world as they know it. We have developed a mythology that somehow guides us into opposition of nature. This is ironic, or tragic, in that we also know life is defined by and dependent up on nature? Perhaps since nature defined life to end in death, we do not trust nature, thus we are born in conflict with her? If true, this insight may give access to the world of human dilemmas in the human condition. It thus presents humans with *the dilemma* of their live, and may well be beyond their reconciliation. Perhaps this is the source of human religions as comforting mythologies, as well as rationalization of why throwing a plastic bottle and cheeseburger wrapper out the window is a sign of strength, not simply being filthy.

Dilemmas are like Joseph Heller's *Catch-22*, where you are damned if you do or you don't, no matter what. It is also like Gregory Bateson's *double-bind that* invites schizophrenia in those caught up in it, especially if they are restricted to use of unaided-rationality. Or like West Churchman's depiction of the enemies of systemic thinking relying on that which is defined as rational, about 10% of Churchman's reality, while discounting or completely ignoring the other 90% in. This is ultimately what those concerned with the environment and our war with its natural governance face. Perhaps there is no way out. Elsewhere I've argued that we can start to resolve this via thinking in *both plus more* terms, where the rational and non-rational are combined to stand on in search of the vastly more insightful *more*. Herein I suggest we may find such in the 5th dimension that humans seem to have no access to.

Myth is here used in the sense of Joseph Campbell. He often lectured how myths are at the center of social-organizational thinking, be it for good or bad purposes. More succinctly, he suggested *myths are public dreams, while dreams are private myths*. Myths organize the elements that define the human condition and then the actions and activities that bring it about. Leading myths become societal stories that lead to satisfying human needs with echoes that expand to deal with human wants. Currently mythology is clearly connected to dreams of an industrial state organized by the sciences of the artificial. As we see how the current sense of industrialization is dangerous to the human context, we may well try to create a new myth. In the current situation we are entering a major dilemma with two aspects to it.

Part I is that nature is clearly not dependent on human wellbeing. Part II is that aspects of being human link back to present danger to nature's wellbeing, perhaps her survival. Arising from religious and cultural myths are stories and mentoring systems that favor ignoring nature or moving on to emphasize the un-natural dimension of life, the artificial. Within these myths are powerful entities that are not normally understandable except via the interpretations of a few humans, generally of the male version, that represent interpretations of nature via such myths as the Garden of Eden to explain nature.

Other humans, also men, offer an opposition myth that allows any to interpret the natural surroundings in a more objective manner, although any wishing to do so must accept the mythology of technology as generated via rational knowledge gained from science. Not that different from a religion this approach leaves us with unaided rationality to deal with that which is not required to be rational. Humans thus lack appreciation for the non-rationality of nature from the choices of the chromosome to the essential need of black holes to allow the cosmos to make sense, even if it is sense beyond rationality. These myths pose problems for humans relating to nature and ever appreciating how their activities deteriorate the environment on which both depend.

The human attitude to nature might best be envisioned as derived from a religion of "homocentricity," sometimes called a "religion of humanism." This religion and its closely held beliefs may well be the definition of the problem of 1978.

> "There is more than an academic reason for writing about the religious nature of humanism, for some of humanism's religious assumptions are among the most destructive ideas in common currency, a main source of the peril in this most perilous of epochs since the expulsion from Eden. Nor is the danger merely a potential one – to be characterized as the figment of a doomsday neurosis, and then dismissed."[13]

---

[13] *The Arrogance of Humanism*, Ehrenfeld, David, New York: Oxford University Press, 1978, p. 4

Ehrenfeld then goes deeper. He seeks the underlying characteristics of humanism as seen in the dominant human myth

Because human intelligence is the key to human success, the main task of the humanists is to assess its power and protect its prerogatives wherever they are questioned or challenged. Among the correlates of humanism is the belief that humankind should live for itself, because we have the power to do so, the capacity to enjoy such a life, and nothing else to live for. Another correlate is the faith in the children of pure reason, science and technology. Although shaken in recent years and the source of much confusion among humanists, this faith continues to permeate our existence and influence our behavior…[14]

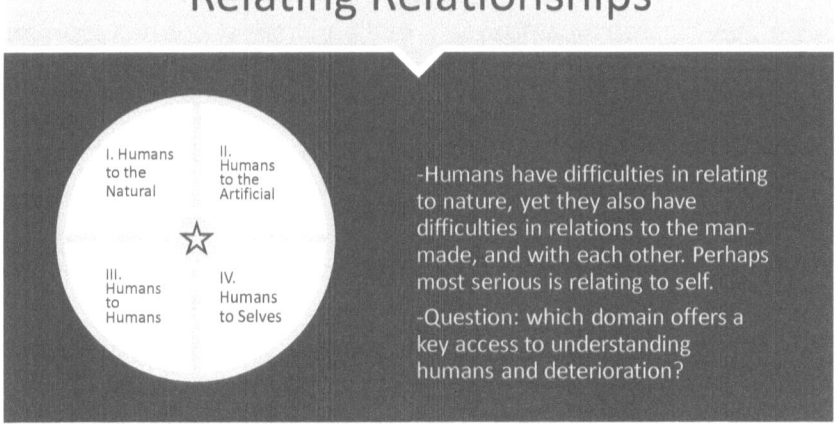

Figure 1.1 Human Relations Quadrants

These are seen with great clarity in the work of Joseph Campbell in his inventory of human behavior that points towards the human passion to rise above nature and move towards an emphasis on

---

[14] (Ibid., p. 5-6)

tyranny, as it arises from the will to leadership in a society via the peculiarities of its culture.

> "They tyrant is proud, and therein resides his doom. He is proud because he thinks of his strength as his own; thus, he is in the clown role, as a mistaker of shadow for substance; it is his destiny to be tricked. ... The hero of yesterday becomes the tyrant of tomorrow, unless he crucifies himself today."[15]

1.2 Deterioration, resulting from Humans wanting to be Artificial

During thousands of years in designing and developing what may be called the human project there has been a consistent desire to develop support systems to satisfy humans needs. Although it was always a bit homocentric, humans recently emphasized the homocentric. In so doing they created a paradox where the current support system for human life has become a major threat to all life. This change is outlined in the following.

On the satisfying of insatiable human wants? Problems of managing consequences of meeting insatiable wants.

A) *The emergence of insatiable wants?* Humans have long enjoyed inventing and organizing machines to meet basic human needs. This has become widely known and accepted. This has come to be called industrialization. Based on its early success, the model expanded to attempt the satisfaction of essentially insatiable human wants. The collective results from this provide the consequences that increasingly challenge humans. All industrialization has some deterioration associated with it. Massive industrialization has massive consequences to its environment, and the conditions of life. Meeting human wants is not like the meeting of "more basic" bio-physical needs

---

[15] Joseph Campbell, The Hero with a Thousand Faces, 1949, P. 289.

of life. Human wants are ill-defined and infinitely expansive. The watchword is "more." Many businesses are based on expanding this more.

Industrialization applies machine logic and mechanization to provision of goods and services. In the beginning these are to meet tangible human needs.[16] Much of the labor required to maintain bio-life has been replaced with machines.

Industrialization responded to a call for more plentiful sources of food, water and shelter, and served to allow expansion of the human population. This called for and allowed an exponentially expanding industrialization. This expansion was then squared with industrialization moving to also meet human wants. Wants are very different from the limitations found in the world of bio-physical needs. They are much more ambiguous, thus more ambitious. Wants lack tangible limits and controls. In essence they are virtual[17] and easily move beyond methods of self-control. They can expand infinitely. Self-regulation, via the thinking of Socrates and Lao Tzu, offers the best form of managing human wants. Social-regulation can be effective in managing bio-physical needs. Socrates talked of this distinction, as did Lao Tzu.

Serious dangers have accompanied the expanding ideas of the industrial and the artificial. Approaching consequences seem deep and dangerous. Dreams of reason have helped spur this development. We see serious threats to systems of life as they evolve on our planet. The systems depend on conditions for life, conditions that have long been deteriorating, but now approach a point of change beyond the capabilities of human

---

[16] Now known as *cybernetics*, industrialization was also in the psyche of humans in Roman and prior eras of civilization creating. Coined by Norbert Wiener in 1948 as "theory or study of communication and control"

[17] Virtual is here used in the sense given it by Susanne Langer in *Form and Feeling*, 1953.

management. The evidence for this in the study was strong. If true, then business as usual will come to represent no business. Even human needs will no longer be met.

B) *Problems of managing consequences of meeting insatiable wants.* If the first challenge, that industrialization emphasizes the problems between humans and nature, proves to be correct, then the second challenge is how humans deal with the changing conditions of life from challenge one. Industrialized changes can be clearly seen as detrimental to continuance of life. How then can or should humans respond to the situation prior to mortality? We know all life is mortal but does it need to be such at the more systemic level, say of a species? In addition, we know of the entropic quality of all the universe and its contents. Entropy was not the concern of the research, although entropic processes emerged as important to the deterioration process being studied. Via entropy there is an essential deterioration underway regardless of human actions, presence or absence. The problem, as confronted in this work, is that human actions, especially those associated with economic thinking for fulfilling human wants, seem only to add to the entropic process.[18] Per Georgescu-Roegen's work we see how virtually all economic thoughts and acts only speed the entropic process. So much so that it human youth begin to see the industrial process as an entropy machine. If all this is so, then how can we hope to govern, regulate, control or even deal with the first challenge as outlined above? This presents us with a second challenge. It is sufficiently serious as to take us beyond human capability to correct the industrial process. If we simply stop industrialization, a process at the center of our definition of the "good life," do we also stop that life?

Thinking in dimensional terms was seem as helpful to explaining the results to some participants in the research. This was where charts

---

[18] The Entropy Law and The Economic Process, Nicholas Georgescu-Rogen, Harvard Press: Cambridge, 1971.

were used to demonstrate how humans seem limited to thinking in one dimension at any time, as depicted by a line with two ends. This seems to have been a limitation through human history as seen in the limits of dichotomies, oppositions, politics, arguments, Catch-22s, ultimatums, etc. Humans tend to formalize conclusions from one-dimensional thinking in two dimensions of presentation. Herein verbally articulated conclusions are generally written as two-dimensional sacraments on sheets of paper by those most educated in two-dimensional legal writing, now known as legalese. Next, we act out our understanding in a three-dimensional reality. The espoused end is enhancement of human life, and, less poetically, adding to the universal entropic process that manages all things as it moves them irreversibly in time into a 4th dimension. This implies that human's best hope appears to be moving regulation from the 2nd dimension into the 5th dimension, where humans cannot go.

If you can understand the above, you are smarter than I am. Regardless of my limits it is obvious that the challenges arise from systemic problems in connections, not those in parts as amenable to reductionistic analysis. Unfortunately, our education is in avoiding or not noticing that which is systemically connected. We continue to rely on industrialized analysis. This continues in the late 1940s development of cybernetic systems that now call for development of AI. The research shows there is no "post-industrial" transition underway. The research also shows this to be an important part of the environmental deterioration problem. The second challenge, how to manage the consequences of gaining intended and unthoughtful results, is large. Can the problem be managed by those who created it via their using the same analytic logic that created it?

Most humans seem to think yes, and support responses being called environmental protection regulation. We can regulate by making its existence illegal, as was done in New Jersey, or, more realistically, pose large threats upon those that create pollution if they do not manage it to make it harmless. We now begin to see from the study that the second, more realistic, option is also not part of any world we inhabit. Regulation begins with funding expensive and extensive research using the best analytic minds available to apply the best analytic models. As a model of science, this is expected to arrive at the best methods of regulating. These have been shown to be effective as they analytical determine pre-determined causes of post-determined effects, all while applying the best of scientific methods from the 19th Century. Problems in this are now emerging.

If the problem is by its nature systemic then by definition it is set up to fail if guided by results of analytic thinking. Study results herein show that not only may it not manage the problem but may well worsen the situation of which the problem is only a part. Another approach is needed. Important herein are questions about values and value systems that lie underneath all of the above-mentioned choices.

Herein I disregard the excuse that humans are incompetent and in need forgiveness. The human attitude towards nature and the supporting actions are clearly derogatory and now sufficiently dangerous to the context of life to require urgent change. What can be done, how should humans change, where should change begin? Let's begin with the dominant problem solver of modern society, regulation. This has become the general means to respond to evidence of a societal wrong being done. From bi-polar beliefs and/or analytically filtered evidence regulation is drawn up by those with limited beliefs, no science and analytic filtration as acquired in law schools. This is done in the cause of creating social regulation against the cause of the effect. Western society is quite proud of the results of this for organizing and improving society. It has been attempted for about a decade in use to slow and then reverse environmental deterioration processes. The evidence for what this brought society comes from the research project mentioned above.

Regulation efforts are seen in the factories, refineries and company headquarters that assisted with the research behind this writing. The evidence shows regulation was too little, done too late, and often seen as counterproductive? My responses come from evidence in a two-year research study of various national systems of regulating environmental protection. Some who helped with the study believe it may now be too late although to others it may appear as too early. Those most concerned were industry representatives who knew most about the role of industrial by-products and how they don't just go away. On the other hand, the lawyers as politicians in the United States, simply disappeared once a law was passed, or commented in the study: "Sure, the law has problems, but we will put it out there for a year or two then bring it back in for repair. It's hard to predict these things." There were agency people that knew more and better. They would point to serious problems for living systems from laws as written from analysis that had been limited. They would comment on the continuous need they encountered in lowering what was the tolerable level of pollution and deterioration.

One member from industry, an American, argued that current industrial practices will lead to fundamental change in our planet's climate. Two regulators, one each from Canada and Sweden, went deeper to argue that we will soon encounter planetary deterioration at an unacceptable level, as well as unresolvable scale. At that point solutions like pollution catchment, limits on population growth, halting destruction of natural terrain, etc. will be irrelevant. It was interesting that in the study no regulators trained in the law ever voiced such a deep concern for the prospects of environmental deterioration.

Humans have come to occupy a parallel world that they have created mostly from and in two-dimensions. It is commonly called known as the world of the artificial. In it we occupy an artificially constructed habitat that we define as superior to living in nature. We often go so far as believe the artificial is superior to living "with" nature. Where from does this human want arise? Is it genetic or acquired via mental constructs? Why do humans feel they want to or even need to be distant from nature?

Perhaps the ideology arises from the mentality of myths. If so, this will be difficult to address in that myths are often the unquestioned untruths of societies. Humans deeply feel they need to oversee their place in the world, a feeling that easily becomes a passion for being in charge of the world as they know it. We have developed a mythology that somehow guides us into opposition of nature. This is ironic, or tragic, in that we also know life is defined by and dependent up on nature? Perhaps since nature defined life to end in death, we do not trust nature, thus we are born in conflict with her? If true, this insight may give access to the world of human dilemmas in the human condition. It thus presents humans with *the dilemma* of their live and may well be beyond their reconciliation. Perhaps this is the source of human religions as comforting mythologies, as well as rationalization of why throwing a plastic bottle and cheeseburger wrapper out the window is a sign of strength, not simply being filthy.

Dilemmas are like Joseph Heller's *Catch-22*, where you are damned if you do or you don't, no matter what. It is also like Gregory Bateson's *double-bind that* invites schizophrenia in those caught up in it, especially if they are restricted to use of unaided-rationality. Or like West Churchman's depiction of the enemies of systemic thinking relying on that which is defined as rational, about 10% of Churchman's reality, while discounting or completely ignoring the other 90% in. This is ultimately what those concerned with the environment and our war with its natural governance face. Perhaps there is no way out. Elsewhere I've argued that we can start to resolve this via thinking in *both plus more* terms, where the rational and non-rational are combined to stand on in search of the vastly more insightful *more*. Herein I suggest we may find such in the 5th dimension, where humans are excluded.

Myth is here used in the sense of Joseph Campbell. He often lectured how myths are at the center of social-organizational thinking, be it for good or bad purposes. More succinctly, he suggested *myths are public dreams, while dreams are private myths*. Myths organize the elements that define the human condition and then the actions and activities that bring it about. Leading myths become societal stories that lead to satisfying human needs with echoes that expand to deal with human wants. Currently mythology is clearly connected to dreams of an industrial state organized by the sciences of the artificial. As we see how the current sense of industrialization is dangerous to the human context, we may well try to create a new myth. In the current situation we are entering a major dilemma with two aspects to it.

Part I is that nature is clearly not dependent on human wellbeing. Part II is that aspects of being human link back to present danger to nature's wellbeing, perhaps her survival. Arising from religious and cultural myths are stories and mentoring systems that favor ignoring nature or moving on to emphasize the un-natural dimension of life, the artificial. Within these myths are powerful entities that are not normally understandable except via the interpretations of a few humans, generally of the male version, that represent interpretations of nature via such myths as the Garden of Eden to explain nature.

Other humans, also men, offer an opposition myth that allows any to interpret the natural surroundings in a more objective manner, although any wishing to do so must accept the mythology of technology as generated via rational knowledge gained from science. Not that different from a religion this approach leaves us with unaided rationality to deal with that which is not required to be rational. Humans thus lack appreciation for the non-rationality of nature from the choices of the chromosome to the essential need of black holes to allow the cosmos to make sense, even if it is sense beyond rationality. These myths pose problems for humans relating to nature and ever appreciating how their activities deteriorate the environment on which both depend.

The human attitude to nature might best be envisioned as derived from a religion of "homocentricity," sometimes called a "religion of humanism." This religion and its closely held beliefs may well be the definition of the problem of 1978.

> "There is more than an academic reason for writing about the religious nature of humanism, for some of humanism's religious assumptions are among the most destructive ideas in common currency, a main source of the peril in this most perilous of epochs since the expulsion from Eden. Nor is the danger merely a potential one – to be characterized as the figment of a doomsday neurosis, and then dismissed."[19]

Ehrenfeld then goes deeper. He seeks the underlying characteristics of humanism as seen in the dominant human myth

---

[19] Ehrenfeld, David, *The Arrogance of Humanism*, New York: Oxford University Press, 1978, p. 4

> Because human intelligence is the key to human success, the main task of the humanists is to assess its power and protect its prerogatives wherever they are questioned or challenged. Among the correlates of humanism is the belief that humankind should live for itself, because we have the power to do so, the capacity to enjoy such a life, and nothing else to live for. Another correlate is the faith in the children of pure reason, science and technology. Although shaken in recent years and the source of much confusion among humanists, this faith continues to permeate our existence and influence our behavior....[20]

These are seen with great clarity in the work of Joseph Campbell in his inventory of human behavior that points towards the human passion to rise above nature and move towards an emphasis on tyranny, as it arises from the will to leadership in a society via the peculiarities of its culture.

> "They tyrant is proud, and therein resides his doom. He is proud because he thinks of his strength as his own; thus he is in the clown role, as a mistaker of shadow for substance; it is his destiny to be tricked."– (Joseph Campbell, The Hero with a Thousand Faces, P. 289)….."The hero of yesterday becomes the tyrant of tomorrow, unless he crucifies himself today." [21](Ibid, p. 303)

1.3 Entropy and Man's Future: Ignore, Deny or Defy

What is this entropy thing? What does it have to do with anything of the lives or humans or processes of nature? As one of the least taught subjects in all universities and most revered laws of science by

---

[20] (Ibid., p. 5-6)
[21] (Ibid, p. 303)

the most revered scientists it is worth understanding something of entropy and its role in in human and natural affairs. When I was Prof Eric Trist's teaching/research assistant in 1974/75 I would offer the following story to his MBA classes, to question their myths about the role of their species in the world. This was to reduce their arrogance implicit in their being accepted into a Wharton MBA program. I would begin with the question: "Assuming there is a grand design in nature, what is nature's purpose for humans existing?"

My often-used response centered on the concept of entropy. It is generally seen as a confusing concept often remarked as:

> Entropy: Something I had no idea about when first told, then began to understand it on second encounter, then knew I would never understand it when I met it the third time. Then, not being able to ever get over it on forth encounter."

I first learned of in via a confused instructor to my thermodynamics class at Iowa State University. For him entropy was the concept that he cautioned us to avoid at all costs, if we wanted to be successful. To me, it became one of the clearest construct that clarified much for me about humans and the universe. Unlike the Iowa State physics instructor, Einstein proposed that:

> "A theory is the more impressive the greater the simplicity of its premises, the more different kinds of things it relates, and the more extended its area of applicability. Therefore, the deep impression that classical thermodynamics made upon me. It is the only physical theory of universal content which I am convinced will never be overthrown, within the framework of applicability of its basic concepts."[22]

---

[22] Einstein, Albert (author), Arthur, Paul (author), Schilpp (editor). *Autobiographical Notes. A Centennial Edition*. New York: Open Court Publishing Company. 1979. p. 31

For Einstein, then Steven Hawking, the 2nd Law of Thermodynamics was sacrosanct. Per Prof Klein, Einstein was said to offer the following insight into entropy, believing it was sacrosanct. When then did humans avoid including it in their economic activities and beliefs on laws of nature? "What must the laws of nature be like so that it is impossible to construct a perpetual motion machine from either the first or the second kind?"[23] This is important to deterioration as most human activities around the ideals of industrialization act as if they are negative-entropy. Many leading scientists have gone deeper in arguing why they agree with Einstein, then Hawking, and feel so strongly about entropy is a supreme law of nature and must be factored into what humans do.

> The second law of thermodynamics is, without a doubt, one of the most perfect laws in physics. Any *reproducible* violation of it, however small, would bring the discoverer great riches as well as a trip to Stockholm. The world's energy problems would be solved at one stroke. It is not possible to find any other law (except, perhaps, for super selection rules such as charge conservation) for which a proposed violation would bring more skepticism than this one. Not even Maxwell's laws of electricity or Newton's law of gravitation are so sacrosanct, for each has measurable corrections coming from quantum effects or general relativity. The law has caught the attention of poets and philosophers and has been called the greatest scientific achievement of the nineteenth century. Engels disliked it, for it supported opposition to Dialectical Materialism, while Pope Pius XII regarded it as proving the existence of a higher being.[24]

Einstein once commented that if someone comes to you with a "neg-entropy" invention you best leave them alone. He did not

---

[23] Klein, Martin, *Science*, Vol. 157, 509, 1967
[24] Bazarov, Ivan P., *"Thermodynamics,"* 1964

go further into the consequences of having a bad understanding or entropy or of humans entering the world of the immoral via knowing of entropy yet moving into making and marketing of products as neg-entropy. In the class in question I would go further to describe how much of what is designed, produced and sold in industrial-based society focuses on, not just the possibility of neg-entropy, but its products being widely available. None-the-less, the universe remains subject to the entropy law and it is not to be defied by economic mythologies.

> The law that entropy always increases holds, I think, the supreme position among the laws of Nature. If someone points out to you that your pet theory of the universe is in disagreement with Maxwell's equations — then so much the worse for Maxwell›s equations. If it is found to be contradicted by observation — well, these experimentalists do bungle things sometimes. But if your theory is found to be against the second law of thermodynamics, I can give you no hope; there is nothing for it but to collapse in deepest humiliation.[25]

Back to the story that needs these definitions and quotation: Why did nature invent humans? Thousands of years ago nature encountered a violation of her entropy law in a pocket of neg-entropy in the earth. It was a clear violation of her supreme rule. She was unsure how to clean up the mess resulting from the violation.

The problem was that much petroleum from dinosaur remains came to be entrapped deep underground, and via entropy it could not be dissipated from a potential to do work and turned into the cold of disorder over time. That storehouse of potential to do work that was fixed in time was in violation of entropy, the 2nd Law of Thermodynamics. What was nature to do to resolve this contradiction to her fundamental law? She arrived at the idea of inventing a being that would go and release all that buried neg-entropy so a natural

---

[25] Sir Arthur Stanley Eddington, *The Nature of the Physical World* (1915), chapter 4

order could be arrived at. Within about 100,000, a very short time, she became pleased with her result – much of the petroleum was being released into the air. This being that solved her problem came to be called humans. She then only needed to await the distribution of petroleum into the air then she would get rid of these humans.

Students listening to this never seemed to laugh. This was and is a simple-minded explanation of much in our world and addressed the human-nature problem. Some express thermodynamics in simpler, more poetic, terms as four laws where the first and second are of most interest in the research described herein. They four are:

> Zeroth: There is a game.
> First: You can't win.
> Second: You must lose.
> Third: You can't quit.
> (Unsourced, simply often quoted in industry energy labs.)

1.4 Deterioration, Beyond the Entropic

The values behind the current state of humankind and its relations to the environmental are consistent with Newton's dream of industrialization based on reason. The concern behind this document are closer to Einstein's thinking and concerns about what men should and shouldn't do. This concern is herein centered on continuation of business as seen in business as usual. As such it is akin to the values behind a Native American proverb:

"We don't inherit the earth from our ancestors, we borrow it from our children."

Such a value, or the lack thereof, seems central to what humans do and the thus crucial to the problems articulated herein. For some reason(s) contemporary human's give emphasis to ownership of property to define their status, then move forward to borrow against the future of that property and those who will depend on it. The most that current humans do is to barrow against the past value of that property to take control of neighboring properties to demonstrate future wealth that isn't, all the while getting others to use it as it deteriorates. Clearly this leads to problems that now begin to be seen in small publications like the "Tragedy of the Commons."[26] Concern is now with general deterioration of and, water and air by the many for purposes of the few but the problem remains.

The deterioration becomes more serious with time leading to life-threatening conditions on the planet as initiated by human acts. Humans have come to ignore or have ignorance of the consequences of their actions, actions derived from an endemic desire for greater and higher results in ever shorter terms. The two-year Stockholm research project was conducted into this concern then sought two ways to regulate it. The project went well beyond studies of the effectiveness of pieces of regulation to examine the chances for success of analytic (short term) responses to systemic (longer-term consequential) difficulties. The results from the two years of work were clarifying yet troubling. This document attempts to present and explain these results.

The research was set up to examine the role of relationships in leading to long-term consequences of human acts. The relationships were between humans, between humans and nature, then between humans and their images of their selves. All the relations were analyzed with a clearly rational emphasis on cause-effect understanding of parts. This non-systemic approach was taken to help understand the mentality behind the actions, not the systemic consequences of those actions. That was examined later. The non-systemic was found to be based in a desire for stability via the values of changelessness. An alternative value set emerged from participants at the edge of operations; those who lived in a world of change. As a sign of there being a better way towards problem resolution the results of the study point to the clarity of views coming from the edges; those who embraced change and practiced fluid management of connections, not parts. Those bound by analysis could only see parts, not connections. Those thinking systemically came to mostly see connections while overlooking behavior of parts. As such, the project focus became critical of standard economic thinking, acting and fixing. on but did

---

[26] "Tragedy of the Commons, *Science*, 1965

examine how humans arrive at valuations; especially what and how they arrive at value of life?

Humans seem to be developing what is herein called the *human project*. In its essence, the current stage of development is seen to be based in Newtonian-directed industrialization values. These seek the mechanical rationality that can be seen in emphasizing causal results from backward analysis of effects. Herein this is seen as 1-dimensional greed as managed by 2-dimensional regulation based on paper. Ostensibly, the purpose of the human project is to supply for human needs with reduced human work all while encouraging humans to seek fulfillment in life through inventing and seeking material wants.

Meanwhile, humans tend to not notice, or not care, about the peripheral costs in the ever-expanding human project's environmental deterioration from one–dimensional thinking as seen in three-dimensional danger to life. This, added to the irreversible nature of natural entropic deterioration, pose serious problems for systems of living order. Early responses to this, by those humans who notice something amiss, is, once again, 1-dimensional ideas set out on 2-dimensional paper to manage the complexities of 3-dimensional deterioration. Those who seem to most understand the situation see all this as *a band aid awaiting surgery*.

The research was set up to improve understanding of the current situation, then to move to propose ideas for changing human values about human relations to their environment and the entities occupying it. Research results raised questions about control over emerging conditions, or lack of any control. Evidence suggested that humans lack control over themselves thus how can they hope to control consequences of environmental conditions they have changed? That became the research question after the research results were written up. Many reviewing the results responded that "tougher regulations and enforcement" were needed. A few argued that we need to await further expansion of current rude experiences from a deteriorating environment, to mobilize political action. Via this pain from "effects," humans would more efficiently work to identify and control the "causes." Then, the effects would be erased and the negative consequences to the planet would be avoided. In this way industrial production pollution and further pollution from use of industrial products would be taken care of. As such the human project could continue. The history of philosophy, science and humanism illustrates that this myth was not to be realized. Neg-entropy would not be discovered and realized.

The research data showed why this myth could not happen. Thus, significant changes to the human project and the values sponsoring it are needed. The roles of the analytic (i.e., the rational) and systemic (i.e., the non-rational) must be changed, perhaps even reversed. Without such the human project will come to halted by other forces.

There were two major research concerns. 1) The first was with the limits in knowledge of environmental deterioration in three dimensions, and the consequences of this in the fourth dimension. Hundreds of industry and university researchers in many countries pointed to the data for this in the project. 2) The second, and perhaps more serious, concern was seen in seriously humorous reliance on one-dimensional thinking to govern two-dimensional regulatory governance. This did not appreciate, nor have any chance to manage, the highly systemic domain of 4-dimensional consequences. It even failed to manage deterioration of the third dimension. Hundreds of governmental and legal researchers in several countries helped describe this dilemma for the human project.

The level of understanding in both problem domains seemed locked into the limitations of traditions in their respective domains. Both seemed to come from Paramedian and Platonic arguments for reality as changelessness. As they said, if it changes it is no more, thus why worry about it? It's like the weather. As such, humans continue to be troubled in conceiving of Socratic, Heraclitan worlds ruled by ideas of nature and natural change. The world of the artificial is paramount to the human project, especially artificial stability.

The science limitation comes from the reductionistic tradition set by Newtonian dissection and analytic methods to seek cause-effect two-dimensional relationships. In so thinking humans avoid thinking of death and related timetable dilemmas. These are of the four-dimensional effects of nature that lie beyond human powers or understanding. Concern for this came to be one of many shortcomings showing up in the research. One researcher pointed out how she felt trapped in the limits of her university education where she went to learn about nature but was instead taught cause-effect thinking was fundamental to knowledge. In this way she jokingly pointed out that what she learned from the fox chasing the rabbit allowed her to know that the rabbit was perhaps the cause of the fox. Prior to graduation she was encouraged to move to the edges of reality and appreciate, or even understand, the systemic phenomena operating there, e.g., nature.

Limitations beyond the simple-minded analytic were found in the second area, the regulatory. Regulation approaches were set up to approximate changelessness in a situation. In this way those having control over the situation could remain in control. The research evidence showed how the values of stability via changelessness were endemic to management of industrialization. The "externalities" of avoiding change were seen in the same dim light. Widely advertised domains of Platonic truth and justice, as the espoused bedrock of regulation, were seldom noted or noticed after graduation from law school. The two soon joined the trash pile containing any ideas of ethics. Ethics were quickly dispensed with in college. Students learned that ethics and the law were two very different domains and they should avoid the confusion of ethics and concentrate on warm certainty in the law as written. Ideas of including a larger setting in a more systemic manner, such as including a wider social group as the problem, were simply side-stepped. More radical ideas such as including laws of nature in laws of man, or even including the natural environment in environmental laws, as the location of the problematique, were avoided.

Throughout the study it appeared that regulation was to maintain the operations of "business as usual." The often-used metaphor by those who knew was we need regulation to "keep the lid on things" until we figure out what is going on and what to do. To accommodate all these contradictions, regulation thus needed to absorb much ambiguity. This was specifically done via developing and relying on legalism as communication to those that expected more. Users and religious adherents of the American approach to the law, i.e., words on paper, and the essential basis to regulation, argued how even if laws are not written clearly they did allow a bit of room for movement; i.e., essential deceit needed in and out of regulator's offices and courtrooms. To non-lawyers this tactic becomes obvious with time. Non-lawyers would easily see that the language of law, as "legalize," was essential to hide what lawyers fail to know and cannot express even in two-dimensions. Knowing this it is easier to why one-dimensional enforcement becomes as clear as it is clearly counter-productive.

Problems with drawing up laws and enforcing them to solve societal problems was seen in capital crime and drug usage expansions attempted during the nineteen-sixties. The same limitations are now becoming noticeable in the environmental legislation of the late sixties and early seventies. Not only is ambiguity not to be avoided in the US approach to writing laws; it is essential to accommodate an almost complete lack of knowledge about a systemically connected terrain.

Thus, both science and regulation are trapped in the limitations of what Gregory Bateson called "unaided rationality." Both had a reliance on concepts like logic and accepted the serious limitations that resulted from using them manage systemic nature.

> To regain our place in the natural world before it is too late, we must give up our simplistic, quantitative science….and learn to 'think like Nature thinks.'[27]

Or, to be clearer about the everyday limitations on human thinking seen in unquestioned frameworks of thought we need on examine the funny basis for the serious concept of logic:

> "Logic; n. The art of thinking and reasoning in strict accordance with the limitations and incapacities of the human misunderstanding. The basic of logic is the

---

[27] *Mind and Nature*, Bateson, Gregory, Bantam Books: Toronto, 1978, inside cover

syllogism, consisting of a major and minor premise and a conclusion – thus:

- Major Premise: Sixty men can do a piece of work sixty times as quickly as one man.
- Minor Premise: One man can dig a post hole in sixty seconds; therefore –
- Conclusion: Sixty men can dig a posthole in one second.

This may be called the syllogism arithmetical, in which by combining logic and mathematics, we obtain a double certainty and are twice blessed."[28]

Moving to the broader context of limitations seen in social regulation, as we now practice it, we need only look at the extensive use of ambiguously drawn and interpreted regulations. One hint of how bad this is can be seen in reliance on 125 plus word sentences, where the writing seems to not know why they enter and certainly have no idea of how to exit. Following are guidelines to "help" those preparing Environmental Impact Statements to send to court and other places:

"Agency procedures shall also specifically include provision for public hearings on major actions with environmental impact, whenever appropriate, and for providing the public with relevant information, including information on alternative courses of action in deciding whether a public hearing is appropriate, and agency should consider: (1) the magnitude of the proposal in terms of economic cost, the geographical area involved, and the uniqueness or size of commitment of the resources involved...[29]

---

[28] *The Devil's Dictionary*, Ambrose Bierce, 1911, pp. 108-9
[29] *Federal Register*, US Government, Vol. 38, No. 147 – Wednesday, August 1, 1973m o, 20, 553.

The above 70-word sentence continues for another 90 words. Therein a humorously strong statement, that this law: "…shall also specifically include provision….", is soon followed by a noteworthy qualifier of: "…. whenever appropriate…." Seeming clarity, using ambiguous sentence structure to wrap around specific double-talk is seen throughout thousands of pages in this and related environmental laws and rules of enforcement.

When the research study results were presented to OECD by Sweden's Government, they used it to denote the "American approach to regulation." The Swedish alternative came from the quotation of the Swedish Minister of Environment: "We Swedes are, it seems, unusual in that we believe the first stage to get citizens to obey a law is to understand it." The US Head of EPA at the time, wrote me a letter of some hostility about this "nasty" comment. Others found the comment informative then insightful.

The study began in 1975 with direct knowledge of wholly ineffective results from 1969 legislation. Clearly, another approach was needed to begin management of harmful human actions on the natural environment, or, to at least prepare for consequences of continuance and mismanagement. Conclusions pointed to some hope in development of the positive nature of environmental appreciation for improving human-nature relations. The common practice in 1975 was based on legalistic punishment for being caught doing what a law deemed as wrong. The first approach was to encourage a search for better understanding and responses to problems in human relations and was called "business as unusual." The second approach was seen to be sidestepping of societal restrictions that were not well understood nor open to legalistic practice but came to encourage more "business as unusual."

Specific difficulties are depicted in some detail in the reporting of the research behind this document as seen in "Environment Protection: Analytic Solutions in Search of Synthetic Problems," 1977. This was published by the Institute of International Business, Stockholm School of Economics and presented by Sweden to OECD in raising questions about the legalistic emphasis in the US approach to environmental concern.

Leadership was found to be a key control factor in the study, especially with those given overriding authority to resolve or create problems. The study found that too much leadership was centered on those with a very limited education in the law as written by humans, i.e., lawyers, and/or in those trained to be on top a hierarchy as nurtured in business school education. On the other hand, those in direct supervision of production and governmental oversight were granted little authority yet illustrated a very different sense of environmental problems. Many impediments to business as unusual were set up in corporate headquarters or central government offices. This created dilemmas in narrowly conceived designs of production processes followed by similar regulatory means to control the negative consequences of it all.

Each model of design of course finds dilemmas but fixating then freezing a single model tends to worsen things as it is deterred from adaptation at the edges. There was much humor in the obvious contradictions revealed in the research, but the cumulative results were of course not funny. This was especially clear in US examples where there was the greatest fixation on one right way. In one state they encountered a problem with what to do with toxic wastes. The lawyers involved had no idea of what to do so they passed legislation that denied its existence. Within two years it had to be rescinded. In another state it was discovered that all wells in a region contained dangerous to life chemical. The seemingly irresolvable problem was dealt with via cutting off future funds to measure water quality.

1.5 In Search of the Artificial

Nature furnishes the external environment. Humans use parts of this environment to gather resources to create their own more private, homocentric environment. This is an artificial environment, one that humans appear to be proud of. Additionally, nature provides humans with their internal and evolving genetic code. From this breadth of relations why then would

humans hold nature in such disrespect. Where would we look for answers to this great dilemma? To address this, we need to look more seriously at the innovative breakthroughs that brought so many benefits and so much power to improving the human condition. This begins with the thinking of an Englishman, Sir Isaac Newton, and his impact on designing an industrial revolution. This brought artificially construed, rational processes to humans meeting human's needs. The process centered on a need to provide for bio-needs but rapidly expanded to meeting large needs associated with human life on earth, i.e., shifting from meeting needs to allow expansion of wants. This address long standing concerns for finding meaning in life. This allowed a means to answer questions such as: why we are here, where from do we come, where to do we go, what matters, etc.

There is clearly a mismatch between natural processes and human activities. In the early 1960s the mismatch became more apparent and was labeled as environmental deterioration. The human response to continuing deterioration was environmental protection regulations. Once regulated, humans continued adding to the initial problem via homocentric economics, seeming to not realize that deterioration and economics were interconnected. Natural resources continued as widely available and freely accessible inputs to an economic mechanism set up to meet human needs then provide for human wants. Most human lives were and still are employed in the entertainment of seeking and meeting wants beyond needs. An economic myth directs and manages the process, where myth is herein used in the non-derogative manner of Joseph Campbell. Via their myth of economic process humans work hard to formulate and attain economic ends. Unfortunately, there are problems in this myth. They used to show up as deterioration. Now they are becoming more serious.

There are serious limitations in the economic and scientific logic of two hundred years ago. These guide the way humans take resources from nature to use as inputs to economic realizations. The cost to nature for providing inputs necessary to what we call the economic process was discounted greatly, then simply disregarded. This began in an attitude towards nature written by men in early biblical teachings and then became firmed up in the later ideologies of Adam Smith and Isaac Newton. In this, there was a fundamental miss-match in human perception and natural reality. The major costs for the mismatch may well be about to come due. Can humans respond effectively, then survive the costs? Now the mismatch between nature and humans predominate economic model is more than simply noticeable. Regulations have not worked and may have worsened the situation.

Somehow humans came to act as if they have a project on the planet. Humans like to own what they walk on and be mission oriented to claim that ownership. Projects are a means to fulfill missions and secure ownership. The most significant project of humans was driven by the idea of the industrial, via Newtonian science, and came to be centerpiece in defining human achievements. This is the human project with a purpose of stabilizing the meeting of human needs. Simultaneously this created a threat to natural systems and their stability. Via a Newtonian logic of rational analysis, mechanistic cause-effect logic, and homocentric domination humans developed in clear opposition to nature and the natural order that we once looked upon as ecosystems. We now see humans trying to redesign genetic codes to replicate natural design, all while working towards creating a system of artificial intelligence to control and manage natural systems and natural intelligence.

Is this good? Based on the experience of industrialization so far, we have reason to be concerned in this direction of development. Can it have a good ending? Are humans capable of managing all this around us since they have yet to manage themselves? What is nature's role in the making of the artificial process and in the longer-term prospects of life on earth? Does nature occupy another dimension in the universe, or she only a struggling force in the third dimension to planet earth?

It's helpful to see how the human attitude to nature has evolved. Beginning in fright, then worship, then respect and finally to seeing nature as a servant to human use. Recently, some shame has surfaced in the human attitude towards nature. Some humans feel badly that humans turned nature into a depository for the backside of industrialization, where the deposits spread through the oceans, landscapes and air. Soon the manly attitude towards nature may well have gone full circle and turned to fear.

There are early signs of a justified fear by humans of nature, in the human perception of her. She is increasingly recognized as supplying the essentials of life. Some humility is returning to humans yet the signs of acting no this are scant. How to state this in a more recognizable manner to humans? One means is to note how humans somehow relate closely to religious metaphors, especially when thinking of that which we do not understand. Thus, we might say humans have "desecrated nature" via industrialization and now might best fear retribution from nature. Moving beyond this what is happening to the environment on which human depend and what best might they do to deal with the consequences of past actions? Or, is it simply too late to manage those consequences?

Even with signs of a human change on the horizon there is little indication that this change will bring a radical difference to our definition of the industrial. Computerization of the artificial will only further enhance its status with humans against the natural. We will still favor a 19th Century Newtonian paradigm of industrialization. It is hard for the human project to change the centerpiece of what defines that project. Industrialization has long supplied the goods desired by man and done so via a 19th Century paradigm of economics supplying human needs while marketing to its ever-expanding human wants. This seemingly guarantees continuation of business as usual even while the winds of a natural disaster approach. How best might humans respond, once they decide they must? Can we find a replacement to the industrial, to Newton, to Smith, to economics and to rediscover the role of the natural of which we are a part?

The role of human activities, especially bio-needs turning to economic wants, was derived from how we met biological needs. That approach left deterioration to the natural in the wake of achievement of the artificial. If nature was found to be important later there surely was an artificial recipe to "fix things." What was once seen as implicitly manageable, via more industrialization, now appears as explicitly dangerous to all life.

Our current best definition for meeting human needs, then moving to ever expanding wants, has turned quite bad and is now irreversibly changing the context of viable life on earth. Perhaps there is time for humans to change their economic values and/or their systems of production, and consumption, and valuation of the results, considering rethinking the human project. The best advice for humans just now seems to be developing an appreciation of nature and the larger cosmic context of life and the forces creating it. Of course, humans do not need to do such. They can continue with a business as usual approach until the context as stage set will become the main actor in the human play. As such humans will witness dramatic change to the essential conditions of life.

This is the context for the thesis presented herein and the driving force behind the research on which it is based. Those I worked with in this study tell me that by about 2020 the man-made impact on the natural environment will be sufficiently large as to be unavoidable and beyond repair. Humans will then experience the consequences of failing to improve their historic conceptions of business as usual. The research posed questions about human-capability for designing a learning-based means to change prior to human-managed change becoming irrelevant. There is little evidence for this possibility. Can innovation via business as unusual become the new standard? Can humans find a way to lessen the values of contemporary industrialization and redefine their vision of future business success to include the well-being of nature? Perhaps not. Options to better meet human needs while redirecting human wants are very exciting, but no one is reaching to develop them. Even adding computerization is little more than digitization of business as usual, faster. The war of the artificial against the natural continues.

Socrates appeared to offer the last best hope on regulatory context in Greece, but we should note how he came to end his life in a regulation event demanding self-inflicted poison. Likewise, Lao Tzu in China of the day offered an optimistic alternative to the normal societal emphasis on stability via control as argued for via Confucius followers. Regulatory leadership embraced Confucian thinking, even if it was unacceptable by most citizens, in that it emphasized stability of what was, not what should be, via central control. Lao Tzu instead gave emphasize to the continuous role of the normative, the becoming of what ought to be.

In 15th Century France Joan of Arc offered humans a different pathway to finding widespread societal leadership and governance. Her actions were consistent with teachings of Socrates and Lao Tzu but came to an end at age nineteen when the religious leaders of the day tied her to a burning stake to reflect upon her open disregard of their regulations. These disharmonies continue to be a part of societal development. In the 1970s an America version of leadership pasted a law to reduce the consumption of scarce petroleum. There were stiff penalties as threats to any who would be caught driving faster than 55 mph. This proved as counterproductive as the legacy it was based on. Some months later it was seen that the average driving speed was then higher than during before the threats were imposed.

Does history show social systems to be wrong in the idea of regulation, or having the wrong leadership with their ideas, laws, regulations, governance, and management? Such questions seem important as modern social systems as they face very serious consequences of the present on the future. Perhaps it's not the ideas of regulation that are at fault but the set of ideas at the center of motivating social systems. A central idea relates to the economics of short-term results achievement that will provide for human needs and wants. Meeting these needs and wants has somehow come to be a fundamental good of social systems. As such, ideas about regulation should not interrupt such economic workings but move into control what are called the externalities of the work. What happens if regulation is not able to control the approaching long-term consequences of humans having achieved an abundance of short-term results?

If industrialization is based on use of tremendous quantities of energy to provide tremendous quantities of goods to meet bio and psycho needs and wants, and the process of meeting those needs and wants becomes the cause of human death, what shall we do to "regulate" the problems thus created? It's not too late to raise this question but may be too late to answer it. Let us hope the human project finds a way to do well and turn from seeking ends that will end badly.

The human project has progressed far since humans emerged from the cave, or so humans have been taught and have come to believe? Humans, as one-time cave occupants, found their way out as portrayed in Plato's "Allegory of the Cave," then found new means to better provide for their needs while expanding a human need to satisfy their wants. Unfortunately, they failed to emerge from the limitations of human relating to each other and their environments as acquired in the cave. Put another way, humans did escape the 2-dimensional restricted on perceiving reality as shadow movement on the cave's walls. But they failed to lose their homage to or attraction of management via the confused clarity of simple-minded concepts of 1-dimensional polarization. Prisoners would sit in their entrapments and learn to pretend they knew reality. This setting provided the necessary and sufficient conditions for life and adherence to the reality of their limited experiences. Later in the human project would be known as culture where humans would accept harshly authoritarian governance to protect culture from change. Its pervasion and perversion were clearly illustrated in Plato's Cave via the sad experiences of any who left the cave and attempted to return to describe the bondage of those remaining in the cave.

The eternal dilemma of human relations to truth was seen in the behavior of those who would bring new knowledge back from the edges of reality to comment on the different reality of the cave. Leadership served as the protector of those left in the cave and the major impediment to their moving to a higher state of knowing. The power of governance and legitimation of regulation thus began and were further developed to instill and preserve the permanence of the culture of the cave. The idea of change as threatening and the governance that protected cave dwellers from it became major impediments to improvement of the human project. Both stood in the way of progression of the human project and the finding of differences that made a more relevant difference to improvement.

Most cave dwellers came to appreciate changelessness and its war on differences that could not be trusted. Leadership of a changelessness culture retained authority by pointing out that new differences were simply wrong, and perhaps evil. Interesting for the study of regulation as presented herein is how that at the edges of known reality could necessarily see how the beliefs of the core were wrong, and often silly. Yes, those at the core of a culture, its leaders and managers, would retain authority via this emphasis on differences out there that might be harmful, or negate the meaning of the culture. This included religions, governments, corporations and even scientific disciplines. The study of regulations illustrates these cultural differences as well as the ominous nature of challenges facing humans in not turning to differences that made a good difference in dealing with bad differentials.

Back to Plato's Cave. Humans continue to accept the ideological strait jacket forms of 1-dimension regulation/leadership noted by Socrates in Plato's Cave. Humans continue to accept a 2-dimensional interpretation of reality as seen in the shadows on the cave ceiling via finding legitimation in writings on 2-dimensional paper that get interpreted by 1-dimentional judges. The notion of moving on to a 3-dimensional governance scheme of virtual managers remains a dream, or unimaginable. This is more than a problem of effectiveness in dealing with the 3-dimensional reality we occupy, but increasingly involves the largely unknown and much unappreciated 4-dimensional entropic reality that threatens three-dimensional life. Humans seem happily uninformed as they move into a crisis while carrying the consequences of their behavior in the 3rd dimension into the irreversible 4th dimension.

To be fair, a few of the "regulated prisoners" did escape the bondage of Plato's cave and did come to experience a 3-dimensional reality beyond their 2-dimensional "Flatland". From this the mental leader of Plato's Cave, Socrates, could sense the pointlessness (A trait of the 0-dimensiont.) of continued 1-dimensional leadership in society based on religions not subject to questioning. Once outside the confines of the cave occupants could marvel at the nature represented by a sun passing through a 4-dimensional timeframe, although this vision made their eyes hurt and caused their minds to become confused. Two thousand years later humans would come to marvel at the 4-dimensional entropic movement of time in nature. While we now begin to see this entropic arrow of time as leading to our non-existence, we now cannot conceive of a 5th- dimensional reality surrounding the entropic passing of something into nothing.

As such, humans continue to occupy caves while making an environmental mess of life in the 3rd dimension as well as using economics to speed up 4th-dimensional entropy. This presents a potentially hopeless situation for the human future. Can human activities be regulated, or their consequences be otherwise resolved? This question grows louder with time and has greatly increased during the past two decades of the past two centuries. Underlying the emerging situation is a deeply seated human belief that nature furnishes human with a storehouse of resources for human use. As such dimensional differences to the realities of the human project and largely ignored as is the wisdom lying in the 5th dimension, a wisdom that may well make humans irrelevant.

Humans came to feel free of biological needs and having to negotiate with nature over them. Humans could relax and not worry about their need for food, water and shelter. Humans could avoid the historic feelings of terror towards natures' variations, vicissitudes and violence. Humans could then move forward to build a homo-centric project on earth, and beyond, and move the human project from meeting needs to satisfying human wants. Human projects could be counted on to simply do better and better without end via human science and technology, without any meaningful restriction. Better and better than more could be the end in themselves. This could become the myth defining the meaningful human end state.

The research this is based on suggests a different sense of the context of humans, its condition, and its probable future for humans. Research carried out with the Petro-chemical industry and its governmental regulators suggest that what humans have done since leaving their caves may well have insured a dire future to the human project. Our best hope now seems to be returning to renegotiating with nature, but in a more ominous manner. Unlike life in the caves, restricted to seeing a 2-Dimensional flatland of images on a cave ceiling, the renegotiation needs to begin from a re-appreciation that there are important dimensions to life beyond the two of flatland. This include the environmental dilemmas emerging in the 3rd-Dimension that call for knowledge from the context provided by an irreversible entropic 4th-Dimension. Since context matters to understanding we must do more to understand the context of the 4th-Dimenion; the nature of the 5th-Dimension and its meaning for humans. Just now our primary emphasis of on the economic potentials found in the third dimension, over which humans believe they have homocentric authority. Crucial to this control is the idea that humans can own and regulate property ownership. Most constitutions are drawn up with property ownership as a central tenant of regulation. This may make sense in the 3rd Dimension but lies between silly and becomes deadly in any 4th-Dimensional fast forward via limited wisdom of the homocentric. To survive, it seems that the human project needs to appreciate the context provided the 3rd Dimension by the movement of the 4th Dimension. As such the 4th Dimension requires appreciation of the 5th Dimension, whatever that may prove to be.

1.6 Can Humans Access the 4th Dimension?

The sad potential in using traditional regulation in a new round of negotiation with nature is suggested herein. It will not be easy. More innovation is needed in the process. It will need to exceed the self-imposed restrictions humans have put on regulation via life in 2-Dimensions and its faith on what is written in a 2-Dimensional legal order. In it, humans have restricted the idea of potential harm to the strict logic found in 2 Dimensions. This is the domain West Churchman described as representing 10% of human reality. It is the same world taught in law school while depicted by Gregory Bateson as that which is within the sad limits of unaided rationality.

We start in the 2 Dimensions portrayed as reality as shadows for those restricted to Plato's cave. As such humans protect themselves from nature via manufacturing industrial-produced homes, manufactured consumer products, and industrialized agriculture as food. Humans can then move to concentrate on inventing new wants, needing new industrial products, and market ever more tangents of love. This process pretends stability yet portents crisis from the limitations of mechanized thinking leading to replacement of innate wisdom by seeking ever more intelligence of the artificial.

This stimulates total arrogance ending in total ignorance. Is there a way out? is a way out necessary? How does nature relate to wisdom?

19th Century Industrialization thinking has become the potential for and the limitation of the human project. Is industrialization the best we can do? Is Newton's approach to industrialization as war on nature the best we can do? If humans remain a part of nature isn't this a war of humans against humanity. Is industrialization of the artificial the best we can do? If so, what is its end point? The model of industrialization criticized herein is from the stability hoped for in 19th Century Newtonian formulated presumptions guiding humans to see nature in a way so that we could control nature. The environmental deterioration results now pose considerable threats to life.

The tenants of Newton used herein begin in how 1) all effects can (even must) be traced back to their causes; then go on to argue how 2) force must be met with counter-force; 3) Euclid's Law of Parallels is fundamental (and it offers visual and static stability in designing an anti-natural, artificial environment); 4) success in human interactions (e.g., economics and other shared behaviors in pursuit of wants) is defined as the shortest distance between two points being a straight line (i.e., Adam Smith); 5) all things are understandable as a hierarchical structure (Herbert Simon's basis for receiving a 1978 Nobel Prize for the economics of Bounded Rationality and his argument for Artificial Intelligence.); and 6) life is neg-entropy (where action in a cesspool exemplifies the potentials in finding negative entropy in crating life as seen in Prigogine's 1977 basis for non-equilibrium thermodynamics and the basis for his Nobel Prize).

These Newtonian ideas operate in the zeroth, first and second dimensions of humanly defined realities. An argument will be presented, based on data from a two-year study of efforts to regulate the Petro-chemical industry, that we need to find a management doorway into the third dimension via an appreciation of the arrow that defines the fourth dimension and then the appreciate the humility necessary to sense a yet to be described fifth dimension, as therein lies the hope of negotiation with the forces of nature. This agenda is as challenging as it seems to be essential to the species.

1.7 To Manage the Human Project in Five Dimensions

Accepting that a human project is underway on the planet dare we ask if it has a mission, or even a discussable direction? Yes, religious and science bibles, such as Darwin's, suggest a purpose and direction for the species but besides using nature and/or researching nature what is the end point? While references these works are not the subject here. Herein we concentrate on the challenges in our utilization of natural resources to meet basic human needs and then evolve to feeling better by realization of the economics of human wants. This is not about economics or finance but the basic industrial processes that economist try to manage without understanding then fall back on finance to fill the gaps is our subject. Just now these are the limiting dimensions to human life on the planet. Finally, how does the human project get beyond these limitations and their consequences?

The ideas that structure our current reality come from a rational tool kit organized around a technological logic, a logic steeped in Newton's cause-effect thinking via Newtonian metaphors cloaked in the ignorance of nature. Behind this you can see a religious attitude encouraging nature's desecration. During the past two-hundred years of an industrial revolution we see where technological development given almost complete credit for advancement of societal affairs. Industrialization of the means of shelter building, food production, transportation and living has become the essence of the human project and its purpose. Crucial to this transformation has been the development of the sciences of the artificial. Imaging the artificial in defining and realization the mechanical has led to the fruits of industrialization, while heightening the war on nature. There is now discussion of the robotization of the human body to follow the mechanization and rationalization of the human mind.

All this had been derived from a continuous accessing of nature's stores of materials for product making, including houses, autos and connecting infrastructures. This is accompanied by ever expanded access to the energy required to make and use the products sought by human needs then human wants. More recently there has been an industrialization of agriculture. All this tends to refine as well as more deeply instills the values behind societies as well as how best to define human existence. All this was done to protect humans from the precariousness of nature via stabilizing natural change.

At the center of industrialization is the human project accessing, refining then consumption of Petro-chemicals. The Petro-chemical industry is at the center of the research on which the thesis described herein is based. It has made Petro-chemicals widely available to society in its development of the human project. In addition, it has recently come to be seen as a centerpiece in human efforts to regulate the cost to nature (i.e., externalities) of having and using these critical fuels of industrialization.

Humans recently began to be aware of unforeseen consequences to gains to the human condition from industrialization. Humans now begin to see consequences to extensive and expanding uses of Petro-chemicals in what we begin to note is environmental deterioration. The benefits of industrialization now appear to have costs as we see significant changes to environmental systems on which life, including human life, depends. This business as usual driving the human project is now beginning to be potentially dangerous to nature and thereby life which humans continue to have a stake in, regardless of emphasizing and greatly expanding the artificial. As such, humans are now expanding the role of regulation of the industrial and its products. One subject of regulation, to reduce the unwanted, has been on Petro-chemical industry. The research reported herein focuses on the aspirations, successes and failures of such societal regulation efforts. As will be outlined in some detail, the role of American trained lawyers in the success and failure of American attempt at regulation is critical to understanding failure. As Will Rogers said decades before: "The minute you read something you don't understand, you can be almost sure it was drawn up by a lawyer." In response the director of environmental concern regulation in another country commented on the 10,000-page USA Water Quality Act and attachments by saying: "We seem peculiar when compared to American lawyers. We believe the basis for a citizen to obey the law is to understand the law.

Therefore all environmental laws in our nation are written on twenty-five pages."

Social systems offer the subject herein. These include nation-states, cities, communities of interests, religions, cultures, political groups, companies, schools and families. The emphasis here is with governmental and corporate systems that negotiate via regulations concerned with consequences of environmental deterioration and its trajectory for the planet.

Much attention is focused on social organizations negotiating over the future conditions of life, but an argument is made herein that the individual actor offers much insight and energy for the discussions, especially as society realizes more the limits to social regulation. Individuals are the basic element of social organizations as well as the source of independent thought and creativity for trying something new when the old fails. When business as usual begins to break down individuals generate the potential found in business as unusual.

The role of the individual is crucial to improving what an organization does when its performance reaches its limits, then breaks down when the context becomes intolerant of its behavior. When an organization reaches its limits, it turns to individuals for repair. An early systems scientist, Andras Angyal, noted that when a system reaches its limits, the parts assume the whole. This is noteworthy in that some contemporary social systems seem to be approaching or at their limits. Organizational limits are herein defined by their relations with and to a context. In the research this thesis is based on context is essential to determining limits.

Since industrialization humans generally turn to regulations for solving problems of systems. This generally involves discussion, note of effects, speculating on cause(s), marking a possible path to solution, then drawing of written laws or rules to manage the detected cause. For example, if too many citizens are seen to be consuming too many mind-altering drugs then laws against their use will be drawn up. Of course, this will exclude the drugs designed and distributed by major drug companies then prescribed to patients by licensed doctors. Only when the first stage fails do humans look at the much larger activities of the drug companies and the doctors they are related to.

One consequence, not considered at the beginning of the regulation, is that the process of governance of drug use will be less than successful thus requiring expansion of prisons to house those who fail to obey the regulation as promulgated. Where a forbidden drug intersects with prescribed drugs the legal process will attempt ignore those said to be legal. To do otherwise makes the legal process unworkable. This model of regulation is largely derived from a Newtonian model of reality and use of its metaphors. Newtonian thinking and Newtonian based regulation is mostly restricted to 2-dimensional imaging that derives its legitimacy from laws as written and emphasizes the 1-dimension that points to the law as written.

Humans sometime raise their eyes and make use of a larger set of resources available in 3-dimensional reality. While it is exceedingly rare, some humans (not those trained to be lawyers) even reflect on the impact of regulation in the 4th-dimension. This is the domain of the longer-term consequences of environmental deterioration. Those who find the 3rd dimension available to them often resolve their problem in need of regulation by moving to another location. Many who begin to experience the consequences of a problem, misuse the 4th dimension to away a solution, or see the problem float away. A few seek solutions beyond cause-effect by looking into the 4th dimension. Based on the research behind this writing there is reason to believe that the more legitimate solutions of problems of consequence are in appreciate of the 5th dimension. To date science cannot find this dimension. It is where there is understanding of the 2nd Law of Thermodynamics as seen to define the 3rd dimension; i.e., that gives time its arrow. Herein most discussion will focus on regulation activities generated in the 1st dimension and implemented in the 2nd dimension, with some 3rd dimensional conclusions suggested.

This document mostly ignores those operating from the pointlessness of the 0th dimension, although some examples of their problem-solving capabilities are given. One is where the state of New York tested many wells on Long Island and found them all polluted and in need of repair. Since there was no known repair at an affordable cost the regulatory issue was resolved via removing the funds for further testing of wells. A similar result came from a New Jersey law saying toxic wastes could not exist in the state.

On occasion, humans face phenomena beyond the capabilities of laws as written, movement in space, and movement in time. This calls for imagining of the 5th dimension of reality, a place human imaging, even imagination, is ill-equipped to enter. This may become important to realize in face of the most ominous situations facing life and living. In this domain the idea of regulation seems trivial, as does the capabilities of governance. As such, other kinds of human conceptualization are required. Needed innovation often begins outside the social system, at the level of the individuals. Social systems tend to favor stability and thus prefer changelessness more than individuals. Throughout human history individuals arise from the organization to propose unorthodox ideas. These individuals are later called leaders but even the idea of a leader being able to resolve an ominous situation may now be diminished. Leadership is now mostly associated with entertainment and/or wealth, and not management of crisis.

These days' societal leaders often create chaos, not resolve it. Thus, humans may want to go light on awaiting leaders to resolve serious social problems. Herein we will not turn against the idea of leaders resolving environmental challenges but will see individuals as those, when stimulated, can generate ideas on improvement that a total system does not.

Individuals are essential parts to an organization yet are viewed as suspect by that same social organization. Those emphasizing the maintenance of an organization worry about those who talk of reconstructing the organization or suggesting they will simply leave it and initiate a new organization. As such the social group is always concerned about what some individuals are up to. This can be seen in how the first group makes use of the latest technology to covertly monitor the second group while the second group uses the same technology to openly communicate with the total organization. When change is needed in regulation this distinction will be important. Opponents to regulation are often seen as anarchists. This is not helpful, nor accurate.

CHAPTER 2

Regulations

2.1 Humans Regulating Humans

ON THE REGULATION OF SOCIAL ORGANIZATIONS AND THEIR MEMBERSHIP

Organizations continually fear their individuals will move into an anarchistic posture, in the French American sense of the term, where chaos is the consequence. Who knows, individuals might destroy the organizational core. They stored capital wealth would thus be disassembled. This sense of anarchy is opposite to the sense originally given by Greek philosophers. Therein it was the individual being co-managed in partnership with nature, as in "the sailboat without rudder." The individual as anarchist as an early warning system stationed at the edge of social organizations that would informs the whole of a need to change. Individuals like Socrates, P. Kropotkin, and M.L. King illustrate the importance of such.

But there are major dichotomies between social systems and their semi-independent members. It is important to understanding these to then understand the dilemmas in social regulation. The difference between the social group and the individual is fundamental to understanding larger issues of governance and where and why they turn to regulation as a tool for problem control. This is just now important as we may be encountering a problem that is not open to regulation or governance. Perhaps only individual appreciation of the problem and their personal role in it can unravel it.

To lower the suspicion of the social system towards the individual members individuals pass through public educated to learn to be subservient to the social group. This is seen as important to the functioning of social organizations. Individuals are often seen as capable of objecting to the social group and are thus a target for social intimidation. Regulation is the dominant means of control. Some individuals are potential anarchists, i.e., as threats to operations of the group. As such, they need to be carefully watched, some must even be imprisoned. Socrates, P. Kropotkin and M. L. King illustrate the essence of the problem posed to a social system by an intelligent and highly moral individual; especially in an immoral society. Such individuals operate at the edge of the social system, and never in its core. Sometimes a system moves to embrace the thinking at the edge to survive but even then, the anarchist stays at the edges. Such people are essential to a social system that needs ominous change and on occasion the human project requires very drastic movement.

Why is this in an introduction to research into regulation of environmental deterioration? As deterioration expands from an acceptance of environmental desecration and the consequences therein the dangers become more three-dimensional and noticeable. Just now we begin to see signs of change in four-dimensions. A new form of response to this seems urgent. At the root of all this is a deeply held belief in ever expanding industrialization, and expansion of the artificial. It is an expanding war against nature where the end is to ever more serve human needs and then move to satisfying human wants. The resulting societal acceptance of natural desecration supports deterioration leading to environmental pollution. The way out will involve a critic of societal acceptance of desecration. This will involve an appreciation of human-nature relations and rethinking of the cost of industrialization. This is best done at the individual level as worker, employee, consumer, shopper and citizen. As individuals like M.L. King have illustrated the societal context is slow to appreciate what is obvious to the individual. Evidence from the research behind this work shows how innovation and improvement is best seen and implemented by individuals, especially those at the edge. Expanding society regulation seems to only worsen a situation in need of change. This change is seen in the consequences of industrialization. The interest behind this paper is with where lies the power directing humans to do what they do, and how can that power be managed to do better?

RESEARCH, TO SEARCH AGAIN, FOR THE THESIS

This writing is derived from a relatively large two-year study done at the Stockholm School of Economics into best means to reverse environmental deterioration that ended with evidence that there were no known means and the consequences for the planet would be severe. Regulation of social systems was the emphasis in that two-year study and will be the focus herein but presented in a way that is less optimistic then the beginning of the study. Global warming, acidification of rain, changing climate conditions, plasticizing of the oceans, etc. offer no reason of optimism in the consequences of human behavior.

Concern herein is with attempts to regulate societal systems to enhance the societal good and reduce the bad. This is a heavy agenda, often done badly and generally directed at individuals seen to be not doing good by societal definition, those of other races, religions or low incomes. Such individuals via regulation are coerced, threatened or simply forced to change their behavior via trivial to serious penalties on their lives. Those who write such laws then set up means and methods to enforce them are at the center of the process. The process has many names but herein we shall call it "legalism." This comes from those at the center being trained in the profession called lawyers.

Our central question herein is: how successful can legalism be in "forcing" individuals to behave in ways that are in opposition to what their culture has trained them to do and be? If teenagers have been taught that they are breaking some unimportant law by drinking and driving, but it's sort of okay if they are careful, drive slowly and don't get caught, or are stopped by an enforcer that is a former classmate, much like happens to their parents, then what is the social harm? Viewed in another way, what then is the value of legalism except to gainfully employ lawyers, where the United States has about five times as many per capital as its trading partners? Then, we might ask which is a stronger regulator of behavior, laws as written and enforced by narrow professionals or cultural behaviors that are widely acceptable in and used to define the culture?

Where the law, as written by lawyers, is unsuccessful are there alternative modes that can work better? Ought they be written by non-lawyers as happens in some other countries, or is there unwritten regulation that works better? Or, is the best hope to practice good for society come from change to the culture and its definition of good?

The next deeper question then becomes: If a set of cultural ideas provides the economic goods and services necessary to a society and goes deeper to define societal success in wants ownership can it be changed? This begins in a perception of what is socially desirable and undesirable, and then how this viewpoint thus relates to any definitions of good/bad in a context seen as relevant, perhaps even meaningful. Context is thus crucial to regulation effectiveness in that it is basic to any and all evaluation.

There is much yet to be known about context and its emerging growth in importance. A few scientists have noted that context seems in motion and with time the movement is becoming more rapid and less predictable. Using time, space or prediction of cycles no longer can keep necessary stability in human context. That work of Emery and Trist in the mid-sixties set the foundation for what is now accepted as a genuine concern for societies. Thinking of our surroundings as a stage set for human acting Emery and Trist suggested that the stage set would increasingly become the subject of the play, not the human actors.

Before concentrating on environments and their emerging turbulence we need to see the variations available to any who analyze: 1) the desirable/undesirable, 2) the good/bad, and 3) the right/wrong. All three have a relationship to cultural world of the artificial but a bio-physical link to the world of nature becomes more noticeable with time. As such we need to improve our ways of including differences in values, morals and operations in are study of regulation methods but not in their segmented analytic sense. They need to be viewed as whole with the parts systemically connected as a network of operations, not a hierarchy. Appreciation must cut across all three not set up in isolation so each can seem to contradict the others. Legalism often relies on this approach as well as adding other methods of ambiguity.

Ambiguity in what is written and what is adjudicated can become crucial to allow the good and right to be undesirable. Analysis via segmentation and reductionism are helpful to future ambiguity, especially where it is used to obscure an ominous event that is approaching. This insight is helpful to see much of what is addressed in this work, but it may raise questions irresolvable by humans.

For shorthand purposes let's assume desirable activities are those seeming to enhance life, while the undesirable seems to denigrate life, and the living. The deeper problem dealt with herein comes from evidence that recent regulation activities set up to control fundamental relations between man and nature, relations growing more dangerous to life with time, are not working.

EVALUATION OF EVOLUTION

The distinction between the good and bad is of course important but will only be referenced herein as a doorway into the darkness posed in Goethe's Faustian Struggle, a battle that says much about the challenges to and limitations of societal regulation. This is where humans generally seek short-term promises while ignoring the long-term consequences of having realized those promises. More poetically, this is the long-standing human fantasy of concentrating on work for short-term rewards while hoping the long-term costs will evaporate, be resolved by new technology, or pass on to unmet or unknown others. For example, via industrialization and extensive use of energy and materials to gain products for human needs it is widely known that there will be and are long-term consequences. These pile-up as environmental deterioration and as they pile up more, and are more ignored, they lead humans into a culture of environmental desecration. This desecration becomes central to an economic process where we alter resources taken from nature for products essential to human needs for food, shelter and security, and then expand on the process to satisfy human wants. In more scientific short form this is where we create products for now via our ideas of negative entropy while rapidly expanding entropy's arrow into the future.

This provides a context for the work presented herein where the work focuses on explicit then implicit difficulties in regulating human dilemmas in their search for the good and bad, then seek ways to govern the differences. Central to the governance as it is now practices are laws that are written and quickly adjudicated, then abdicated. The record of success in solving problems via regulation is questionable at best, nonsensical on average, and deadly at worse. Unjust laws, written with analytic precision about small parts of very large wholes can lead to problems larger than those initiated the laws. They can lead to warfare, as well as an uninhabitable context for life.

FOUNDATION OF REGULATION'S PROBLEM

Interest is with regulation efforts to manage individual activities to induce the species to do well by doing the good. At the center of this is the question can humans be effectively managed if they have free will, or belief in expressing it? Or, is free will the key to individuals rethinking who and what they are in breaking away from the idea of "follow the leader" no matter how mistaken he is? Regulation, is viewed herein, is seen as a human response to a challenge arising from leadership that has led wrongly and governed mistakenly. This is especially apparent where regulation is based on laws written in an esoteric manner by people trained in law schools to pretend what they cannot know to protect the community that does not understand. This was clearly illustrated in some American refineries in a non-American location that were far cleaner than the same kind of refinery was in America. In America the water quality laws and attachments were written on ten thousand pages. In the other country all environmental laws, including water quality, were written on twenty-five pages. The success in reducing environmental deterioration in that country was remarkable. When asked, the Head of environmental quality in that country was asked why they restricted their laws to twenty-five pages. His response: "We are funny about regulations. We believe the first stop to obeying a law is to understand it." His American counterparts were upset with this response they called "naive." The dilemma for the Americans so commenting was that the later results in the non-American facilities were far better than what the Americans felt to be "sophisticated".

Special emphasis is herein on an emerging class of relationship difficulties that appear beyond human methods of control. Current definitions of leadership seem incapable of adequately describing the difficulties except to say they seem to arise from nature and might have been initiated by industrial activities. Humans are gradually accepting that the difficulties pose a danger to systems of life but in the longer term. Many describe such difficulties as being complex but are being worked on to make them understood. This depiction seems unhelpful in that the research explicitly seeks to describe the effects then move to the causes. Seldom are they discussed as systemic difficulties. Complexity is often in eye of the beholder, and not intrinsic to a lightly understood systemic subject. When we posit that our relationship to another human is complicated, we usually mean he/she is wrong, but we don't want to say so. We imply that the relation contains a network of culturally incompatible issues that we avoid unraveling, as we know of no solution therein. It may be the same in human-nature relations in that we fear the economic consequences of no longer seeing nature as a store house of resources for our willful use, or a dumping ground for that which humans have used.

The class of these challenging relations includes how humans have related to nature and then, how nature is redefining her relations to humans. Humans have long ignored nature via a culture defined by industrialization. This did not involve complexity but did involve ignorance based on past cultural beliefs from such wisdom as that suggested in biblical advice such as: "go forth and use offered resources." Now humans meet the consequential feedback from nature, but with no known means to manage the consequences from the human environment. Research behind this thesis shows regulations applied to this problem area were someplace between ineffective and exacerbating of the challenge to find resolution.

Relations can always be "complicated," even complex, but this mostly implies the relations in question are outside the current capability to understand them. In some instances, this can be explained as a viewer desiring to see an analytically stable hierarchy instead of seeing a systemically organized network in constant change. This is not a criticism of colleagues but a suggestion we carefully consider Gregory Bateson's depicted of a limitation built into modern human thinking. This is the limited thinking process he titled: "unaided rationality."

There is a more reflective process that seems to emerge in the youth, those pre-teens that sense the arrival of a new pattern of relations. It is as if they come from another world, not one that humans own as their human project via a contemporary culture of knowing what is and isn't reality. The emphasis on rational meaning as sent to us in thoughts of Confucius, Plato, Kant, et.al., now seem insufficient to the challenges of emerging relationships of the systems we occupy. As such, regulations are a doorway into another place, not the means to control the place we now believe we occupy. Most human endeavors, such as attempts at regulation, must be based on learning at various levels. Bateson's model as paraphrased in Figure 2.1 shows its importance.

There are many categories of relations involving humans. Some are between humans and humans, often labeled the social. Others are seen to exist between humans and nature where previously the relation was battle between humans and nature, where we look on it with pride as the industrial was destined to release humans from the needs given us by nature. Now, with less pride over time, some humans note that the relationship was a Faustian Bargain of the long-term payment for some short-term gains. The gains were freedom from needs, access to fulfilling wants and the human project headed towards happiness. The longer-term consequences were

<u>Human Learning, or not, Comes in Five Levels</u>

Zero learning - No learning takes place here. The activity is characterized by simple and direct responses, which, regardless of whether they are right or wrong, are not subject to any change or correction. (For example, there is a command and control simplicity, where hierarchical orders are given and taken without question.)

Level 1. learning - This is change in aspects of specific responses. Correcting errors of choice is allowed, but only within a narrow range of alternatives. (For example, alternatives to a set of project specifications are allowed, or given.)

Level 2. learning - This is change in the process of Level I; such as making a corrective change in the set of alternatives from which a choice is made or change in how the sequence of experiences are punctuated. (For example, there is a moving between assignments, or learning to do a variety of jobs)

Level 3. learning - is change in the process of Level II, e.g., a corrective change in the system of sets of alternatives from which choice is made. (We shall see later that to demand this level of performance of some men and some mammals is sometimes pathogenic. This could involve redefining the sexual habits of men in a protestant community, or to have those building nuclear power stations to switch to photovoltaic stations.)

Level 4. learning - is a change in Level III, but probably does not occur in any adult living organism on this earth. Evolutionary process has, however, created organisms whose ontogeny brings them to Level III. The combination of phylogenesis with ontogenesis, in fact, achieves Level IV. (This would involve people learning to not go to war, to achieve a new relationship to nature.)

Figure 2.1 Learning Types

environmental pollution and deterioration that would close the entire human-nature relation. A third relationship is becoming as disheartening as the second. It is where humans as individuals confront themselves, their nature, their own character and what it means. Even with the aid of shopping, drugs and entertainment the meaning is largely found insufficient. This is the world of the psychological.

Regulation is supposed to resolve problems in these categories. There are laws against humans hurting each other, except maybe for few restrictions on use of guns, and laws against environmental pollution being put in nature and some drugs put into humans. Closer examination shows serious shortcomings in this process of regulation. For example, in 1972 it was agreed in the US that there was a serious problem in pollution passing into water systems from industrial production facilities. The laws were primarily written by Senator Muskie and his staffers. When they all were interviewed they pointed out that: "Sure we knew there were problems in the National Water Quality Act we drew up, but we decided to simply get something out three to deal with problem, then in a " year or two drag it back in and fix it based on knowing more about it." This seems okay, except in 1978 we still await its "suitable repair." Except for sending industrial facilities to other countries little has been accomplished in water quality improvement, or even stabilization.

There are many problems within and between these categories with some of them very serious, even deadly. Humans often resort to regulations out of fear of consequences from problems, simply to get hold of the problems as they see them. The general objective is to stabilize the context needed for life; i.e., to gain back control of that which seems to control the human project as it is contemporaneously defined. This process is not necessarily bad but if it is designed via analysis, as based on analysis, and deemed analytically beneficial it leads to deeper instability and hopelessness. In the research that the thesis herein is based on the following example was found. In the early seventies water pollution was found to be a significant threat to life and human well-being. The Environmental Water Quality Act was framed passed and implemented. Senator Muskie and his staffers were central writers of the Act. When interviewed he and his staffers argued: "Sure, we know it is not the solution for water pollution now occurring but we want to just get something out there to see how it works and then drag it back in and repair it in a year or two when we know more" of how to do it. It awaits repair.

Much evidence for success/failure of regulation can be gained for the three areas via inquiring into the relations between humans and their artificially constructed environments. These include the industrial framework within which most humans live and define their success at life. It certainly includes the industrial plants and energy organizing facilities on which the industrial project depends, but also includes the organization of products from those plants and the energy use such projects require. This includes enlightened design of man-made environments to inspire independence within collective forms of social organization. It also includes the attempts at regulations in all the above, including building materials laws and their enforcement. Relative to the thesis mentioned in the opening we even see problems in governance of that which humans understand or should understand since they created it. Instructive of this point US Supreme Court cases on building products regulations. They conclude in their review of this area this it is the most corrupt area of regulations they have seen. Perhaps they say this about all areas they study? Regardless, please take note that there are serious problems in laws, regulations and governance everywhere. Many of these come from the limited knowledge of the legal professionals trained to manage such as abstractions. This is not what is covered in this document. The concern here is with emergent issues that are not appreciated, not those issues of judicial conflict as humans have come to understand the role of regulation in the human project.

Humans take greatest pride in that which rises above the limitations and restrictions of nature as they perceive nature. While also being part of nature humans seem to be working on a project to control and even eliminate nature. There is a growing reliance on this are of relations between humans and their artificial environments, especially the computerization of human activities. Surely regulation will be applied in these areas of human relationships and their governance.

Difficulties in relations can be depicted in various way but generally rely on economic, political, judicial and personal terminology applied within and/or between the subject areas. Most recently, difficulties in human relations with the natural environment have emerged in human consciousness as of potential importance although presumed to be less important than economic relations. During times of drastic societal conflict, e.g., wartime, the emphasis is with man to man relations. After war the emphasis moves to the consequences of that war and attention centers on the psychological and then its relation to the ethical. As the consequences of man-nature relations become more apparent this area of difficulty is likely to be more a focus and a greater target for resolution via regulations.

2.2 Perceptual Environments leading to the Conceptual

Langer's comments give insight to two ideas, both of which we encountered previously: the idea of conception, and the idea of perception of things. This set of distinctions is crucial to this dissertation and the research it is based on. An appropriate starting point for examining the significance of conception, perception, rationality, and non—rationality lies with the model of C. G. Jung for categorizing people. The model is based on four functional typologies by which consciousness obtains its orientation to experience feeling, thinking, intuition, and sensing. Jung's definitions follow.

1. Feeling — "When I use the word 'feeling' in contrast to 'thinking,' I refer to judgment of value - for instance, agreeable or disagreeable, good or bad, and so on. Feeling according to this definition is not an emotion."

2. Thinking – "...people who used their minds were those who 'thought' - that is, who applied their intellectual faculty in trying to adapt themselves to people and circumstances."
3. Intuition – "In so far as intuition is 'hunch,' it is not the product of a voluntary act; it is rather an involuntary event, which depends upon different external or internal circumstances instead of an act of judgement."
4. Sensing – "(Like intuition, sensing is) more like a sense—perception, which is also an irrational event in so far as it depends essentially upon objective stimuli, which owe their existence to physical and not to mental causes."[30]

For Jung, feeling and thinking are dominantly rational functions used for "ordering" and are the product of voluntary mental events. Intuition and sensing, on the other hand, are dominantly non-rational functions used for "perceiving" and are the products of involuntary human events initiated by the physical world. Rational functions are triggered by the human mind, while non-rational functions are triggered by the environment. Both aspects are important for regulation in complex environments. Jung's summary of the four functions outlines the importance they could play in social regulation,

> Sensation (i.e., sense perception) tells you that something exists; <u>thinking</u> tells you what it is; <u>feeling</u> tells you whether it is agreeable or not; and <u>intuition</u> tells you whence it comes and where it is going.[31]

The appreciative mode of regulation developed within the dissertation rests on the integration of all four functions. Jung thought that everyone tended to emphasize one or the other of the functions. By including a wider set of individuals in a regulation process the conditions for accommodation of all four functions are enhanced. Grounding the mode of regulation in negotiation enhances the potential for interactivity between the functions. This should enhance

---

[30] C, G. Jung, 1964, p. 61.
[31] Jung, 1964, p. 61.

the potential for integration of the functions. This takes the social regulation system well outside the traditional realm of limited human rationality. On the other hand, some individuals are strongly advocating movement towards a <u>more limited</u> sense of rationality for dealing with problems like environmental deterioration. One example of this, which tended to typify a large section of the governmental thinking within the U.S. version of environmental protection, is offered by the proceedings of a Congressional Committee looking into regulatory problems in controlling environmental pollution. (Their discussions were dealing with obstacles to effective rationalization of problems in the environmental protection domain; e.g., economic, administrative, conceptual, etc.)

> Foremost among those obstacles is EPA's attitude toward its statutory responsibilities. Often it has been too timid... The range and strength of EPA's opposition suggests the need not only for EPA to pursue its mission more aggressively, but also for Congress to provide additional means by which EPA's activities and opposition can be monitored... Finally, EPA should adhere more closely to its statutory mandates.[32]

The individuals making the previous comment had been reacting to evidence given about dilemmas which were building up in the environmental protection regulation efforts to that date. One bit of evidence, presented from a Federal Court decision, which they had found especially distasteful was,

> Questions involving the environment are particularly prone to uncertainty. Technological man has altered his world in ways never experienced or anticipated. The health effects of such alterations are often unknown, sometimes unknowable. While a concerned Congress has passed legislation providing for protection of the

---

[32] "Federal Regulation and Regulatory Reform," an Oct. 1976 report of proceedings from the House Oversight Subcommittee, pp. 150—151.

> public health against gross environmental modifications, the regulators entrusted with the enforcement of such laws have not thereby been endowed with a prescience that removes all doubt from their decision-making. [33]

The point of departure here is towards enlargement of the view of rationality, or failing in that attempt, to include, within a social regulation process, enough of the non—rational factors so that their characteristics can be accommodated. The limits of strict rationality are proving to be too restrictive to accommodate the multifaceted events we perceive in the empirical world. This is in accord with the idea of U Thant (1971) that we must radically change our present systems which are based on rigid divisions, where, "No rigid system, however well-established on a few sacrosanct principles, is able to cope with all the problems of our diverse, complex and constantly changing society."[34]

The conceptual environment, as it is used here, refers to Rapoport's (1974, p. 51) sense of the "symbolic environment." The perceptual environment in turn refers to his sense of the "physical environment." In the physical environment, man's actions are not that different from other animal's interactions with their environments.

> Overall, however, man's interaction with the physical environment differs only quantitatively, not qualitatively, from corresponding interactions of other animals with their environment. A house is but an elaborate nest, A superhighway is an improved cow path...
>
> The other environment, the symbolic one, has no analogue in the non-human world. There are no precursors among animals of epic poems, monuments, preferred stock, protest marches, confessions, astronomy, or astrology.

---

[33] Ibid., p. 149, originally from ETHYL CORP. v. EPA.
[34] Toronto, Canada, Globe and Mail, May 25, 1971.

Clearly, the degree to which man has been able to modify his physical environment (for better or for worse) is intimately related to certain features of his symbolic environment, to science, for example. The symbolic environment deserves careful examination as, perhaps, the most important determinant of the human condition.[35]

The conceptual (symbolic) environment contains the psychological landscape and the assorted structures which man places or finds there. Dostoevsky concentrated on this landscape so extensively that he hardly mentions the physical landscape. The perceptual environment in turn relies on the physical landscape, where man also places and identifies structures. Man-made and natural structures found in both landscapes are important to social regulation. A thesis is advanced here that current modes of regulation limit themselves to the physical environment, in that it is more tangible and implies more certainty, especially the man—made portions of it. The importance of moving into the psychological environment is seen from the large role it plays as a factor inducing change, where to be viable a mode of regulation must be able to accommodate change.

Dimensional Behavior:
0 Dimensional – Pointless
1 Dimensional – A Point, Singularity, very limited
2 Dimensional – Flatland, the Word as Written, Printed Leadership
3 Dimensional – The Box, Space absent Time, Hierarchy, Promissory Leadership
4 Dimensional – Entropic, Outside Human Control, Negotiated Leadership
5 Dimensional – Differences that Matter, Wisdom, Outside Entropy

Table 2.2: Beyond the Context of Climate Change

---

[35] Rapoport, 1974, p. 51.

Individuals and organizations expend considerable resources attempting to control natural phenomena and their dangers as posed upon mankind. Herein, is a thesis looking in the opposite direction. It examines current modes of regulation and concludes that they are not very competent in management of limiting the effect of human acts on nature. More important to humans is a related thesis that no mode of regulation can control the mostly autonomous relations from humans upon nature resulting in what we now call environmental deterioration. The ostensible purpose of this control has been to increase the opportunities to satisfy human needs. The thesis of this paper raises questions as to how well current modes of regulation can accomplish this. The paper also attempts to enlarge the purpose of regulation to include larger systems of life processes beyond man—made ordering.

> ... [It] is indeed true that we have created an ungovernable world, in which the natural order and a man—made order are blended as never before into a system which can be neither interpreted by natural nor governed by man-made laws.[36]

2.3 Attempts at Regulating Humans

Two major pathways await humans in search of future success in relating to nature and the environment managed by nature. The challenge behind the work outlined herein is to discover evidence for which is timelier and offers more hope for beneficial change. 1) First is to institutionalize the means for humans to redefine self-interest via the dictates of environmental interest around different variables; variables beyond the limits of the Faustian Tragedy. 2) Second is give more energy to the traditional manner of improving within the limits of Faustian negotiation but then lessen the consequences via broader and harsher punishment to those with the most loses piled highest around them. In other words, this would be expanded governance of

---

[36] Vickers, 1970, p. 122

the state via tougher regulations and harsher enforcement of the most noticeably bad humans.

The first approach is based on significant self-learning to achieve contextual appreciation. Humans tend to learn best via experiences that are most rude and pose the highest danger. This is of course a dilemma in that it always requires the threat of more time being needed than humans have available. We are not very good at finding leadership that can manage this dilemma and this time around the cost side of the dilemma is much more significant.

As such it is most likely that humans will turn to guaranteed failure in the second approach. Those with the resources can avoid, and the rest can ignore it. The expression used for this damage control, as found in the study, was that "More regulation is sort of acceptable, especially if my lawyers can help me get around it or delay its impact on me and my work." This is coming to be the essence of business school teachings in courses on "strategic management." This will worsen the situation in the mid-term but maybe can serve to make the first option more viable in the longer term. Perhaps the terror seen from results of those trained in a Harvard B-School model of strategic management can then give legitimation to something we might call "consequential management." This would be fundamentally different. It would require appreciation of consequences of results achievement in a manner that would enhance seeing the downside of those flawed results.

Relations between humans and nature will undoubtedly become rude, but hopefully will enhance learning in ways that can bring more rapid change to the necessary. Even now, in 1978, we see ominous environmental conditions approaching but little sign of needed response being apparent. Maybe we can only await the rudeness that allows us to better appreciate the differences between the good and bad, as well as the right and the wrong ways. Much of history shows a heavy bias towards reliance on the omnipresence of the bad to seek or create the good. The approach presented herein is quite different from the tradition of science in using causal thinking to set up analytic models to find the bad, via articulation of effects, then elimination of the cause. In this case we humans are the cause. Will we thus eliminate ourselves? Will punishment finally be found to make humans better? There is no record of it having worked previously.

Humans have long had trouble with appreciation of the good, or even defining it. This is seen in Plato's Republic, Goethe's Faust and American leadership. None-the-less it seems that their remains a 90% bias towards societal problem solving via the punishment tradition. The statistical tradition of business research is part of this bias and is just as wrong. The opening question is: Is it better to complement and encourage the good or criticize and punish the bad? All statistical samples show how the second is more successful, but never why. This is from where comes the regulatory bias for problem seeking and solving. It is supported by not understanding the statistical mean.

Criticizing, then punishing, what was done is shows via statistical sampling to be more effective in getting participants to do better. If someone is complemented for doing good, without a regulatory requirement, the evidence shows that they almost always do less good the next time. If what was just done seems good, or better than usual results, then via the law of the mean that actor will be necessarily pushed down towards the mean via the next action. On the other hand, if someone does bad and is criticized for being bad, the statistical odds will favor their doing less bad the next time, due, again, to movement upwards towards the mean. Using "next-time results" to thus decide on options to take for improvement almost always fails. This project avoids such logic and the legalistic thinking it supports, as well as finding its highly predictable limitations on progress.

Perhaps the "waking up" option is most urgent, prior to encouraging right and/or discouraging wrong but that is not the subject herein. How best to help human appreciate an approaching storm by educating them is important but not our subject. Besides, past research shows that humans tend to learn best via rude experiences in the beginning of the storm. Once it seems too late, humans can quickly respond. History illustrates how humans primarily respond via option b above with option a coming later as part of societal education. In most instances option b, encouraging humans to stop doing bad, involves governance with its structure resting on regulation. This has become the favored societal choice in modern times. As such, regulation is the focus herein as a problem-solving activity. This is not done with a sense of optimism that regulation can avert the ominous situation now approaching the conditions of life on earth but to argue that current approaches to regulation seem assured of failure. Something more appreciative of the problem faced and more robust in the human response may well be needed. This may be a different form of regulation or a shift towards option a, a broad encouragement of humans to consider the good and innovatively work towards it. It is hoped that an explicit failure of the traditional of regulation will redirect humans to experiment with option a. The normal long timetable for this approach can be greatly collapsed.

2.4 Regulation Options: A) To manage the bad or B) To seek the good

Option b) emphasizes the doing of good. Option a) emphasizes punishing the bad. Society often elects option a) to avoid significant change, even when it is widely felt that society itself is bad. This is like changing oil in a car that ought not to be on the road. If the guiding principles of a society emphasize the doing of what comes to be bad, then can there be much hope for use of regulation to change their values to force them to do good? Probably not. Doing the good while avoiding the doing of the bad will be profound to any continuation if life on the planet, or so the research results on which this writing is based imply.

In simple terms continuation of life on this planet is based on the actions of humans while they live on the planet. Humans now emphasize strategic management in that they have come to believe longer-term strategies are more powerful than results achievement in the present. In that the definer of strategic thinking argued that strategy is deceit and to be successful with strategy one must not be transparent of honest then this thinking may simply bring higher dangers to the long term. It would seem humans need to replace the strategic management that replaced results management with consequential management. Those actions have consequences. Herein the results of human actions come with aspects of environmental deterioration where the processes surrounding environmental deterioration have consequences beyond the intended results. These are mostly referred to as "unintended" consequences, not because they are not known but they are mostly ignored and said to simply be "the price of progress" for the human project. Perhaps we can look closer at the definition given to progress prior to perhaps clarifying the sinister end to the human project, and humans?

It is unclear how to best to accomplish the first, to encourage the good in humans. Most societies introduced religious as vehicle to argue for and expand on the good side of mankind. dilemma therein was it attracted preachers and teachers, as well as many of the followers that were predisposed to the bad thus found the atmosphere of preaching the good an ideal place to practice the bad. The good generally exist outside religious precepts and education. Perhaps we are best served to not bother those who quietly demonstrate the doing of good as if they were unaware of the bad? Relative the second approach, the "encouraging" of humans to not do the bad they have a will to do. This is the world of governance, of regulation, and of leadership. Much more can be said about this world, then asked of it. As such learning of regulation is the emphasis of what follows via question such as: 1) what is regulation, 2) are there different approaches to it, 3) are some more successful at deterring the bad then others, 4) does it ever encourage those doing good to shift towards the regulated bad, and 5) can regulation ever work to worsen that which it intends to better.

CHAPTER 3

Changelessness and Change

Change is an aspect of the more encompassing concept of difference, where change is difference over time. Confronting the meaning of change outlines the basic function of regulation: to provide and enhance a sense of stability.

> The word change is in everyone's mouth, usually in a context which implies something either welcomed or inevitable. The word instability is seldom heard. Yet instability, not change, is the challenge of our time; stability, not changelessness is its primary need. It is essential to distinguish these two ideas, change and instability; for though they overlap, they are radically distinct.[37]

Regulation, both biological and social, should provide a structure for change to pass through. In its most desirable sense, regulation should provide progressive growth through adaptation to new environmental conditions, while still retaining a base for commonality of expressions and meanings. For socially meaningful regulation during conditions of environmental change, man needs to consider two domains of required ordering.

---

[37] Vickers, 1970, p. 121

1. Man-Made Order: Here man is the primary regulator, with ordering systems such as technology, techniques, laws, values, and communications, all of which rely on a commonality of human effort.
2. Natural Order: Here the primary regulation effort is beyond man's capabilities, although he does have some success in interpreting some of the components of natural order. One season turning into another, flood into drought, and life into death represent some of these orders.

Some of mankind's most recent developments in working to make the natural order more understandable have themselves generated complexities which impair human understanding. The steady increase in cancer related to increased use of chemical and biological agents, illustrates one area of emerging difficulty.

The history of mankind is keyed into incidents of interpreting natural phenomena followed by development of technology to better use nature. Associated with this have been social—organization processes in the realm of institution design which were making effective use of man's growing knowledge. Numerous intellectual disciplines and social organizations have been created to use specialized knowledge in many areas (e.g., laws of locomotion, mechanics, materials). These efforts have allowed for a vast increase in the variety and quantity of products available for man to insulate himself from natures' uncertainties. The problems that are now occurring point out that some of these products contain their own uncertainties. Perhaps of more danger though, is the possibility that the products which have offered man insulation have also isolated man. The isolation of man from nature may well have encouraged an estrangement between man and nature. This estrangement may also have entered man to man relations. (Considering man as part of nature would have predicted this event.)

As humans, we exist within a thin fabric of natural and man-made systems of order. During an earlier period of history man relied on non-scientific methods of relating to the natural order. Even though man felt that he could not then directly control natural processes, he felt he could indirectly participate in them by gaining favor with the "gods" in charge of nature (e.g., Sun "god," Rain "god," etc.). The offering of sacrifice was one dominant mode of "regulating" nature. Social orders were built around this mode of regulation, with prominence given to those men with the greatest potentials for communicating with the "gods," e.g., priests.

Through the efforts of men like Kepler, Copernicus and Galileo, it was demonstrated that some natural processes could be explained with scientifically reasoned knowledge. Man's perception of communication with nature was moving into the realm of tangible, direct control. The age of priests was being replaced by the age of scientists. Now we are discovering that mankind's reduction of uncertainties in our direct relations with nature might be responsible for increasing uncertainties in nature's indirect relations back to man. The environmental pollution aspects of the 1960s was one indication of the impact of the uncertainties.

The theory of regulation advanced in this paper does not advocate abandonment of human powers of scientifically rational thought. But it does advocate an inclusion of more of the non-rational domain of human understanding so that at least the limitations of current views of rationality become more clearly explicated.

Some of mankind's most recent developments in working to make the natural order more understandable have themselves generated complexities which impair human understanding. The steady increase in cancer related to increased use of chemical and biological agents, illustrates one area of emerging difficulty.

3.1 Changelessness, a Human Preference, against Natural Change

Humans have a general tendency to resist change. Leaders of social groups are often chosen in a social group by promising ways to avoid change, or even reverse changes. Common to most leadership was how they believed things were not so bad for them personally, and if substantial change took place the chances of them remaining in a good position were not good. They might not even continue as leaders. This came to be an important aspect of the structure for social responses to the second challenge.

Political and social science researchers tend to lessen the chances for construction change. They are even more timid then leadership and followership in social organizations. They warn us about the repercussions of "too radical" of change. Difference, for them, is acceptable, but seldom differences that make a difference. They generally find out that just now it's too early to motivate humans to seek significant changes in how humans define life and living; i.e., man-nature relations. Their attitude continues 2,500 years of arguing for reason over emotion, via such as Parmenides, Plato, Aristotle and Confucius in their tight logic to see then manage reality. Their logical emphasis on the rational, which has obviously become the predominant view of humans. It has provided for humanistic responses to challenging difficulties and generally comes to stand on the idea of changelessness as synonymous to reason. They go on to argued how change is unreal in their world; if something changes then via simple rationing it is no longer there. Thus, settle down. Why allow touches of romanticism and the emotion to obscure reason, and embrace change? In this way nature becomes defined and then treated in a peculiar way.

Bio-physical researchers, are, on the other hand, more emotional about their subjects of interest, and definitions of reality. Change is their definition of life, while changelessness is, of course, death. They side with philosophies of Heraclitus, Lao Tzu, and Kropotkin, and then 20th century scientists such as Einstein and Hawking in arguing for some emotion in passing above the strict rationality of Newton and his followers.

For Einstein and Hawking the entropy law and the change it governs in the 4th dimension, time, is far more fundamental to understanding the universe than Newton's belief in gravitational permanence. As such, this mentality is predisposed to see the arrival of the first challenge mentioned at the outset while Newtonian followers resist seeing it. Efforts to avoid seeing the change processes behind the first challenge, and even working to maintain ignorance of it, suggest a high probability of bad consequences in the second challenge.

Some scientists in climatological research areas,[38] which is part of the first challenge above, now suggest it is too late for humans to appreciate change enough to undertake modification of the humanistic traditions. Some historians side with them. They argue how the argument for why it's too early often shows up as evidence of why it's too late.[39] Goethe summarized the approaching consequences of Plato, et.al., in their attitude and how it would lead to an obvious end to humans via their emphasis on rationality and its sister, arrogance.

> "Man is accustomed to value things to the extent that they are useful to him, and since he is disposed by temperament and situation to consider himself the crowning creation of Nature, why should he not believe that he represents also her final purpose? … Why should he not call a plant a weed, when from his point of view, it really ought not to exist? He will much more readily attribute the existence of thistles hampering his work in the field to the curse of an engaged benevolent spirit, or the malice of a sinister one, then simply regard them as children of universal Nature, cherished as much by her as the wheat he carefully cultivates and values so highly."[40]

Two hundred years later Robert Pirsig expressed Goethe's concern as a basis of

---

[38] Hawking, Stephen, "I have noticed that even people who claim everything is predetermined and that we can do nothing to change it, look before they cross the road." From lectures, then published in his book, *Black Holes and Baby Universes and Oher Essays*.

[39] R.G. Collingwood, *The Idea of Nature*, Clarendon Press: London, 1946, and *Essay on Metaphysics*, Gateway Press: Chicago, 1972.

[40] Johann Wolfgang von Goethe, "An Attempt to Evoke a General Comparative Theory" in *Goethe's Botanical Writings*, Bertha Mueller, trans. Honolulu: University of Hawaii Press, 1952, pp. 81-84)

Challenge I above, before suggesting a synthesis of reason and emotion, which he labeled as the classical and the romantic, in order to avoid an impending catastrophe between humans and nature.

> Phaedrus remembered a line from Thoreau: "You never gain something but that you lose something." And now he began to see for the first time the unbelievable magnitude of what man, when he gained power to understand and rule the world in terms of dialectic truths, had lost. He has built empires of scientific capability to manipulate the phenomena of nature into enormous manifestations of his own dream of power and wealth – but for this he had exchanged an empire of understanding of equal magnitude: an understanding of what it is to be part of the world, and not an enemy of it.[41]

Challenge 1 comes from a rapidly expanding deterioration of the natural environment coupled to rapid expansion of the artificial environment. This endangers the context and its conditions that support life on the planet. The cause appears to be study expansion of the way humans strive to meet their needs and wants during the past two centuries. The industry and business conduct associated with this poses serious threats to systems of life on our planet. These appear to be far more dramatic than those suggested by Darwin in his *On the Origin of Species via Natural Section*. We now see that his articulation of the human project and life surrounding it relied on much that was artificial, i.e., a bias towards the evolution of humans, not the balancing requires in life's landscape (1859). Just now it would seem we need to take the second more seriously, making it the ultimate context for evaluation and scientific discourse. In so doing, relationships take center stage while industry and business become support actors.

Challenge 2, with deeper knowledge of challenge 1, thus occupies center stage in the unfolding human drama. Instead of a concentration

---

[41] Pirsig, Robert, *Zen and the Art of Motorcycle Maintenance*, New York: Morrow, 1974. Introduction.

on how nature is set up to select certain characteristics of certain species we would turn to questions of human-nature relations. As such we would revisit Rachel Carson's concern, not via the arrogance of humanism but as how does the current attitude of humans to nature bring us to a *Silent Spring* (1962). Carson's central concern, of semi-autonomous human actions endangering collective relationships between humans and their environment as supporter of their life, did lead to change. Unfortunately, the social institutions took a business as usual approach. Humans design environmental legislation, protection and enforcement. US educated lawyers follow the analytic script set down in the US Constitution. The whole called governance is divided into interest groups that will fight with each other in a continuing search for truth. As such, the US approach to regulations began in ignorance of Carson's appeal to be more holistic in relating to the natural environment, and less segmented then divided into interest groups. In the US cases in the research it was found that to be interested meant you were segmented and arguing from a interest; usually the interest that paid for the speaker's wellbeing.

Carson saw the problem in segmented human vision, not in nature. As such she saw where systemic connections as the definition of life being broken and returning to life as harm. Even worse, the legislation empowered the mental weaknesses of lawyers working via the restrictions placed on 2-dimensional papers after 1-dimensional arguments of a point. Their analysis seemed to enhance deterioration. EPA's award-winning pulp and paper plant in Florida, used in the research. Illustrated the difficulty of business as usual legislation and enforcement. That plant was deemed to have the cleanest air coming from production while the harmful chemicals were being collected and deposited nearby in a landfill next to a swamp. They eventually spread into the water supply, but that was being managed under other legislation and regulators.

Since the composing of environmental laws, as limited by human logic in the early 1970s, humans continued to rely on <u>business-as-usual</u> approaches to managing the expanding dilemmas from business-as-usual relation to nature. As such, the essence of what had created the problem was thus used to generate its solution.⁴² This is called the "legalistic" approach. It relies on a 19th Century Newtonian business as usual science model of reductionistic analysis. Herein rules are drawn up, the government funds research consistent with the rules and then uses enforcement as threats, via cause-effect science, to continue with anti-natural logic seen in unnatural legislation.⁴³ Since Carson's articulate of the relationship problem man-nature relations have become more precarious. They now include consequences of human acts to come back and harm humans, not just the natural context on which life depends. The wrongfully conceived legislation will most likely lead to evidence to be used against any government (societal body) interference in a social interpretation of going back to "Darwin's way.⁴⁴"

The second challenge now calls for research into why and how humans attempt to research the systemic relying on results of the analytic, then trusting rules written in legalisms that mostly mask the growing crisis from deeper development in the first challenge. As such humans attempt at regulations provides the focus herein. Potential results from its current pathway seems at least as ominous as what it

---

⁴² Senator Ed Muskie and a staffer were interviewed relative to their logic for writing the early environmental protection laws, especially the 1972 "US Water Quality Act."

⁴³ This logic runs in parallel to changes in scientific method, in moving away from positivism as the basis for the physical sciences. (*Methods of Inquiry*, West Churchman and Russell Ackoff, 1951. It was the same in 19th Century Legal Positivism arguing with 20th Century Legal Realism. The later legal Realists objected to a pretend objectivity of the former legal formalism with their positivist conservatism. Realists went on to point out that positivist judges were guided by blindness, or corruption, in believing in their own objectivity. They were shown to have private views on a case as well as not being socially neutral towards a set of cases. The same came to be built into writing of environmental laws, by ill-trained lawyers, then judged by ill-prepared judges interpreting, in the best light, what they didn't understand. Carson's concerns became lost under all this context. Polluters came to show disrespect to all of the above.

⁴⁴ Via case law this came to be interpreted as "survival of the fattest," to augment the interpretation of the science of Darwin's central idea, "survival of the fittest."

attempts to regulate. Research brings light on a long history of human failure in regulating nature, each other and themselves, going back at least, to limitations outlined by Confucius and Plato.

Perhaps it's too early to discuss regulation of a situation when humans only begin to see its ominous aspects? Humans only begin to realize the consequences of deteriorated human to nature relations in a deteriorating environment. Later, there will be more of a focus on results of a long-standing conflict human conflict with nature. Eventually they will discover how it arises from a longer conflict with each other necessary, stemming from inner conflicts with themselves. As such, humans will need to reconcile relationships in several important paradoxes. An early one will be how they relate to the natural processes that give support to continuance of life, while also prescribing their own mortality.

Not resolving the essence of the first challenge, human-nature relations, will halt the evolution that improvements in meeting that challenge hope to manage. Humans must learn to resolve consequences of their earlier actions in ways that do not exacerbate the initial challenge.

The first challenge, living through consumption of context, is briefly introduced here. The second challenge, to learn to manage continuance of life, is presented in considerable detail. The second includes management practices known as planning, governance, regulation and survival. Leadership is deemed as important to these; in that it defines them. From research presented herein humans need rethinking leadership. New forms seem needed. Practices most effective in reducing deterioration were seen governed by a very different mindset, one not taught in any schools.

We have become used to the long-standing arguments between dictatorial and democratic forms of leadership. Due to the nature of environmental challenges there is growing evidence of a need for a third model. Therein, the major role of leaders is to encourage traditional followers to assume responsibility for their own actions, in that the consequences are therein initiated and cannot later be reversed. This calls for a very different form of regulation of self, one where the effects of threats from the social group will be avoided.

If environmental problem causes are widely distributed, then eliminating and/or managing them may also need to be decentralized. From early concern about authoritarian leadership this idea was well stated twenty-five hundred years ago in China.

> "A leader is best when people barely know he/(she) exist, when his/(her) work is done, his/(her) aim fulfilled, they will say: 'We did it ourselves.'" (Lao Tzu)

The challenge from deterioration arose from the consequences of processes designed in support of humans meeting their bio-needs, e.g., food, clothes and shelter. Early responses to these needs were compatible to context. Later developments began to create a new context. These began to pose problems for the surrounding environment, problems that gradually expanded into the natural environment. Perhaps the consequences of this phase of human development were manageable via space and time. The far greater threats to the larger definition of life arose when production processes were greatly expanded in order to meet the more endless domain of human wants. These were different than bio-needs. They grew from human psycho desires for meaning in life; meaning that could counter-balance or obscure the human awareness of their mortality. Human wants, as programmed by human desires and despondencies, leads to desires without limits. Humans often use "things" to keep from seeing mortality and its implied meaning.

The human response has come to be called "industrialization." The mechanization of materials, processes and men to produce things. This relates to the first challenge mentioned above. The consequence of this is shown to have measurable deterioration consequences for the context of life. As a result, the situation of the environment that supports life is highly problematic. Humans now attempting to find a way to change industrial process is the second challenge, which is the primary subject of the following book.

The concept of industrialization was key. It began in a rather simple-minded manner, in design to meet basic bio-physical human needs. This began with farming then moved to factories. Via the questionable ethics of consequential marketing and strategic management the potentials of the industrial were noted then greatly expanded into the infinite negotiation with human wants. As such the practice of the industrial as unpinned by the rules of mechanization has grown into the single greatest threat to conditions necessary to continue life on earth. Something is wrong with the business model behind this. Herein you will find research on business as usual and how those most familiar with its shortcomings begin to favor examples of business as unusual. The first challenges arise out of the idea of humanism as a driver of the human project on earth. This is defined as:

Humanism – the religion of humanity," in the Oxford English Dictionary, or with more elaboration of the consequences of this attitude in Webster's Third New International Dictionary:

> "…a doctrine, set of attitudes, or way of life centered upon human interests or value:
>
> As a: a philosophy that rejects supernaturalism, regards man as a natural object, and asserts the essential dignity and worth of man and his capacity to achieve self-realization through the use of reason and the scientific method… b: a religion subscribing to these beliefs."[45]

From such a religion there will be difficulties, a major one associated with "religious acts" in need of correction but how will such be undertaken? This introduced the essence of the second challenge, and the emphasis found herein. It differs linguistically from the first yet stems from the same problematic base. It questions the low level of quality given 1st order results from industrialized business then goes deeper into the high and growing level of threat to life emerging in 2nd order consequences of the same business. The industrial was to be a rational process relying on machine thinking to save human labor and feed a business model to remove scarcity and restricted access to the physical dimension of life. It has instead become the greatest

---

[45] Webster's Third International Dictionary

threat to continuance that humans have ever seen. The challenge then becomes one of how to encourage a different model of the industrial and business as usual that that change the fundamentals of both. We see increasing signs that the usual is not working thus how best to encourage the unusual, the experimental, the difference that will make a difference?

We must first examine the social order. Herein we will do this via questioning of the legal order in society as set up to provide constancy and predictability. This area is commonly known as regulation. It is a means used to manage societal action via legal order established via threats to members of society.

There are additional challenges in how industrial and regulation processes are designed and governed. To date both have been managed with some pride via human values associated with analysis. Analysis underlies the cause-effect thinking that used reductionistic methods to segment reality so that causation can be ascribed to parts. Regulation of those causes follows the same non systemic values. Most modern industrialized nations are proud of this model. They tend to not notice that using the same logic to control a phenomenon as was used to create it tends to only work when it's not needed to work. This dilemma emerged from the research reported herein. This led of a call for a new mode of governance more in line with natural process then processes of the artificial. The largely ignored second is increasingly coming to rely on greatly improved knowledge of the partially ignored role of the consequences of the first. The first involves improved understanding of the harmful consequences of industrialization. The second requires greater success in efforts to regulate, i.e., control, the elimination of consequences and manage those that can't be eliminated.

Clearly, industrialization has become important to support meeting human needs. The key question becomes is there a replacement to or better form of industrialization that poses less danger to life? Next comes the challenges of how best to encourage the societal change that clarification of the first challenge calls for. A better support system of human needs is needed. Then a better means to manage such support systems is also needed. The first challenge comes from production, the second from regulation. This has traditionally been the activity of regulation, as primarily derived from lawyers. Just as with industrialization, its tradition is structured via mistaken beliefs and anti-systemic thinking. And, as with industrialization its repair must find and use more effective ways to detect and manage consequences, not just collect results.

The two challenges seem clearly linked in subject matter and methods. Both are heavily reliant on machine-age thinking, reductionism into parts, seeking cause-effect relations between parts, and avoiding the systemic connections and relations between all things.

> Example:
>
> We know humans have a need to communicate. They so do with their environments, their selves and each other. Industrialization provides many reasons for and pathways of direct and indirect communication while continuing to develop new means and reasons for communicating. Humans like to go out into nature to commune thus they remove sections of nature to provide roadways so individuals can drive their cars to visit nature. Additional means of communication are necessary for contemporary economic exchange, but also come via a cost to the larger environment and its systems of life. The emerging question becomes: How might we reduce the environmental costs of business as usual and reduce the irreversible consequences that cannot be eliminated?[46]

---

[46] This was the subject of a 1974 thesis in City Planning titled: "The communications alternative: From moving mass to moving ideas." University of Pennsylvania, Department of City Planning. Behind the thesis was concern for more rapidly increased entropy via ever expanding uses of mass and energy.

Herein, I will argue for a more fluid and less static approach to seeing the above and developing responses to it. This will be presented as a negotiated order to industrialization and its regulation. It is to work beside or simply replace the norm of industrial production and societal regulation developed via legal orders. How do we negotiate humans out of their individual autos driving to secure goods that built their self-esteem while leaving the environment with dangerous costs? Are there ways to communicate that are more economical, more efficient and offering of greater potential delight? Many fixed laws stand in the way of change. Many of those in the means of industrialization are derived from Newton. Many of those in the methods of regulation are derived in the writings of Plato and Aristotle.

Are we ready to negotiate with building ultra-high-speed transit that has shifted from Newton's straight lines as the shortest distance between two points, to Einstein's rule of seeking the path of least resistance? Then, will we continue to rely on fixed ideas related to regulations applied via the effects of threats?[47] Will a more expansive police and lawyer force imposing threats and punishment on those who disobey become more successful than it was in stopping midnight dumping of New Jersey toxic wastes, or national laws that required 55 mph speed limits to save fuel?[48]

Those wishing to respond to the first challenge might see how it arises from a human tendency towards the short-term and away from the resulting issues from the longer-term. With early industrialization it was clear that there were pollution side effects from producing goods as well as from their use. It was assumed that this would not be a major problem, as there seemed to be lots of land, and anyway with time humans could develop new mechanical processes to overcome the harm if it became significant. Then, the problem became very significant with time as responding to human wants as well as bio-needs was included in the industrial agenda. This expanding agenda became "infinite industrialization." The long-term consequences

---

[47] *The Effects of Threats*, George Kent, Ohio State University Press, 1967.
[48] Prior to the threatening law the average speed on 65 mph roads was 70. When the law became 55mph the average speed dropped accordingly, then, with time, the average rose to 75 mph.

became infinite as well. This might be summarized as a very large-scale Faustian Bargain with humans giving away much of life on earth for the short-term rewards in negotiating with human wants.

The second challenge addresses the image of the end-state of the Faustian Bargain, where the longer term becomes realized then humans seek corrective action, i.e., find and regulate the causes of the consequences from the effects of industrialization. There is a dilemma in this second challenge: The same model used to become industrialized is being used to attempt control over its consequences. This model relies on segmenting reality into parts to be carefully analyzed[49] into cause-effect chains of mythological determinism. The guiding myth worked well to motivate industrialization, but encounters difficulties in managing the realistic consequences.

The essential argument from this research is that we have not taken environmental deterioration very seriously to date. The deterioration mostly arises from desecration ideas towards nature. Where we have experiences harmful consequences, we have turned to the lawyer's approach to problem solving called legalism. Evidence shows how this often exacerbates the consequences, not control them. More effective in dealing with the fluid nature of man-nature relations is appreciation. Legalism seeks a legal order. Appreciation requires a negotiated order. It is more natural and more difficult for humans. In the research chats with those helping provide information it emerged

---

[49] This can be seen as reductionism and segmentation of an entity (e.g., human) and its environment leading to an anti-systemic attitude. Angyal cautioned us to always keep the human and its environment in a whole, that he called the "biosphere." He believed: "...the two (the human and environment) are interacting parts, not as constituents which have independent existence, but as aspects of a single reality which can be separated only by abstraction." (*Foundations for a science of personality*, Angyal, Andras, A Viking compass book: New York: 1941) In his work Angyal illustrated how the emphasis on segmentation, even as abstraction, created individual and social schizophrenia. To add to this weakness in science we see how cause then effect thinking weakens science. Some leading scientists (e.g., Sagan) suggest that in the universe effects can precede their causes, thus reality is much more interesting.

that the subject area may have a dimensional problem, that may have no solution.

The deterioration problem clearly acts out in a 3-dimensional space (environmental pollution and wilderness destruction) and then accumulates in the 4th dimension (further deterioration via entropy plus more). The best resolution would appear to lie in the next higher dimension, that may be the 5th, where humans have no apparent access. Thus, we are trapped in human activity paradoxes of the 3rd dimension, beginning with a feeling of hunger and seemingly ending in flushing a toilet. Nature and her rules provide the context for human activities while humans have a passion to ignore those rules or make them irrelevant to life. The results seem irresolvable, especially considering the subject of focus herein. We deal with this situation via 1 dimensional ideas-fixed in 2-dimensions on paper. Via these rules of law, e.g., constitutions, humans manage their frustrations and expenses from 0 dimensional points, or even occasional pointless with time. Our situation of life is becoming dire. We need to do better. Can we? The following reports on research into this question.

I sincerely thank those many individuals in private companies and public agencies who helped address the questions raised herein. The final reporting came down to ten companies and then concentrated on two nations with the most distinct differences in governance.

3.2 A Prognosis for Human Deterioration

The magnitude of the impending situation was seen as more ominous by those at the edges of where the problems begin, not those managing systems from the center. The same limitations were seen in the centralized optimism about regulation methods undertaken by central government, especially the almost blind optimism found in the framers of legislation, such as seen in an interview with a US Senator that had framed the US Water Quality Act. The ideas of allowing and doing more experimental approaches to facing the consequences of continuing problems were seen in those at the edge of a company's operations, where they reference a need for business as unusual. The research reports present examples of business as unusual from both business and government people. Both groups were concerned about the dangers to life on earth of failure.

Research results show change in human values and activities are needed. These are presented herein via the idea that we need to experiment to discover, in Gregory Bateson terms, differences that make a difference. We begin with relations of men to various entities, including self. It is obvious that the new businesses will need to be unusual and organized around different in ways that improve the situations of which they are a part.

The problem area is outlined via some unusual differences in that the current depiction of the problem seems to be unsuccessful. Serious aspects of the problem area emerged during the last decade and were then met with efforts at what was called environmental protection. This was where aspects of the larger human environment were seen to be harmed by human actions thus the response to the harmful effects came to be called environmental protection. This was where our environment was to be protected from us by us for us. The dominant means was via social regulation to punish or deter the humans seen as responsible for the human acts against the environment. This presumed continuation of business as usual with tangential laws set up to manage aspects of the business. This has not worked. The research behind this reporting goes deeper into from where the problem comes and then asks if there are other opportunities for humans to manage their relations to their environment.

At the most general level the problem is labeled environmental deterioration where it arises from the human ability to take advantage of their environment while ignoring the consequences. in order to better understand human responses. Much relates to current use of regulation to resolve societal problems to see if man help manage the emerging problem. Is regulation the most effective approach to managing problems that are systemic in nature and not well understood, nor appreciated? Current modes of social regulation predominantly attempt to restrict the undesirable characteristics of mankind. As such they are seriously limited in their ability to appreciate problems that are systemic. Are there alternatives to management of systemic societal challenges; e.g., threats to human existence.

An empirical research project was used as a focus in the dissertation. It was directed at the subject of human actions in industry and business leading to environmental deterioration. The inquiry dissected the issues of degradation of the environment via man to nature relations to see where the major impediments for change lay. As such the subject is conceptually described via four types of manly relations: man-to-nature, the man-made environment to the natural environment, man to other men and man to himself. No disrespect is intended towards women as the term men is used as an abbreviation of mankind in general, although it is obvious that much of the problem investigated in this research is derived from manly thinking. This four-part conceptual system is given specificity in the empirical focus on a variety of attempts to control pollution side-effects from industrial production facilities with emphasis on Petro-chemical production and use.

The empirical evidence is only outlined in this document. Those interested should consult the three volumes that reported on research results that were the basis of the dissertation. Those reports are under the titled "Environmental Protection: Analytical Solutions in Search of Synthetic Problems," Volumes I, II and III, published by the Institute of International Business at the Stockholm School of Economics: Stockholm, Sweden, 1977, Hawk, David.

The following is an attempt at conceptual realization of serious difficulties facing life on the planet; based on such we may see a better chance at survival of our species. Foremost are difficulties encountered in the US approach to carrying out environmental impact statements (EIS's) said to protect the environment. These illustrate limits in current operation of US environmental protection. From early warning signs in doing EISs the research was expanded to a global setting with an emphasis on industrial production and focus on Petro-chemical production and use. This was to set the stage to understand the effectiveness of current thinking about man's relation to nature.

Conclusions point to serious difficulties in how men related to nature and then in how they attempt to resolve the consequences via regulation, with an emphasis on the use of the mode of regulation I come to call Legalism. It and the analytic frameworks derived from cases was seen to be highly inappropriate to describing or even seeing the complexity. An alternative mode of regulation was seen to be needed and was seen to be emerging. Herein that more systemic mode is outlined and proposed for wider experimentation. Early indications show it to have been more effective in managing systems of networked problems beyond those artificially segmented. It is based on the need for appreciation of a setting followed by a more fluid approach to management of change. It attempts to create a negotiated order much like what is metaphorically seen in the science of fluid dynamics. It was seen to be more consistent with natural processes while leading to their further appreciation.

Conceptually this document can stand alone. The empirical basis is in the Institute of International Business, Stockholm School of Economics research reports.

3.3 The Problem Area

> As human society makes greater and greater demands on the earth's resources, the margin for error in the management of these resources decreases. As a result, a more and more interdependent, elaborate and fail—safe organization is required to prevent the system collapsing at the first perturbation. This need to prevent catastrophic breakdown could result in either a 1984—type social system rigidly structured and designed to "police" the activities of the individual to ensure the survival of the social organism as a whole; or a more sensitive complex system based on intricate models; or the world may "solve" its problems by war, famine or anarchy.[50]

The opening portion of the quote presents one stimulus for the problem area, while the closing portion implies a limited set of responses. The opening suggests a problem in man-to-nature

---

[50] Kneese, 1977, from the introduction.

relations, as explicitly seen in how the man made relates to nature. The closing part of the statement in turn suggests a poverty in man-to-man relationships. The man to nature and the man to man problem area distinctions are linked to the additional domains of <u>man-to-man</u> and <u>man-to-self</u> problem areas to compose an interlocked set which better defines the general dissertation problem area. The man to man social—organization and regulation aspects will be the eventual emphasis in the dissertation in that man's greatest potential for altering the others is felt to lie there. This is not to diminish the importance of the remaining three sets of relations, as they contain many variables crucial to man to man relations.

Man-to-nature relations gives insight into the values underlying man to man relationship problems. They also suggest entries into man-to-self difficulties. A sign of inter-locking shortcomings in value systems is seen in everyday phenomenon that is widely approved while seeming strange upon reflection. One example is the planting of "plastic trees".

The <u>Los Angeles Times</u> of February 8, 1972 described the efforts of County officials to install over 900 plastic trees along the medium strip of a major street. The trees were plastic because the depth of concrete planter boxes was not potentially enough to sustain real trees. The decision-makers also felt that real trees would not remain healthy in the location once they were planted. Two values are emerging here: that trees were felt to be needed and that they needed to be plastic duplications of real trees.

This "planting" activity does not present much of a definite conclusion about man to nature relations, except that it initiated considerable reaction from many organizations in the U.S. which presented their conclusions. Of special interest was an article in <u>Science</u> (1973, 179, p. 446) titled, "What's Wrong with Plastic Trees?" which lent strong support to the "planting" activity on the grounds that it "satisfied human wants." The evidence in the article implied that man's view of the world is, and should be <u>homocentric</u>, and that his relations with nature are satisfactory with that view.

Pursuing the homocentric value—set further, one can argue that most of the policies and institutions that were established to deal with environmental deterioration typify the homocentric attitude. <u>Satisfaction of human wants</u>, as a guiding value, appears throughout the legislative statutes for environmental protection. The most referenced, and perhaps the most significant, paragraph in the important 1969 National Environmental Policy Act (NEPA), is Section 102, Item (C). The responsible party shall

> include in every recommendation or report on proposals for legislation and other major Federal actions significantly affecting the quality of <u>the human environment</u>, a detailed statement by the responsible official on… (my underlining)[51].

With the "human" environment as the point of departure it is a short step to limiting discussions to impacts on humans throughout the follow-up court actions involving lawsuits against implementation of environmental policies. For example, the Supreme Court case of the U.S. vs SCRAP in 1972 points out that, (the Justices were noting the Interstate Commerce Commission's defense):

> Inasmuch as we conclude that our actions herein will neither actually nor potentially significantly affect the quality of the human environment, we have not included in our report an extensive formal impact statement.[52]

It now seems that unless environmental values can be tailored as to how they impact human wants, the courts cannot entertain them. Further, unless it is shown that endangered species are important to man's "biological" survival, it is difficult to justify halting a construction project which clearly satisfies human wants. To illustrate that an alternative approach is needed, Ian McMillan, a naturalist, writes on the California Condor as an example of human attributes beyond wants via looking at how Dubos views the situation,

---

[51] NEPA, Washington, D.C.: US Government, p. 2.
[52] The ICC's report, Ex Partee No. 281, at 314, Sept. 27, 1972.

> The real importance of saving such things as condors is not so much that we need condors as that we need to save them. We need to exercise and develop the human attributes required in saving condors; for these are the attributes so necessary in working out our own survival.[53]
>
> Conservation is based on human value systems; its deepest significance is in the human heart. Saving marshlands and redwoods does not need biological justification any more than does opposing callousness and vandalism. The cult of wilderness is not a luxury; it is a necessity for the protection of humanized nature and for preservation of mental health.[54] (Dubos, 1972, p. 166).

What does this have to do with planting plastic trees on a California street? It has been stated elsewhere that since Earth Day of 1970 our social value systems have exhibited a marked change. No longer do we value nature as an object of conquest, but we now consider it as something which man has deteriorated and now needs enhancement. I hypothesize that planting plastic trees in California is in line with the enhancement value as is our current mode of social regulation for environmental protection. A major difficulty is that current environment values are based on a continuing homocentric attitude to man—nature relations, except that man is now acting more benevolently. I further hypothesize that this does not represent an appropriate value change in that it will not correct dysfunctions in man's relations to nature. We require, instead, a value set which is in the interest of nature as well as man.

Laurence Tribe (1975) also criticizes plastic tree planting by hypothesizing that such phenomena are not a feature of man's industrial revolution mentality of the past, which has now been

---

[53] In Dubos, 1972, p. 165
[54] Ibid, Dubos, 1972, p. 166.

replaced with a new attitude of conservation, but a confirmation of the continuation of the industrial age value system.

> The perpetually green lawn and the plastic tree, far from representing the outcroppings of some inexplicable human perversion, are expressions of a view of nature fully consistent with the basic assumptions of present environmental policy. These assumptions, which are implicit in developing uses of policy analysis as well as in emerging institutional structures, make all environmental judgment turn on calculations of how well human wants, discounted over time, are satisfied.[55]

Evidence that his hypothesis might be true can be seen in the underlying conditions of a homocentric attitude. One characteristic of a homocentric viewpoint is that it leaves man with the limits of human reason. Doing so excludes the potential for dealing with the non-rational, of the softer values. To date, hard values determine the final decision logic. Hard values deal with economic efficiency through terms like employment, tax revenues, GNP, etc., and technical feasibility looks to: safety, capacities, project life, etc. Soft values on the other hand deal with less well understood areas of natural and biological systems, life styles, and aesthetical issues.

Another limitation of the homocentric approach is that it short circuits the dialectical means—ends process. This is where humans initiate a process with some idea of an end, but until the means begin to be specified, it is ambiguous. Through specification of a means, a new end might arise, leading to different means, leading to a different end, etc. Both ends and means involve values, where the specification process should result in mutual value adjustment of each through learning. This continual adjustment should be very much to the benefit of man and man's relations to the natural environment, but that it tends not to be is seen from the human tendency to simply turn means into ends in a short-circuited, reverse linear process. Relating

---
[55] Tribe, 1975, p. 719.

the homocentric approach to another portion of the means—ends problem shows the human tendency for everyone to simplify the situations he is part of by <u>centralizing the world around himself</u> so as to pursue his own ends. Emery and Trist (1973) call this tendency "segmentation," and describe it as a response to complexity.

Another problem with the homocentric approach relates to its use in the social domain of man to man values and relations. Emery and Trist term this phenomenon "dissociation," where it entails moving the short distance from man as the center of the world, to a select group of men as the center. Some have described this phenomenon as ideological boundary construction and maintenance (e.g., Goldman, 1972).

Another characteristic of the homocentric perspective Is that it heightens the difficulties which humans have with conflicting goals. This should not be a disadvantage to humans, but too often the complexity induced by conflicting goals leads to maladaptive behavior. Artificial goal selection criteria, as will be pointed out by the empirical evidence in chapters three and four, gives illustration to this tendency and lays a basis on which to build an alternative for social regulation. Specification of conflicting goals can illustrate a need for consensus on overriding objectives that can then accommodate a wider range of goals.

Building on this logic, an overriding value set is described in this paper that might be used to widen strictly homocentric viewpoints. The overriding values stem from a sense of life forms beyond humans while including man's potentials within the view. Man is present, but not necessarily at the center. Tribe speaks of one aspect of such a view,

> What has been omitted is, at base, an appreciation of an ancient and inescapable paradox: We can be truly free to pursue our ends only if we act out of obligation, the seeming antithesis of freedom. To be free is not simply to follow our ever—changing wants wherever they might lead. To be free is to choose what we shall want, what we shall value, and therefore what we shall be. But to make such choices without losing the

thread of continuity that integrates us over time and imparts a sense of our wholeness in history, we must be able to reason about what to choose - to choose in terms of commitments we have made to bodies of principle which we perceive as external to our choices and by which we feel bound, bodies of principle that can define a coherent and integrative system even as they evolve with our changing selves.[56]

In order to transcend the shortcomings of homocentricity we need to instill ourselves with a sense of reverence for whatever lies beyond human manipulation and control. That we do not now recognize this in industrial societies is pointed out by plastic trees and environmental policies which rely on man's utilitarian needs as the point of departure. Plastic trees do provide an aesthetic resemblance to natural trees, and they do offer decoration and shading, but they do not symbolize the infinite potentiality of nature and life. Environmental policies drawn up in simplistic legalistic terms provide some recognition of the difficulties in current man to nature relations, and do offer a well-defined approach, but to date they have not resolved the difficulties. Perhaps of even greater concern, they diminish the social concern directed towards the difficulties, at a time when it is so necessary.

The groundwork for an alternative mode of social regulation is laid within this paper where that mode involves the <u>appreciation</u> of the larger context which each man is an individual part of. <u>Negotiation</u> is relied on to resolve the differences between individuals. The objective of regulation is the <u>integration</u> of partial processes into desirable wholes. This does not exclude the power of human consciousness from the vital place it occupies, but it does attempt to enlarge the area of consciousness of humans.

---

[56] Ibid, Tribe, 1975, p. 729

CHAPTER 4

Regulation of Relations and Change

Social systems provide the subject for the paper. Of partilcu1ar interest are the regulation means used by social systems to deal with difficult relationships between humans and the natural environment and between individual human beings. Many of the difficulties relate to some form of ambiguity within the situations where interactions occur. One viable means for social systems to control ambiguity is through <u>social regulation</u>. Regulation offers an organizing structure for a situation which can provide a sense of stability against the destabilizing forces of vagueness, uncertainty and change.

Much of mankind's history is written regarding the successes of respective modes of social regulation. Although considerable individual achievement can take place during "turbulent" times, when social regulation has failed, it is here assumed that greater achievements are possible when social regulation provides for a minimum stability so that interactions might have continuity and long-term meaning. This assumption is in line with the central thought in the Chinese curse stating, "May you live in interesting times." Stabilized human interaction allows potential for enough uncertainty, without that induced by the movement of the ground beneath the situation as well. There are many modes available for man to regulate a situation's ambiguity, but each mode tends to contain its own destabilizing forces. This is in part due to how the regulation mode accommodates natural changes which occur in all situations, and in part due to the inherent potential for changing a situation contained by each human actor. When a mode of regulation tries to deal with these instabilities through becoming deterministic, it tends to lose its adaptive capacity and may introduce other destabilizing forces.

The predictability offered through <u>formalization</u> is a valuable feature of man's rationality and underlies the basic potential of the concept of regulation as we currently understand it. The difficulty of such understanding is seen in the dysfunctions of current modes of trying to formalize situations. The dysfunctions can be seen in relationships between: man, and nature, man and machines, man and man, and man and himself. One means to understand this situation is by considering two alternative paths for man to stabilize a situation: a) structuring the situation so that individuals with choice capabilities can act, or b) structuring the individuals' choices directly. <u>Values</u> are an important structuring means for both paths of regulation, and in both cases help to indicate system tendencies.

> The demands for survival in a particular environment should place value on certain kinds of preparatory behavior at the expense of other; changes in the conditions of survival should induce changes in these values or goals. The direct study of what is valued should therefore enrich the predictions that would be made from study survival conditions alone.[57]

In order to use values to regulate a situation a common definition of what the values which structure "ought to be" is required so that each individual actor can act out the achievement. This is like the "mobilizing idea" concept for social cohesion. On the other hand, if individuals' values are structured directly only a definition of what "must be" and the powers of enforcement are required. In the first instance actions are implicit in the values, in the second values are implicit in the actions.

Of interest in defining what "ought to be" are the "softer" values which tend to end up in the realm of aesthetics. In order to research

---

[57] *Towards a Social Ecology*, Emery and Trist, 1973, p. 20.

the potentials for social regulation through structuring a situation with values of what "ought to be" the current social situation of <u>environmental deterioration</u> was selected. This effort was to pose an alternative mode of social regulation to what this researcher feels is in increasing drift towards structuring individuals instead of situations with social regulation. The structuring of individuals is being increasingly encouraged through formalized codes of conduct which are instilling a <u>legalistic</u> definition to social interaction. The alternative posed here is a structuring of settings so that the social interaction process may be left to the free—will properties of the individuals most dependent on the situation in question. This mode of social regulation is termed <u>appreciative</u>.

4.1 Regulation of Relationships

Of the numerous types of relationships which form the world as humans know it, some lie between man and the physical-technical realm of existence and others between man and the social-psychological realm. Human life depends on both realms, where a minimum level of <u>stability</u> is crucial for meaningful conduct in each. Physiological and psychological stability appear to have been important during mankind's history where both depended on stability in the physical environment. Stability of the physical environment was generally a precondition to social stability and psychological stability. When natural forces would modify the physical environment via climate or resource changes, man would either move to a new location, modify his lifestyle, or become extinct. Since drastic changes in nature occurred relatively infrequently with respect to the human life span, such changes were not a daily concern.

The point of departure taken in this paper is that a large share of mankind's current dilemmas can be explained in terms of dysfunctions in man to man relationships. Through the careful design of our modes of social regulation we can organize human actions which allow advantage to be taken of human potentialities, while also enhancing the stabilizing conditions in the other three areas of human relations: man, to nature, man to man-made and man to self.

In the following four subsections (1.4-1.7) the relationships of man are examined in a manner which helps later development of an alternative mode of social regulation. The final portion of this chapter identifies two "splits" which man has generated through his separation of the life space into the four areas.

Of the numerous types of relationships which form the world as humans know it, some lie between man and the physical-technical realm of existence and others between man and the social-psychological realm. Human life depends on both realms, where a minimum level of <u>stability</u> is crucial for meaningful conduct in each. Physiological and psychological stability appear to have been important during mankind's history where both depended on stability in the physical environment. Stability of the physical environment was generally a precondition to social stability and psychological stability. When natural forces would modify the physical environment via climate or resource changes, man would either move to a new location, modify his lifestyle, or become extinct. Since drastic changes in nature occurred relatively infrequently with respect to the human life span, such changes were not a daily concern.

As man gained more knowledge about and control over the natural environment, he could insulate himself from many of the instabilities and uncertainties of nature. Recently though, we have begun to lose some of this assuredness towards regulating stability in the physical world. Especially during the past two decades, mankind has seen the instabilities increase where the instabilities are of several varieties; the two dominant ones are: 1) Through rapid changes induced by man in the physical—technical realm, a quicker turn-around time of adaptability is needed, or other definitions and varieties of adaptation are required; and 2) Where man could previously <u>move</u> as a mode of adapting to environmental changes (in the social as well as the physical sphere), he now is seeing that option closing down. While man appears to be in a self-exciting dilemma of generating conditions which require more adaptation, the options for adaptations are diminishing.

The point of departure taken in this paper is that a large share of mankind's current dilemmas can be explained in terms of dysfunctions in man to man relationships. Through the careful design of our modes of social regulation we can organize human actions which allow advantage to be taken of human potentialities, while also enhancing the stabilizing conditions in the other three areas of human relations: man, to nature, man to man-made and man to self.

In the following four subsections (1.4-1.7) the relationships of man are examined in a manner which helps later development of an alternative mode of social regulation. The final portion of this chapter identifies two "splits" which man has generated through his separation of the life space into the four areas.

4 Domains, their Relations & Challenges

Domain	Activity	Challenge
1 Natural	Man to Nature Relations	Appreciating non-ownership in 5D
2 Artificial	Man to Man-Made Relations	Conflict over Ownership in 2D
3 Human	Man to Man, Social Relations	Managing Reality in 3D
4 Psychological	Man to Self Relations	Understanding Entropic in 4D

TABLE 4.1: HUMAN ACTIVITIES

A portion of the problems in each quadrant can be attributed to a belief that each was distinct and could be so treated, but more serious problems have arisen in the areas of the two "splits." Human action within the natural-technical area was viewed as one-way control, (man over nature), and not interactive regulation. Activities in the social-psychological domain were viewed from the perspective of accomplishments of controlling nature with technology. The split between the physical and the social is the "regulatory split."

The ecological split, which mankind has become more familiar with during the past fifteen years, is due to the precepts which divide man and his man—made environments from nature and man's natural self. In all cases each quadrant is continually exposed to "differences over time" or change. The dominant concern of regulation is with change, and how best to provide stability during change, i.e., dynamic stability; thus, regulation is involved in one way or another with all four quadrants. Man's purpose now is to organize and redesign the regulatory activities of all four areas so that they can be integrative and not disintegrative.

In each of the quadrants, deterministic, reductionist and mechanistic reasoning has been used to "explain." Where regulation was relied on, it centered on cause-effect relationships and not complex multi-variable interrelations. We now are becoming aware of the necessity for deriving alternative modes of analysis and alternative modes of regulation which can accommodate more of the complexity of life. For example, a resolution of dilemmas in man to nature relationships would entail some modification of relations between man and the man-made environment. In turn, dealing effectively with the man to man-made environment involves reorganizing man to man problems. In social psychology (Angyal, 1941) illustrates the difficulties of understanding social and individual situations with traditional analytic methods. Systems theory has attempted to deal with these difficulties, but a viable mode of social regulation which can integrate the activities in each of the four areas has yet to be developed. The current modes of social regulation deny the connections between the four areas of regulation activity illustrated in Figure 1.

Recent activities for regulating man's relations to the natural environment concentrate on the relations between the human built environment and the natural environment. A case is made in this dissertation that such a concentration must be widened to include how man designs the built environment. Most design, in turn, relies on collective human activity, i.e., social relations. Many of our recent regulation activities illustrate how we are attempting to control man's design of the built environment, but these efforts are useless without recognition of the importance of man to man relations.

Problems in Area I deal with <u>natural ecology</u>. Area II is popularly termed <u>environmental design</u>. Area III contains recent attempts to develop theories of <u>social ecology</u>, and Area IV looks to theories of <u>mental ecology</u>.

Geoffrey Vickers (1970) provides an interpretation of the breakdown of regulation similar to the four domains listed previously, except his Area I is termed, "man—environment regulations," his Area II is termed, "economic regulations," his Area III is termed, "political regulations," and his Area IV is simply termed "appreciation." His concept of appreciation, which concentrates on the man-to-self area, forms the basis for a more integrative system of social regulation, one which can include all four areas. As Vickers describes the area of appreciation and what it involves:

> A fourth is the appreciative field, the inner coherence of that system of interests, expectations and standards of judgement which orders our lives, guiding action, mediating communication and making experience meaningful.[58]

This concept fits into the concept of "life space" as developed by Kurt Lewin, where,

> The "life space" (is) the person and the psychological environment as it exists for him. We usually have this field in mind if we refer to needs, motivation, mood, enmity, ideals.[59]

Although Vickers makes appreciation more of an evaluative concept than Lewin's life space, life space helps us by denoting a boundary zone for defining the limits of perception, and the potentials for conception, so that they may better be integrated.

Evidence that the perceptual and conceptual environments are not now integrated in industrialized nations can be seen through contradictions between environmental protection values and current government policies in many western industrialized nations. Individuals are protesting and fighting for greater controls by government over factors in their perceptual environments (such

---

[58] Vickers, 1970, p. 155
[59] Lewin, 1951, p. 57

as power plants, pollutants, chemicals, etc.), so as to decrease their physiological risks. The same individuals are demanding more freedom from governmental control in their own conceptual world activities (freedom of information about government activities, privacy of individual information, and other things).

Vickers discusses another perspective on current dilemmas in the collective domain of social regulation.

> The capacity of political societies for accepting regulation is being eroded by several factors. The capacity for collective response is dulled, when the situation which should evoke it is not present to experience but is a mental construct, based on uncertain predictions. It is further dulled by those policies of collective security which cushion the individual against even such present experience as he might otherwise have. It is further limited by the need for greater consensus and by the increasing vulnerability of that consensus to the resistance of protesting of predatory minorities, which deny the opportunity needed for the gestation of innovation. These factors... create, as it seems to me, a wild and growing disparity between the least regulation that the situation demands and the most that it permits.[60]

The implication in much of what Vickers says is that a viable mode of regulation is in existence, although he never explicitly states this opinion. The viewpoint of this dissertation goes beyond Vickers' criticisms about the varieties of regulatory skills available in industrial societies and points out how the modes are lacking qualities as well. To apply current regulation modes more strenuously could even increase the instabilities in society and between man and nature. Increased force does not seem to be a suitable substitute for lack of knowledge in the environmental deterioration area. The thesis within the remainder of this dissertation questions the deterioration concept

---

[60] Vickers, 1970, p. 93

itself. A tentative suggestion is posed later that current societies are more engaged in <u>environmental disintegration</u>, than deterioration. If so, then perhaps we require more of a response of <u>integration</u>, than enhancement of the environment.

In the following chapter the characteristics of current dominant modes of social regulation are outlined as well as an introduction to the need for an appreciative mode of regulation. Appreciation is felt to better allow for the integration of a growing number and variety of parts which make up complex societies.

4.2 Type I: Regulation of Man to Nature (Technology's Domain)

During the 1940s and 1950s the physical environment appeared to be coming under mankind's control. The effective organization of man's inwardly centered "conceptual world" was allowing control of much of the outwardly centered "perceptual world." The secrets of nature were being unveiled by man for man's inspection.

The nature of the atom had been subjected to a tentative interpretation; a task mankind had pursued for the previous twenty-five hundred years. Many believed that this interpretation would release many beneficial powers for mankind's needs. The 1945 bombing of Japan cast grave doubts over such a belief, but Atoms for Peace under Eisenhower was one attempt to get man's attentions back on the human-need track. Nuclear proliferation during the past few years is showing The Atoms for Peace Program to have been ineffective in regulating man to man relations. As Albert Einstein had forewarned, "The unleashed power of the atom has changed everything, save our modes of thinking, and thus we drift to unparalleled catastrophe" (Russell, 1959, Introduction). Man's capacity for self-regulation had not kept pace with his abilities for controlling nature.

Man's predicament was extended even further through significant advances in the less ominous (at least so initially) areas of micro- and macro-biology, organic and inorganic chemistry, and other realms of physical science. Breakthroughs had emerged in the design and development of synthetic replacements to natural materials found to be in limited natural supply. Man's technical insulation from the uncertainties of nature seemed assured.

4.3 Type II: Regulation of Man to the Man-Made (Technique Domain)

This main is the essential home of the industrial. The is the mechanical process for producing that which humans know they need and feel they want. It is what harvest the raw materials from the surrounding environment, refines them where needed, and enters them into the assembly/production process, and finally transports them to the users. This also includes the infrastructures needed to link the parts of the industrial system as well as connect to the consumers, then connect consumers to each other. Examining the myth of architecture illustrates one area of needed change to business as usual. Architects are taught to create monuments to themselves in the pattern of Ernst Becker's "immortality projects." As such they defy entropy and change. Thus, other, newer buildings must be built for new values and uses. Perhaps the best way out from this is found in Lars Larrup's "Building Unfinished."

Design and construction of infrastructures meant to connect provide another major area for rethinking regulations. Extensive building of highways, airports, water and sewerage lines, and power and communication lines have a large impact on the natural environment. All this should and can be changed to limit deterioration.

The advances in the technical domain were gained through a system of mechanical design that the "free-will"-exhibiting humans did not naturally fit into. This called for the "design" of social systems more suitable to a machine world. Techniques were needed to help man adapt to the machine world. One well-known adaptation technique came through Frederic Taylor's form of social organization called "Scientific Management". Just as a narrow rationalistic logic had been used to successfully control parts of the natural world, it was used to fit man into the machine world. The vast number of "pieces" in the large industrial machines required rational, central control; so too did the human "pieces" via foremen and a hierarchical system of managers. Industrial machines demanded a degree of predictability which humans did not naturally exhibit; thus, techniques were used to cause humans to behave more predictably. Regulation through strict training was the order of the day. Men had to be scheduled to fit the operating characteristics of machines.

All this seemed worth the price to most men. Advances had been made and were continuing to be made in the production, distribution, consumption and disposal of increased quantities and varieties of materials and products. All of these "things" were adding to increased human well-being. But somehow dilemmas began to emerge from this productive network. Contradictions between quantity and quality of products were emerging. Various role models for each individual were emerging as conflictual as well. The mixture of values involved in one individual being producer, consumer, and a resident living in the midst of pollution from the other two activities, generated personal and social dilemmas. Conflicts between man and his manmade environment were becoming serious.

4.4 Type III: Regulation of Man to Man (The Social Domain)

The consequences of implementing a social organization system along the lines of the technological imperative were proving counterproductive for both the social and technical spheres. As technical components became more sophisticated they could replace human work (a phenomenon which is not without disadvantages itself), but then they required a more sophisticated form of human work. This required more comprehension of the total process and responsibility for that process by everyone, which was in opposition to the organization of the industrial mode of operation. Cracks were beginning to appear in the accepted rational of the technological imperative. A few social scientists noticed these cracks. Kurt Lewin's (1951) development of "Field Theory," Angyal's (1941) development of "holistic approaches" to social psychology, and Bertalanffy's (1950) "General Systems Theory" were three examples of responses to the situation. The more recent development of Emery and Trist's (1973) "socio-technical systems" concepts combined the works of many of the previous pioneers to study the organization of work. It appeared that questions of man to man relations, and how the relations effect technical and natural systems, were being raised.

Man had created a man-made world to insulate himself from the uncertainties of the natural world, but the insulated world was becoming uninhabitable in many respects and was restricting man to man relations. Man's forms of social regulation began to be wholly inadequate for this situation. The dysfunctions of social regulation began to crystallize during the 1960s with a significant blow to man's rational pride dealt by the ecological crisis. The traditional mode of human operation was proving to be dysfunctional to the development of alternative technologies and techniques, to interpersonal human relations, and even to the natural environment which all life forms depend upon. This last feature did most to rudely remind mankind of his limits to autonomy and human independence.

This situation called for a collective response. Unfortunately, the legalistically rational mode of social action did not seem to be adequate for the situation. As Sir Geoffrey Vickers stated the human dilemma of the 1960s:

> Looking back over history, the rational mind of the eighteenth century declared the human condition to be a triple slavery and promised it a triple emancipation. Men were enslaved by economic want, by political domination and by religious superstition. Trade and technology would free them from the first, democratic institutions from the second and science from the third. Freed from tyranny by nature, men, and Gods, free men, it was assumed, would need no more regulation than human reason would supply.[61]

---

[61] Vickers, 1970, p. 183

It was beginning to appear obvious that regulation arts beyond those of formal rationality were in order.

The theory of regulation advanced and developed in this dissertation attempts expansion of these limits. Strict human reason seems, in many ways, to be counter to many interpersonal relations, and in some ways counter to man to nature relations.

All these dilemmas were combining to form a self—exciting chaotic system that was outrunning man's conceptual powers to regulate. Essentially, the activities of the conceptual mode of man to control the perceptual world were generating phenomenon in the perceptual world beyond man's conceptual abilities. The needs of man in this realm are clearly stated by Susanne Langer,

> Man lives not only in a place, but in space; not only at a time, but in History. So, he must conceive a world and a law of the world, a pattern of life, and a way of meeting death. All these things he knows, and he has to make some adaptation to their reality. Now, he can adapt himself somehow to anything his imagination can cope with; but he cannot deal with Chaos. Because his characteristic function and highest asset is conception, his greatest fright is to meet that what he cannot construe.[62]

4.5 Type IV: Regulation of Man to Self (Psychological Doman)

Langer's comments give insight to two ideas, both of which we encountered previously: the <u>idea of conception</u>, and the <u>idea of perception</u> of things. This set of distinctions is crucial to this dissertation and the research it is based on. An appropriate starting point for examining the significance of conception, perception, rationality, and non-rationality lies with the model of C. G. Jung for categorizing people. The model is based on four functional typologies by which

---

[62] Susanne Langer, 1942, p. 287

consciousness obtains its orientation to experience feeling, thinking, intuition, and sensing. Jung's definitions follow.

1. Feeling — "When I use the word 'feeling' in contrast to 'thinking,' I refer to judgment of value - for instance, agreeable or disagreeable, good or bad, and so on. Feeling according to this definition is not an emotion."
2. Thinking – "...people who used their minds were those who 'thought' - that is, who applied their intellectual faculty in trying to adapt themselves to people and circumstances."
3. Intuition – "In so far as intuition is 'hunch,' it is not the product of a voluntary act; it is rather an involuntary event, which depends upon different external or internal circumstances instead of an act of judgement."
4. Sensing – "(Like intuition, sensing is) more like a sense—perception, which is also an irrational event in so far as it depends essentially upon objective stimuli, which owe their existence to physical and not to mental causes."[63]

<u>Figure 4.1 The Jung Typologies</u>

For Jung, feeling and thinking are dominantly rational functions used for "ordering" and are the product of voluntary mental events. Intuition and sensing, on the other hand, are dominantly non-rational functions used for "perceiving" and are the products of involuntary human events initiated by the physical world. Rational functions are triggered by the human mind, while non-rational functions are triggered by the environment. Both aspects are important for regulation in complex environments. Jung's summary of the four functions outlines the importance they could play in social regulation,

> Sensation (i.e., sense perception) tells you that something exists; <u>thinking</u> tells you what it is; <u>feeling</u>

---

[63] C. G. Jung, 1964, p. 61

tells you whether it is agreeable or not; and intuition tells you whence it comes and where it is going.[64]

The appreciative mode of regulation developed within the dissertation rests on the integration of all four functions. Jung thought that everyone tended to emphasize one or the other of the functions. By including a wider set of individuals in a regulation process the conditions for accommodation of all four functions are enhanced. Grounding the mode of regulation in negotiation enhances the potential for interactivity between the functions. This should enhance the potential for integration of the functions. This takes the social regulation system well outside the traditional realm of limited human rationality. On the other hand, some individuals are strongly advocating movement towards an even more limited sense of rationality for dealing with problems like environmental deterioration. One example of this, which tended to typify a large section of the governmental thinking within the U.S. version of environmental protection, is offered by the proceedings of a Congressional Committee looking into regulatory problems in controlling environmental pollution. (Their discussions were dealing with obstacles to effective rationalization of problems in the environmental protection domain; e.g., economic, administrative, conceptual, etc.)

> Foremost among those obstacles is EPA's attitude toward its statutory responsibilities. Often it has been too timid... The range and strength of EPA's opposition suggests the need not only for EPA to pursue its mission more aggressively, but also for Congress to provide additional means by which EPA's activities and opposition can be monitored... Finally, EPA should adhere more closely to its statutory mandates.[65]

---

[64] Jung, 1964, p. 61
[65] "Federal Regulation and Regulatory Reform," an Oct. 1976 report of proceedings from the House Oversight Subcommittee, pp. 150—151.

The individuals making the previous comment had been reacting to evidence given about dilemmas which were building up in the environmental protection regulation efforts to that date. One bit of evidence, presented from a Federal Court decision, which they had found especially distasteful was,

> Questions involving the environment are particularly prone to uncertainty. Technological man has altered his world in ways never before experienced or anticipated. The health effects of such alterations are often unknown, sometimes unknowable. While a concerned Congress has passed legislation providing for protection of the public health against gross environmental modifications, the regulators entrusted with the enforcement of such laws have not thereby been endowed with a prescience that removes all doubt from their decision-making.[66]

The point of departure here is towards enlargement of the view of rationality, or failing in that attempt, to include, within a social regulation process, enough of the non—rational factors so that their characteristics can be accommodated. The limits of strict rationality are proving to be too restrictive to accommodate the multifaceted events we perceive in the empirical world. This is in accord with the idea of U Thant (1971) that we must radically change our present systems which are based on rigid divisions, where, "No rigid system, however well-established on a few sacrosanct principles, is able to cope with all the problems of our diverse, complex and constantly changing society."[67]

The conceptual environment, as it is used here, refers to Rapoport's (1974, p. 51) sense of the "symbolic environment." The perceptual environment in turn refers to his sense of the "physical environment." In the physical environment, man's actions are not that different from other animal's interactions with their environments.

---

[66] Ibid., p. 149, originally from ETHYL CORP. v. EPA.
[67] Toronto, Canada, Globe and Mail, May 25, 1971.

> On the whole, however, man's interaction with the physical environment differs only quantitatively, not qualitatively, from corresponding interactions of other animals with their environment. A house is but an elaborate nest, A superhighway is an improved cow path...
>
> The other environment, the symbolic one, has no analogue in the non-human world. There are no precursors among animals of epic poems, monuments, preferred stock, protest marches, confessions, astronomy, or astrology.
>
> Clearly, the degree to which man has been able to modify his physical environment (for better or for worse) is intimately related to certain features of his symbolic environment, to science, for example. The symbolic environment deserves careful examination in its own right as, perhaps, the most important determinant of the human condition.[68]

The conceptual (symbolic) environment contains the psychological landscape and the assorted structures which man places or finds there. Dostoevsky concentrated on this landscape so extensively that he hardly mentions the physical landscape. The perceptual environment in turn relies on the physical landscape, where man also places and identifies structures. Man-made and natural structures found in both landscapes are important to social regulation. A thesis is advanced here that current modes of regulation limit themselves to the physical environment, in that it is more tangible and implies more certainty, especially the man—made portions of it. The importance of moving into the psychological environment is seen from the large role it plays as a factor inducing change, where to be viable a mode of regulation must be able to accommodate change.

---

[68] Rapoport, 1974, p. 51.

4.6 Rethinking Regulation, To Encourage Business as Unusual

Individuals and organizations expend considerable resources attempting to control natural phenomena and their impacts on mankind. The ostensible purpose of this control has been to increase the opportunities to satisfy human needs. The thesis of this paper raises questions as to how well current modes of regulation can accomplish this. The paper also attempts to enlarge the purpose of regulation to include larger systems of life processes beyond man—made ordering.

> ... [It] is indeed true that we have created an ungovernable world, In which the natural order and a man—made order are blended as never before into a system which can be neither interpreted by natural nor governed by man-made laws.[69]

To analyze the complex blend of natural and man-made systems they are here organized into four areas of regulation activity, with man a participant in each. Figure 1 illustrates the relations between the far areas. The looping symbol is drawn on the figure to illustrate the direction of historic effect. Area I reference to the major base of operations during the industrial revolution. Area II refers to the domain of techniques developed to resolve difficulties in Area I. Man's operations in both Area I and Area II relied on a scientifically technical paradigm of control, which had consequences for Area III. But it was later discovered that man to man relations rely on more than is explained through reason. Combinations of problems in domains I, II and III pose dilemmas for human activity in Area IV (man-to-self relations). None of these quadrants is completely distinct from each of the other three, but for descriptive purposes they are conceptually considered as separated.

---

[69] Vickers, 1970, p. 122.

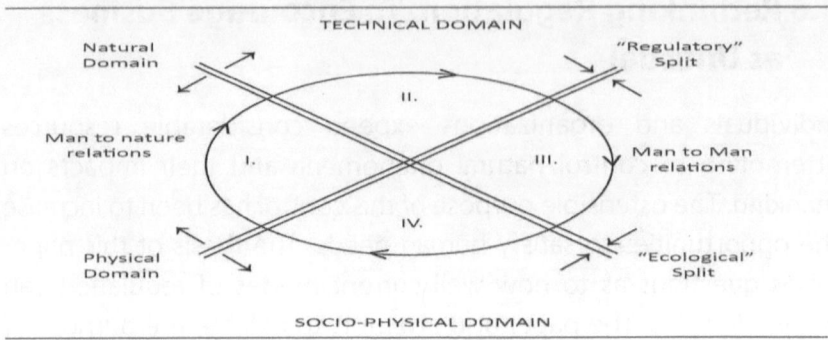

Figure 4.4 THE RELATIONSHIPS

A portion of the problems in each quadrant can be attributed to a belief that each was distinct and could be so treated, but more serious problems have arisen in the areas of the two "splits." Human action within the natural-technical area was viewed as one-way control, (man over nature), and not interactive regulation. Activities in the social-psychological domain were viewed from the perspective of accomplishments of controlling nature with technology. The split between the physical and the social is the "regulatory split."

The ecological split, which mankind has become more familiar with during the past fifteen years, is due to the precepts which divide man and his man—made environments from nature and man's natural self. In all cases each quadrant is continually exposed to "differences over time" or change. The dominant concern of regulation is with change, and how best to provide stability during change, i.e., dynamic stability; thus, regulation is involved in one way or another with all four quadrants. Man's purpose now is to organize and redesign the regulatory activities of all four areas so that they can be integrative and not disintegrative.

In each of the quadrants, deterministic, reductionist and mechanistic reasoning has been used to "explain." Where regulation was relied on, it centered on cause-effect relationships and not complex multi-variable interrelations. We now are becoming aware of the necessity for deriving alternative modes of analysis and alternative modes of regulation which can accommodate more of the complexity of life. For example, a resolution of dilemmas in man to nature relationships would entail some modification of relations between man and the man-made environment. In turn, dealing effectively with the man to man-made environment involves reorganizing man to man problems. In social psychology (Angyal, 1941) illustrates the difficulties of understanding social and individual situations with traditional analytic methods. Systems theory has attempted to deal with these difficulties, but a viable mode of social regulation which can integrate the activities in each of the four areas has yet to be developed. The current modes of social regulation deny the connections between the four areas of regulation activity illustrated in Figure 1.

Recent activities for regulating man's relations to the natural environment concentrate on the relations between man's-built environment and the natural environment. A case is made in this dissertation that such a concentration must be widened to include how man designs the built environment. Most design, in turn, relies on collective human activity, i.e., social relations. Many of our recent regulation activities illustrate how we are attempting to control man's design of the built environment, but these efforts are useless without recognition of the importance of man to man relations.

Problems in Area I deal with <u>natural ecology</u>. Area II is popularly termed <u>environmental design</u>. Area III contains recent attempts to develop theories of <u>social ecology</u>, and Area IV looks to theories of <u>mental ecology</u>.

Geoffrey Vickers (1970) provides an interpretation of the breakdown of regulation similar to the four domains listed previously, except his Area I is termed, "man—environment regulations," his Area II is termed, "economic regulations," his Area III is termed, "political regulations," and his Area IV is simply termed "appreciation." His concept of appreciation, which concentrates on the man-to-self area, forms the basis for a more integrative system of social regulation, one which can include all four areas. As Vickers describes the area of appreciation and what it involves:

> A fourth is the appreciative field, the inner coherence
> of that system of interests, expectations and standards

of judgement which orders our lives, guiding action, mediating communication and making experience meaningful.[70]

This concept fits into the concept of "life space" as developed by Kurt Lewin, where,

> The "life space" (is) the person and the psychological environment as it exists for him. We usually have this field in mind if we refer to needs, motivation, mood, entity, ideals.[71]

Although Vickers makes appreciation more of an evaluative concept than Lewin's life space, life space helps us by denoting a boundary zone for defining the limits of perception, and the potentials for conception, so that they may better be integrated.

Evidence that the perceptual and conceptual environments are not now integrated in industrialized nations can be seen through contradictions between environmental protection values and current government policies in many western industrialized nations. Individuals are protesting and fighting for greater controls by government over factors in their perceptual environments (such as power plants, pollutants, chemicals, etc.), so as to decrease their physiological risks. The same individuals are demanding more freedom from governmental control in their own conceptual world activities (freedom of information about government activities, privacy of individual information, and other things).

Vickers discusses another perspective on current dilemmas in the collective domain of social regulation.

> The capacity of political societies for accepting regulation is being eroded by several factors. The capacity for collective response is dulled, when the situation which should evoke it is not present

---

[70] Vickers, Geoffrey, *Freedom in a Rocking Boat*, 1970, p. 155.
[71] Lewin, 1951, p. 57.

> to experience but is a mental construct, based on uncertain predictions. It is further dulled by those policies of collective security which cushion the individual against even such present experience as he might otherwise have. It is further limited by the need for greater consensus and by the increasing vulnerability of that consensus to the resistance of protesting of predatory minorities, which deny the opportunity needed for the gestation of innovation. These factors... create, as it seems to me, a wild and growing disparity between the least regulation that the situation demands and the most that it permits.[72]

The implication in much of what Vickers says is that a viable mode of regulation is in existence, although he never explicitly states this opinion. The viewpoint of this dissertation goes beyond Vickers' criticisms about the varieties of regulatory skills available in industrial societies and points out how the modes are lacking qualities as well. To apply current regulation modes more strenuously could even increase the instabilities in society and between man and nature. Increased force does not seem to be a suitable substitute for lack of knowledge in the environmental deterioration area. The thesis within the remainder of this dissertation questions the deterioration concept itself. A tentative suggestion is posed later that current societies are more engaged in <u>environmental disintegration</u>, than deterioration. If so, then perhaps we require more of a response of <u>integration</u>, than enhancement of the environment.

In the following chapter the characteristics of current dominant modes of social regulation are outlined as well as an introduction to the need for an appreciative mode of regulation. Appreciation is felt to better allow for the integration of a growing number and variety of parts which make up complex societies.

---

[72] Vickers, 1970, p. 93.

CHAPTER 5

Introduction to the Theory

5.1 Complexity and its Regulation

Social regulation responses to complexity form the emphasis of this chapter. Two Ideal responses and two empirical responses, from the countries of Sweden and the United States, are collectively compared in terms of the properties of each. The dissertation involves evaluation of the appropriateness of each response for <u>complex societal problems</u>, which Ackoff (1974) has referred to as a "system of problems," or a "mess." The crucial property of messes (such as terrorism, pollution, crime, poverty, etc.) is that they entail systemic properties which do not allow easy analytical dissection. Ackoff's sense of <u>system</u> is relied on for identifying the properties of the complex societal problems which social regulation attempts to deal with.

> A system is a set of two or more interrelated elements of any kind... Therefore, it is <u>not</u> an ultimate indivisible element but a whole that can be divided into parts. The elements of the set and the set of elements that form a system have the following three properties.
>
> 1. The properties or behavior of each element of the set influences the properties or behavior of the set taken as a whole...
> 2. The properties and behavior of each element, and the way they affect the whole, depend on the properties and behavior of at least one other element in the set...

3. Every possible subgroup of elements in the set has the first two properties: each has a non-independent effect overall. Therefore, the whole cannot be decomposed into independent subsets. [73]

Although a system is a whole which can be divided into parts, it is assumed in the theory, that it makes a great difference to the result of an analytical effort <u>how</u> the divisions are made. To analyze a human body in terms of cubic inch parts would not aid the understanding of many problems within the body. Similarly, to analyze an environmental deterioration problem in terms of part per million (PPM) pollution tends to obscure the systemic properties of the problem.

Another feature of complex societal problems is that they should not be thought of as "more than the sum of the parts." Angyal clarifies this point in his distinction between <u>aggregates</u> and <u>wholes</u>,

> Wholes, however, cannot be compared to additive aggregations at all. Instead of stating that in the formation of wholes something more than a summation of parts takes place, it would be more correct to state that summation does not play any part whatsoever in the formation of whole in aggregates... It is significant that the parts are added; in a system it is significant that the parts are arranged (Angyal, 1941, p. 256).

This means that the term "part" means something completely different in a system than it does in an aggregate. In an aggregate the parts are objects, while in a system the parts become "positional values," (Ibid.). Taking this one step further, "The system cannot be derived from the parts; the system is an independent framework in which the parts are placed."[74]

Another feature of complex societal problems to add to the properties in Ackoff's definition is that they are <u>dynamic</u>. Within

---

[73] Ackoff, 1974, p. 13.
[74] Ibid., p. 257.

a static system the elements have one positional value, while in a dynamic system the overall system and the individual positions can take on a variety of positions.

Thus, to deal with complex societal problems in a manner which allows the formulation of a response, four aspects must be accounted for: 1) the <u>unit of analysis</u> with respect to the system being analyzed, 2) the <u>positional values</u> of the system elements (the units of analysis), 3) the <u>dynamic properties</u> of the elements, and 4) the <u>whole</u> which they form through their positional values. (The third and fourth are dealt with in Chapter Five of the dissertation in terms of system tendencies towards <u>integration</u> and differentiation, where differentiation poses the danger of disintegration.)

The two idealized responses are <u>legalistic</u> regulation and <u>appreciative</u> regulation.

The legalistic response is specification, prior to an action, of rigidly delineated rules which are put into writing to ensure consistent application to all parts of the system. The specifications are based on a projection of current difficulties into the future, with the emphasis on the control of only those difficulties outlined. The sovereignty lies with the written law. Facts are most critical.

The appreciative response also includes specification of rules for behavior but relies on the specification to be somewhat ambiguous and to be directed toward <u>changing</u> the conditions of future environments, not to adapt to existing environments. In order to encourage the retention of sovereignty with each of the participants in the appreciation process, most of the rules are not put into writing. Values as well as facts are critical to this response.

In the ideal sense legalism relies on <u>legislation</u> to insure <u>legal order</u>. Appreciation relies on <u>negotiation</u> to insure <u>negotiated order</u>. The United States' environmental protection approach to regulation approximates the conditions of legalism, while the Swedish system tends towards the appreciative mode yet contains some elements of legalism. This thesis and the implications from it form the subject matter of the remainder of the chapter, but first legalism and appreciation need to be placed in a historic context.

5.2 Formal and Informal Problem Solving

Others have furnished distinctions like legalism and appreciation, but almost all appear to denote a more general distinction between formal and informal approaches to problems. Each approach represents more of an attitude towards problems than a solution, thus attitude characteristics become important in identifying the significance of each approach. The formal mode relies on characteristics of 1) explicit meanings, 2) rigid action tied into a specific time frame, 3) structuring through official sanctions, 4) definitive responsibilities, 5) expressed relationships, and 6) dependence on unambiguous facts and exclusion of ambiguous facts. The informal mode to problematical situations relies on characteristics of: 1) implicit meanings, 2) dynamic processes in an open-ended time frame, 3) unofficial sanctioning, 4) shared responsibility, 5) spontaneous relationships, and 6) inclusion of ambiguity.

Burns and Stalker (1961) have made a distinction between "mechanistic" and "organic" systems of management and organizational structuring. They rely on eleven characteristics to define each type where their mechanical characteristic of "specialized differentiation" relates to formal and their organic characteristic of "continual redefinition" relates to informal approaches. A difficulty with their distinction, in terms of this dissertation, lies in the implications of the terms. Initially, both imply a concentration on only the collective aspects of the entity. Whether it is a composite machine, or a completed organism, the individuation processes are left in the shadows. (Integration is an important concept for the thesis of this dissertation, but as will be described in Chapter 5, integration is a dialectical concept involving individuation activities as well as collective actions.) The second difficulty centers on the implication of mechanism (from "mechanistic"), being distinctly different from organism (from "organismic"). The implication is that a mechanism is simple, static and dead, while an organism is complex, dynamic and alive. Susanne Langer discusses the dangers of the mechanism-organism distinction.

By "mechanism" I mean any process we understand in terms of physics and chemistry. The complexity of such processes is beyond the imagination of anyone who does not know self-sustaining rhythms and dialectical exchanges of energy, forms and qualities evolving and resolving, sub—microscopic elements - already highly structured - merging and great dynamisms emerging. The commonsense tenet that such products of nature cannot attain feeling, awareness, and thought loses its cogency when one is confronted by the actual intricacies of chemical and electrochemical organization. The bridge of organism arises of itself, and the conviction that "extended substance" cannot think and "thinking substance" cannot have material properties appears as a medieval doctrine handed down to modern philosophy in Descartes' famous dictum, and with no firmer foundation than his word.[75]

Amitai Etzioni (1961) makes a distinction between "prescriptive" and "contextuating" types of control, which more closely approximates the characteristics found in formal and informal modes. Although the terms begin to designate a similar distinction to what is required in the theory developed here, Etzioni's development differs from this one in that he relies heavily on the concept of "power" in his theory, and how power is used. His three alternative modes are: coercive, remunerative and normative, where all three are based on control through external manipulation. Concentration on power tends to detract from the essential qualities of internal appreciation upon which the appreciative mode of regulation depends.

Gilbert Ryle (1953) sets the stage differently by returning to Aristotle's inauguration of formal logic and its alternative of informal logic, which Ryle calls "general philosophy." Ryle claims that formal and informal logic deal with two different types of problems, each with its own type of thinking.

---

[75] Langer, 1967, p, 274.

> The technical problems in the theory of the syllogism have a strong resemblance to the problems of Euclidean geometry; the ideals of systematization and rigorous proof are at work, questions of switches and shades of significance are barred, false moves are demonstrable fallacies. The problems in, say, the theory of pleasure or perception or more responsibility are not like this.[76]

Churchman and Ackoff (1950) fill in the stage more completely, where the formal and informal approaches to ordering are symbolized in the philosophy of science as "formalism" and "intuitionism."

> The formalists claim that mathematical method depends on proceeding according to explicit rules, or operations. The operations are specified in terms of certain <u>abstract</u> symbols which, as far as the formalist is concerned, need have no reference to the empirical world. The fundamental requirement is that no contradiction be deducible within the system.[77]

On the other hand, the speculative intuitionists claimed that,

4. Mathematics has not only a formal, but also a nonformal meaning.
5. Mathematical objects are presented immediately to the thinking mind: mathematical knowledge is therefore independent of experience (Ibide, p. 297).

Although the mathematical formalists have similar characteristics to the formalists described in this paper, the mathematical informalists (intuitionists) are not like the sense of informalism developed in this dissertation. This is understandable since both approaches mentioned are from the domain of mathematics, which is a formally oriented domain from the outset. In addition, neither rely on knowledge

---

[76] Ryle, 1954, p. 111.
[77] Churchman and Ackoff, 1950, p. 296.

through experience, which is critical to the informal approach developed here.

The American pragmatists, along the lines of James, Pierce, and Dewey, begin to illustrate a clearer sense of the role which the informal characteristics can take in decision-making processes.

> The pragmatist, using the results of psychological experimentation, claims that intuition does not provide elements of knowledge; if anything, it provides wholes. The pragmatist asserts, further, that intuition is never pure but is always affected by and dependent for its validity on non-formal knowledge. He also asserts that there are no ultimately simple operations of the kind sought by the formalist. Consequently, he seeks a reorientation of formal science based on the recognition that formal science has the function of providing means of testing the value of intuitively suggested solutions to problems considering assumptions and observations.[78]

This relates to the typologies for viewing the world as posed by Jung and presented in Chapter 1 of this dissertation.

> These four functional types correspond to the obvious means by which consciousness obtains its orientation to experience. Sensation (i.e., sense-perception) tells you that something exists; thinking tells you what it is; feeling tells you whether it is agreeable or not; and intuition tells you whence it comes and where it is going.[79]

And returning to the pragmatist's view of these,

---

[78] Ibid., pp. 320—321
[79] Jung, 1964, p. 61.

> The pragmatist asserts that a complete theory of scientific method will find that all four of the functions which Jung enumerates are essential in the process of progressing toward truth. But it will also find that no function alone is sufficient to establish the truth.[80]

Jung distinguishes between viewpoints which are <u>ordering</u> (rational) and <u>perceiving</u> (non-rational), which relates to the conceptual and perceptual environments described in Chapter 1. Combining the characteristics of the rational and the non—rational helps in overcoming some of the dilemmas in dealing with complex situations. Forrester (1971) (as quoted in Hawk, 1977) helps us examine the situation. If, as Forrester has stated, complexity is <u>counter—intuitive</u>, does the philosophical converse, formalism, provide for an adequate alternative to structure complexity? Or, more precisely, <u>does formalism give an adequate account of the complexity of a situation</u> requiring regulation? The thesis advanced here would answer no.

That some form of conceptual ordering of complex situations is critical was pointed out in the previous chapter in a quote from Langer, "Because his characteristic function and highest asset is conception, his [man's] greatest fright is to meet that which he cannot construe" (Langer, 1942, p. 287). That individual in current societies might be having difficulties in conceptualizing complexities is indicated by several people from several perspectives: "shifting values to beyond the stable state" (Schon 1971). "The break-down of regulation systems through self—exciting processes" (Vickers 1970), and social—organizational complexity (Emery and Trist 1973). But the question of how best to order this complexity remains.

The objective of the informal mode of social regulation is to bring regulation into real time and not have to rely on <u>ex post</u> regulation, which the pragmatic method tends to do. A means to doing this is to include more of the non—rational perceiving functions, sensation and intuition, in the decision process. This tends to place more reliance on experience through immediate interactive involvement, but as Ackoff has noted, "Increases in the rate of change of technology have

---

[80] Churchman and Ackoff, 1950, p. 317.

decreased the effectiveness of experience as a teacher. It is too slow" (Ackoff, 1974, p. 5). The resolution of this apparent dilemma – relying on experience at a time when the conditions requiring it are the conditions which make it too slow - lies in a distinction between types of experience. The type of experience mentioned by Ackoff seems to be of the traditional individualistic type where everyone relies on his/her interactions with the environment. The type of experience relied on in informal regulation is <u>experiencing others experience</u> in a manner that approximates the ideal of social learning which is to build an integrated body of knowledge. This <u>meta—knowledge</u> is not that different from the historical idea of mankind developing by passing information on from man to man. In specialized industrial societies with multiple language systems there are obvious difficulties in passing on information.

Both the rational and the non—rational domains of human understanding are envisioned by this author as integral parts in the appreciative mode of social regulation. Appreciation relies on the additional concept of negotiation. One of the first discussions of the term "negotiation" that was helpful to the dissertation came in an article titled, "The Hospital and its Negotiated Order," by Anselm Strauss and others (1963). Negotiated order emerged as a description of the regulation system used in the complexity of a hospital setting, where the complexity was related to:

> ...a profound belief that care of patients calls for a minimum of hard and fast rules and a maximum of innovation and improvisation. In addition, in this hospital, as certainly in most others, the multiplicity of medical purpose and theory, as well as of personal investment are openly recognized: too rigid a set of rules would only cause turmoil and affect the hospital's overall efficiency.[81]

It is important to note that one major item holding the negotiation process together was that the hospital held a single, although

---

[81] Ibid., p. 103.

ambiguous, goal; "The goal is to return the patients to the outside world in better shape."[82]

This set of conditions sounds like the conditions of environmental policy which forms the basis of the empirical aspect of this dissertation and its theory. The negotiated order concept is developed in much greater detail in Chapter 6 but before that development, a great deal more of the theory of general regulation approaches needs to be presented, as well as the empirical research which helps to structure the theory.

The empirical aspect of the research, as outlined in Chapters 3 and 4, shows the U.S. System of Regulation to be like the formalistic approach of legalism. The Swedish System is found to be similar, in some respects, to the informal approach of appreciation. In the remainder of the chapter, the definitions, the comparative model for evaluation, and an outline of the empirical evidence from the research are described.

5.3 Definitions

<u>Complexity</u>

A systemic multiplicity of interactive and dynamic relationships between the parts of an entity and the relationships of these parts to the whole of the entity.

<u>Order</u>

The degree of lawfulness governing the relations between the parts of an entity where the laws can be either physical laws or social laws between purposeful systems.

<u>Legalism</u>

A mode of formal regulation, which is derived from some of the principles of formal logic from Aristotle. In all cases the systematic presentation of the rules of syllogistic inference is present. All

---

[82] Ibid. p. 104.

regulation of the legalistic variety should contain a major and minor premise leading to a conclusion.

Appreciation

A mode of informal regulation, which is derived from general philosophy and due to the dialectical concepts involved, it does not allow reduction into distinctly discrete categories. (In Chapter 5 dialectical concepts are further described.) Appreciation is the interpretation of self and the environment of self through an evaluative process including: facts, values, ideologies and relations between these (Vickers, 1970). Appreciation allows a better approximation of the richness of a complex environment, which I feel is now required for a mode of regulation since, as Vickers put it,

> [As] creators of a multiple, enduring inner world, men have become free to develop multiple enduring interests - for example, the interests of all the sciences. Possessed by multiple interests, they develop multiple expectations; and these generate multiple aspirations, constituting standards by which to judge what is and might be.[83]

Legislation

A dominant component of the legalistic mode which entails the written enactment of rules for behavior that are bound in a single time frame, directed towards regulating future occurrences, as designed on past occurrences, and justified by worst case scenarios. This term is developed further in Chapter 6.

Negotiation

A dominant process of the appreciative mode which entails the process and the fact of the agreement on rules for behavior, which are not written into statutes. A time frame is involved in the agreement, but it is implicitly directed towards regulation of future occurrences,

---

[83] Vickers, 1970, p. 197.

as based on joint agreement of what activities would be in the best interest of all parties involved in the negotiation. The justification comes from joint movement towards a commonly agreed upon objective, which may be ambiguous, but appears to be in the interest of the parties involved and their environment. This term is developed further in Chapter 6.

LEGAL ORDER	NEGOTIATED ORDER
• Adversary pleading	• Explanatory
• Based on threats	• Promissory
• Relies on adjudication	• Group decision making
• Relies on perfect information	• Relies on imperfect information
• Induces simplicity	• Retains complexity
• Assumes constant values	• Requires value adjustment

<u>FIGURE 5.1: PROPERTIES OF TWO REGULATORY SYSTEMS</u>

<u>Adjudication</u>

A third type of decision making which relates to legislation but aids in clarification of negotiation. All three forms involve <u>participants</u>, all contain <u>values</u>, and all lead to <u>outcomes(s)</u>. Negotiation involves participants, contains values that are in motion through the process, and results in outcomes that are characterized as non-zero sum. Legislation involves participants, but the outcome of the process does not rely so heavily on the specific types of values in the situation, nor their changes, but upon the mass/size of the participants favoring the outcome. Adjudication, on the other hand, also involves participants, but the outcome relies on the strength of the values of the participants involved, not the size of the group. Legislation involves only a two-sided choice of yes or no, thus it represents a zero-sum situation. Although adjudication involves the selection of one item in an infinite field, only one set of individuals, of a single individual, makes the choice. Thus, conflict about values continues after the decision.

<u>Environment</u>

An important concept throughout the paper, but difficult to define without regard to the entity which an environment reacts with.

> It is, in principle, impossible to draw any line of separation in space between organism and environment because organism are not static structures separable in space but are opposing directions in the biological total process.[84]

Angyal goes on to distinguish between environment and "external world," where, "The external world can be called environment only when and in so far as it is in interaction with the organism."[85]

Ozbekhan (1974) goes beyond the idea of the environment to try to identify changing environments,

> Recently the word "environment" has been judged somewhat too static. Consequently, changing environments are, therefore, increasingly referred to as <u>situations</u>, which connotes a temporal dynamic environment made of conjecture of events.[86]

For this dissertation, environments will be thought of as the context half of the system-context distinction. This follows the development of Angyal that environment and organism are opposing directions in a "biological total process." In the previous chapter a further distinction was made between perceptual and conceptual environments, which remains for this definition; the only difference is whether an idea or an object form the "object."

Various senses of the term "environment" are included in the subject area of the dissertation. Four of them are developed here and further discussed in following chapters.

<u>Environmental deterioration/quality</u>

---

[84] Angyal, 1941, p. 92.
[85] Ibid., p. 97.
[86] Ozbekhan, 1974, p. 7.

Environmental deterioration was the stimulus for the social activities which this dissertation uses as its subject matter. Deterioration is a qualitative characteristic which denotes a degrading of the object. It can be defined in terms of the converse called "environmental quality," which should result from an enhancement of the total object of discussion. Unfortunately, the current environmental social policies towards the physical environment have come to be reduced to several discrete categories of deterioration/quality.

> Environmental Quality - A catch—all covering pure air, clean water, fertile soil, beautiful architecture, soft music, no dangerous pesticides or radiation, no starvation, survival of all present species of human, animal and plant life, and social cement (so that all men love each other and share in order to avert crime and other undesirable items). Since it is immediately obvious that we cannot hurriedly have such ideal environmental quality, the next best thing is to see to it that the environment meets certain criteria and standards of quality. These are to be found under Air Quality, and Water Quality.[87]

This author feels that the logic behind this definition is unfortunate, but that it approximates the operations of achieving environmental quality in industrialized nations today. Reviewing the operations of environmental deterioration regulation during the past eight years illustrates how mankind did not think it could achieve the idealized quality which the environment should have, but it did try to achieve what it thought was expediently possible.

Environmental protection/control

The most common response to environmental deterioration has been to "protect" the environment. This implied benevolence on mankind's part is problematical, in that it allows continuation of the homocentric

---

[87] Encyclopedic Dictionary of the Environment 1971.

point of view which helped generate the initial deterioration. Most countries in the industrialized world now have installed protection departments in their governmental systems, but there is little evidence that this has resulted in any significant value change on the part of the societies of each country. The homocentric attitude remains prevalent in environmental protection activities, at least in the United States.

In Sweden, a slight shift in values might have occurred, although some think the Swedes exhibited a nature—centered value, set historically (Tomasson, 1970, p. 273). In Sweden, there was more emphasis on control of man and his relations to the environment, instead of protection of the environment, but even this emphasis was not enough to confront the dysfunctions of environmental deterioration (Nyberg, 1976).

The point of departure developed in this dissertation is that deterioration is a difficult distinction. It calls for a response that enhances and enhancement comes from the aesthetic domain. This generates difficulty at the outset in arriving at a common social objective for resolution of the problem, in that aesthetic issues tend to be a property unique to everyone. (Such an objective is necessary for negotiation to function properly.) As such, the problem area is retitled <u>environmental disintegration</u>, which calls for a response of <u>environmental integration</u>. Integration, which is discussed and developed in Chapter 5 offers an easier objective for a society to hold in common.

<u>Goals/objectives</u>

According to Ackoff, goals are "objectives whose attainment is desired by a specified time within the period covered (by the plan)."[88]

Ackoff further clarified goals in 1971 when he stated that,

> The <u>goal</u> of a purposeful system in a situation is the preferred outcome that can be obtained within a specified time period.

---

[88] Ackoff, 1970, p. 23.

> The <u>objective</u> of a purposeful system in a particular situation is a preferred outcome that cannot be obtained within a specified period, but which can be obtained over a longer time period.[89]

Results and consequences

Ozbekhan continues with the clarification of goals and objectives and connects them with the concepts of results and consequences,

> In the case of purposeful systems, acts are directed toward pre—figured results which are called <u>goals</u>. The consequences of attaining goals should rationally be envisioned as the <u>objectives</u> of the action. If, as it often happens, they are not, it means that the thought processes underlying and motivating the action were exclusively directed towards results, and the consequences were ignored.[90]

Ozbekhan describes one example where consequences were ignored, for the sake of achieving results, which turns out to be another description of the environmental deterioration situation.

We have only recently come to understand that technological or industrial civilization such as ours have emphasized goals, i.e., immediate or intermediate "results" while ignoring the consequences that are caused when such results are attained. But the ability - one is tempted to say talents - we have developed for reaching results incrementally, seems to have proved very costly, for the consequences of our success, obtained within the framework of a purely techno—utilitarian outlook, have now created a situation that is defined by the worldwide "mess" which, earlier on, I have called the <u>problematique</u>.91

Regulation

---

[89] Ackoff, 1971.
[90] Ozbekhan, 1974, p. 8.
[91] Ibid., p. 8.

The act of bringing an object under the actor's control, according to rule, with the use of negative and positive sanctions. In social regulation both the regulators and the regulated are human. (In the later chapters of this dissertation this definition of regulation is expanded beyond the limits of external sanctioning.)

5.4 Postulates

Four postulates form the basis of the theory of regulation developed in this dissertation:

1. Industrialized societies are engaged in a process where the social and the technical components and their interrelations are becoming increasingly complex for the members of the societies.
2. If the same societies are to continue collective functioning, an ordering system is essential for commonality of meanings and actions within the society.
3. The current preferred mode of bringing order (preferred as demonstrated by frequency of use) into complex social situations relies on legalism, where the objective is legal order.
4. Even though legalism may have social legitimacy as the preferred mode of regulation, it is deficient in ordering complexity.

Postulate 4 forms the rationale behind development of an alternative mode of regulation. The alternative attempts to be more adequate in regulating complexity through reliance on behavioral phenomena, such as interpersonal relations, intrapersonal capabilities, and the arts of appreciation, plus other items which contribute to the process of negotiated order.

5.5 Hypotheses

Hypothesis I

The legalistic response for bringing order into complex situations is inappropriate with respect to the following.

A. It is unable to account for an adequate proportion of a complex situation, because the descriptive model which legalism relies on is inadequate for complexity.
B. It tends to further enhance the detrimental characteristics of the conditions generating complexity initially.
C. It offers a mistaken impression, to the wider society, that a dysfunctional situation has been summarily and effectively dealt with.
D. It is a maladaptive response, in that as the mode is being pursued with increasing specificity, to match decreasingly specific problems, it functions less well, but each time the blame is put on lack of specificity, etc....

Hypothesis II

The appreciative response for bringing order into complex situations is appropriate in that:

A. It avoids the legalistic problem of creating a superordinate model of quality of life as a qualified article, in that it can function without that specificity;
B. It can adequately accommodate a large enough portion of a complex situation to allow a description that approaches the reality of the situation;
C. It allows the wider society to have a better notion of the success/failure of the regulation in real time;
D. It tends to be an adaptive response in that it allows a wide range of activities from the distinctly discrete to the ambiguous; and does not require material meant for one to be placed in the other.

Note: The formal aspects of Hypothesis I are self-clarifying which illustrates one considerable advantage which formalization allows, while Hypothesis II relies on negotiation for clarification of its boundaries and operations. Negotiation is the crucial variable for appreciation, where negotiation requires the following:

1. Recognition of the role of appreciation systems for the social elements and social systems involved in the regulation process. Vickers' book[92], develops this requirement.
2. "Movement" of appreciation systems through learning, understanding and acceptance. Bateson's book,[93] and Argyris and Schon's book on <u>Organizational Learning</u>, describes the importance of the learning requirement.
3. A recognition of the fundamental difference in social strategies between the society increasing its chances for survival by instilling redundancy in the social systems through a) redundancy of parts or b) redundancy of functions. Through the first response each social element becomes highly specialized in one functional area, while in the second response each element learns multiple functions. Emery and Trist's book,[94] describes this distinction fully.

According to Rapoport (1966, pp. 18—21), the necessary and sufficient conditions for the occurrence of negotiation come from the following four assumptions.

1. "Mixed motive": Both common and conflicting goals must be available to the parties negotiating. If there are only common goals the process would be discovery, not negotiation. If, on the other hand, there were only conflicting goals, there would not be a basis for the negotiation.
2. "Power Present": Abilities must be present within the negotiation to either make, or allow, things to happen.
3. "Imperfect Information": Some uncertainty or vagueness must be in the negotiation situation to allow room for potential joint development and movement between positions.
4. "Non—Zero Sum Nature of the Encounter" The outcome of the negotiation must be different than zero. The initial situation has been redefined through the process.

---

[92] <u>Value Systems and Social Processes</u>, 1968
[93] <u>Steps to an Ecology of Mind</u> 1973, p. 250
[94] <u>Towards a Social Ecology</u> (1973)

Based on these four assumptions, we can further assume that the following four elements must be present in negotiation (these are supported in Zartman's book, 1976, pp. 8—10):

1. <u>Participants</u> in the process.
2. <u>Values</u> - of each participant in the process.
3. <u>Outcome(s)</u> - to the process.
4. <u>Change in position</u> — implying a change in attained value of the outcome. (Without this, the process is discovery.)

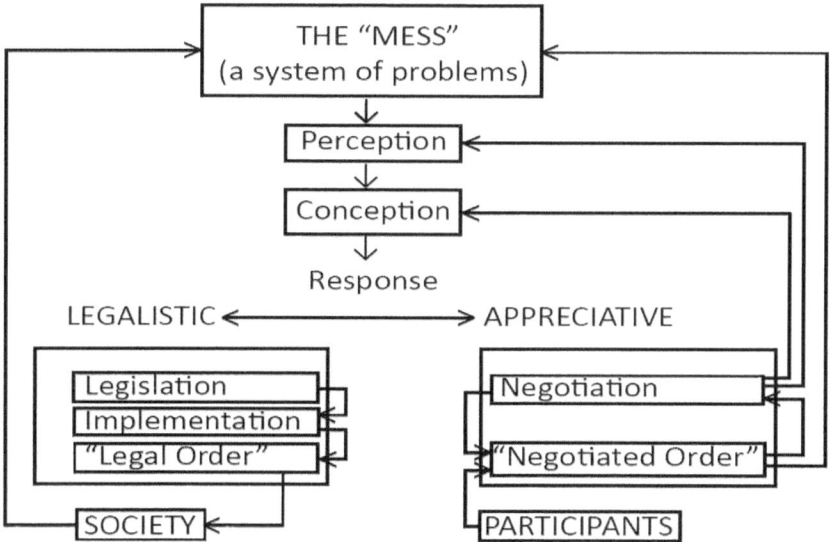

Figure 5.2. Theoretical Model

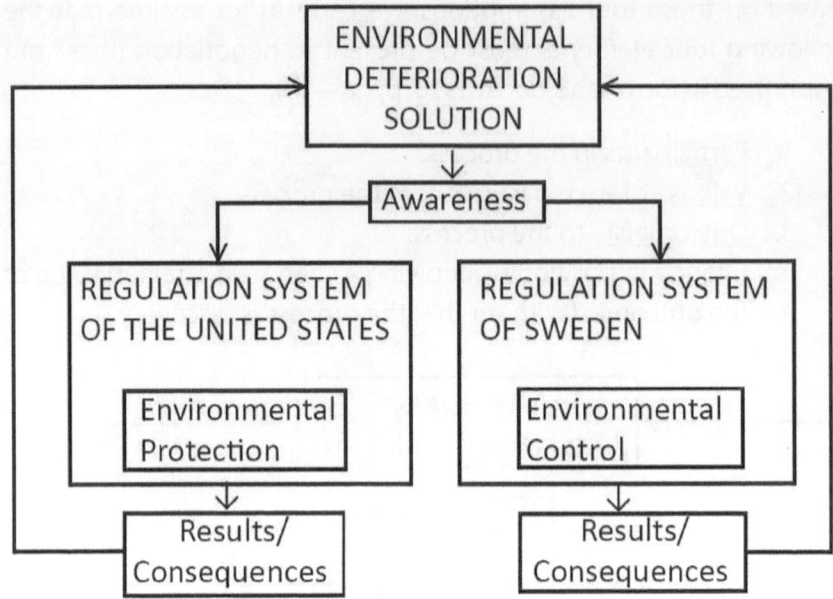

Figure 5.3 Empirical Model

Considerable elaboration on negotiation is presented in Chapter 6, where each of these assumptions and elements are discussed as variables with potential for "explaining the process of negotiation." It is concluded in Chapter 6 that none go much beyond simple correlation regardless of how extensively they have been developed.

Hypotheses Modeling and Testing

In what follows it should be carefully noted that the models of legislation and negotiation represent ideal types, and not the empirical process of either, although the dynamics of ideal types allows insight into the complexity of the empirical cases. Figure 2.1 presents the theoretical model; Figure 2.2 the empirical model.

The "mess" in Figure 2.1 introduced here, requires some further clarification here. This term, introduced by Ackoff (1974), describes a situation which transcends the situation of normal problem solving where there are at least two unequally efficient courses of action to an outcome and where doubt exists as to which is best. In a mess, the problem lies in a situation which is not well enough understood to allow such prior explication. Even where components of the situation can be analytically reduced to "problems," the problems have systemic characteristics which do not allow solution in isolation. In addition, a mess tends to be dynamic and to contain many participants representing a wide range of interests.

Five questions are required to relate the theoretical constructs to the empirical "facts." Beyond the traditional problems of mapping theory to experience for testing, there are additional problems with pure—chance influences; such as cultural factors differing between Sweden and the U.S. How these influences were controlled is described in the following chapter on the research method and its characteristics.

These questions help clarify the basis for the two hypotheses:

1. Are the properties of "The Mess" similar to the properties of "The Environmental Deterioration Situation?"
2. Is "The Environmental Deterioration Situation" similar in Sweden and the U.S.?
3. Do the properties of the U.S. system for environmental regulation have close similarities to the properties of the "Legalistic" response to the mess?
4. Do the properties of the Swedish system for environmental regulation have close similarities to the properties of the "Appreciative" response to the mess?
5. Is negotiated order of the appreciation mode a more effective response to the mess and its complex characteristics than the legal order (of the legalistic mode)?

The first two provide the base for the other three questions, which gauge the relative effectiveness of the two modes of bringing stability into social situations defined as messes.

Question 1

Messes are characterized as having:

- multiplicity of parts
- multiplicity of relationships between parts, and the whole
- dynamic movement of the whole as well as the parts
- numerous decision makers
- ambiguity
- The Environmental Deterioration Situation is characterized as having:
- numerous elements, such as: air, water, soil, built environment, music, chemicals, radiation, food, survival, etc.
- numerous complex interrelations between the elements (for elaboration on this see Vickers, 1970); now the relations are appearing to have systemic characteristics (see Ackoff, 1974; Ozbekhan, 1974; Hawk, 1977)
- self-exciting tendencies of the entire situation (see Vickers, 1970)
- the decision makers include all producers and consumers in the world

Answer to Question 1: The Environmental Deterioration Situation has similar properties to a Mess.

Question 2

Is the Environmental Deterioration Situation similar in Sweden and the U.S.?

Since Sweden has only eight million people and is about the size of California, there are some difficulties in comparing the environmental deterioration situation between a small (Sweden), and a much larger country (U.S.). On the other hand, both countries are part of the Western industrialized world which rely on very similar patterns of production and consumption to form quite similar lifestyles (at least materialistically). There are differences in consumption patterns (the Swedes rely on only 60% as much energy consumption per capita), but much of that difference can be explained through the Swedes making more efficient use of similar commodities. In both the U.S. and Sweden, you find extensive use of: automobiles, single-family houses, chemicals, plastics, artificial food additives/preservatives, nuclear power, etc.   In the research many difficulties in traditional comparisons were avoided by basing the study on physical production facilities which had similar raw material inputs and production outputs, so that the "cultural traits" could be greatly reduced. (In the next chapter this is explained in detail.)

Within the limitations of the research, the following conclusion is appropriate.

Answer to Question 2: That the phenomenon of Environmental Deterioration is similar in Sweden and the U.S. Support for this thesis, at a more general level beyond specific facilities, is given by: Lundqvist, 1974; Westerlund, 1976; and Goldman, 1972.

Question 3

Do the properties of the U.S. system for environmental regulation have close similarities to the properties of the "Legalistic" response to the mess?

The Legalistic Mode of Regulation is characterized as having:

- a major premise, a minor premise, a conclusion (the syllogistic inference as based on formalization)
- simplification through reduction
- based on static values
- a reliance on adjudication to resolve the dilemmas
- a considerable reliance on statutory (written) laws
- The U.S. System of Environmental Regulation is characterized as having:
- a belief that the dysfunctions of a society must be taken care of by formal legislation; a belief that environmental deterioration is a dysfunction; a conclusion that if laws are instituted the dysfunction will be corrected. Evidence of this is seen by looking at one Congress (from two staff members):

More than 2,000 bills related to environmental quality were introduced in the 91st Congress. Of these, 121 became public law out of a total of 695 bills signed during both sessions. The thrust of the legislation was to take a point—by—point approach to the environmental issue, dealing with specific aspects of larger problems.[95]

- the basic value system is a static homocentric view of the world which permeates the laws, the litigation, and the environmental review of man—made activities. For evidence of this refer to the previous chapter.
- the "clarification" of the statutes (another phrase for resolving the dilemmas) comes through extensive court litigation of most parts of each environmental law. For evidence of this refer to the 1977 Research Report for the "Chronology of Court Cases in the U.S. System." Where the courts cannot accommodate the dilemmas, they are resolved outside the "formal" system through sometimes illegal acts (e.g., indiscriminate dumping of toxic wastes, etc.).[96]

Answer to Question 3: That the U.S. System of Environmental Regulation Is Legalistic.

Question 4

Do the properties of the Swedish system for environmental regulation have close similarities to the properties of the "Appreciative" response to the mess?

The Appreciative Mode of Regulation is characterized as having:

- a non—formal logic approach to complexity
- dynamic values
- a reliance on interpersonal relations to resolve dilemmas
- a reliance on non—written laws (e.g., norms)

---

[95] Brezina and Overmyer, <u>Congress in Action</u>, The Free Press: N.Y., 1974, p. 23
[96] Hawk, 1977.

- The Swedish System of Environmental Regulation is characterized as having:
- The properties of being inquisitive, explanatory and requiring broad-based decision-making.[97]
- Limited resort to legal statutes with almost all the environmental areas being included in one, fifteen-page law. An implicit reliance on keeping the guidelines for action within people's heads. The reason for this, as stated in interviews, was, "When you put guidelines down on paper, they become too difficult to modify and they imply mistrust."[98]
- A recognition that uncertainties are inherent in an attempt at regulation and they must be explicitly accommodated. For evidence of how this is handled in the Swedish system see[99] where a passage from the Swedish law is translated to illustrate how, "When events surrounding a permit change, the permit should be changed."

<u>Answer to Question 4: That the Swedish System of Environmental Regulation tends, in many respects, toward the appreciative mode of regulation.</u> The difficulty in clarifying which direction it is heading comes from it containing some aspects of the legalistic approach. For example, some aspects of formal logic occur in the Swedish system which have led to some legalistic conclusions (e.g., that sophisticated specialists located in the central government could forcibly direct policy for local government in order to improve environmental quality. The basis for the direction was similar to formal logic (see Hawk, 1977).

The difficulties in specifying the appreciative mode of regulation without an empirical mode that accurately fits it will be dealt with in Chapters 5 and 6. The comparison within Question 5 also must deal with the shortcomings of the Swedish mode not having all the characteristics of the ideal appreciative mode.

Question 5

---

[97] Hawk, 1977, pp. 21-32
[98] Hawk, 1977, p. 21
[99] Hawk 1977, p. 31

Is the negotiated order of appreciation a more effective response to the mess and its complex characteristics than the legal order?

Since the Swedish system of regulation only approximates the appreciative mode, it is difficult to arrive at a definitive answer to this question, but a careful comparison of the results of the Swedish versus the U.S. system of environmental pollution regulation, and the contributing properties of each system, indicates an answer of "yes" to Question 5.

On the following page the previous questions are summarized. In the remainder of the chapter an <u>outline</u> of empirical research information is given which compares the results of the U.S. system of environmental regulation with the Swedish system. This information preempts some parts of Chapters 3 and 4. Chapters 3 and 4 are only an outline of the information in the 1977 Research Report (Hawk, 1977), as the report is a self—standing document which should be referred to.

Summary of questions; leading to conclusions about an alternative mode of regulation:

6. The Environmental Deterioration Situation does qualify as a Mess.
7. The Environmental Deterioration Situations of Sweden and the U.S. do have similar characteristics.
8. The properties of the U.S. Environmental Regulation System do tend toward Legalism, with legislation toward legal order.
9. The properties of the Swedish Environmental Regulation System do tend toward Appreciation, with negotiation toward negotiated order, although some elements of the Legalistic approach are identifiable in the system.
10. The negotiated order approach of appreciation is a more effective response to the complex characteristics of a mess.

The difficulty in showing that the Swedish System is clearly Appreciative turned out to be to the advantage of the research. In the cases of the research where the properties of the legalistic mode of regulation were clearly found, there were clear dysfunctions in achieving the goals of the regulatory system. The examples of this are discussed in Chapter 4, but, in brief, they deal with the following: where one negotiating party repeatedly relied on the "letter of the law" to make his argument; where a central government/business authority insisted in taking the "tried and true" method of pollution control because its results were more certain; where one of the negotiating parties resorted to adjudication to resolve an apparent dilemma and where the various conceptual categories of the physical environment were given too strict an interpretation. (This last one was where air pollution clean—up was emphasized with total disregard for the resultant solid waste residue.)

5.6 Evaluation

Since the Swedish Environmental Regulation System tends toward the Appreciative mode of social regulation, and the U.S. System approximates the Legalistic mode of social regulation, a comparison of the results/consequences of the two systems should give an introductory evaluation of the desirability of each mode for "mess" type problems which have systemic characteristics.

As a reminder, results are the goals desired within the period planned for, while the longer-term results of achieving these goals are consequences. Before laying out some of the results/consequences of the two systems, a general outline is given of how each system has reacted to specific operational areas.

<u>Design of the legislation</u>

The U.S. system relies on extensive sets of statutes which are meant to dovetail together, allowing the regulators a finely meshed web which ideally can account for considerable complexity. In the U.S. system there are eight major environmental areas, and each is further sub—divided.

The Swedish system has one major statute of approximately fifteen pages, which integrates all eight of the major U.S. areas of the environment. Unlike the U.S. statutes, the law is nonspecific, written in ordinary layman's terms, and allows for future dilemmas by letting the negotiators rework an agreement if time should prove the agreement inappropriate.

Environmental impact review

The U.S. system relies on "environmental impact statements," which are extensive analyses of the separate areas of the environment; specialists in each of the areas are responsible for these reviews.

The Swedish system relies on a less well—integrated (at least in terms of the analytic documentation), inquiry processes of individuals representing a wide array of interest groups, with the final decisions made by people with a generalist's point of view.

A major distinction in this very important domain of reviewing the impact which a man—made project will have on the environment is that the Swedish tends towards a "redundancy of functions" approach, while the U.S. relies on a "redundancy of parts" approach.[100]

Societal view of the problem's "cause"

In the U.S. system there is an emphasis on certain elements of the society as being responsible for the dysfunctions of environmental pollution and that they must be summarily dealt with in order to "solve" the problems. This "cause" of the problem is best dealt with by forcing the "elements" to do more than is currently considered feasible. (This is called "technology forcing.")

In Sweden there tends to be a view that the dysfunctions lie within the social image of "life—styles" and the value set which it is based on. Hedlund and Julander (1977) elaborate on why this is so, and what it means for Swedish society.) This lessens the tendency toward undue simplification and an attack on parts of the problem, where considerable resources are expended but meager solutions result. The current difficulty in the Swedish system is that, recently, it is tending to show signs of the expert/specialist taking over the problem responsibility, like the U.S. trend. Following are comparisons of the properties of the Swedish and U.S. systems (from the 1977 Research Report):

---

[100] Emery and Trist, 1973, p. 71

The U.S. System

- Perceived from inside the system as being very resilient to change
- Perceived by the major stakeholders (those with a stake in the situation), as resistant to change
- Perceived by the major stakeholders as beyond their understanding.
- Relies on narrow—based and detailed expert decision making, with low public participation.
- Segmented, superficial and dissociative in responses to complexity.[101]
- Heavy reliance on the technical—fix approach.

The Swedish System

- Perceived from inside the system as being very fragile.
- Perceived by the major stakeholders as flexible.
- Perceived by the major stakeholders as very difficult to understand, but potentially comprehensible.
- Relies on broad—based expertise for decision—making. (Looking at the National Franchise Board shows this well).
- Low in public participation, as measured by turn—out for public inquiries on project environmental review.
- Hesitant about the high technology approach to resolution of the problem (they prefer the term "appropriate").

Another means to compare the two systems is in terms of the permitting process, where a potential polluter must gain a permit to carry out an action which might result in a pollution outfall or might impact the natural environment.

The following figures illustrate the differences between the two systems for permitting. In Sweden, there are five possible routes, and one is selected. In the U.S., there are at least five routes, all of which must be taken, and where there are several permits possible within each of the five.

---

[101] Emery and Trist, 1973, pp. 60—67

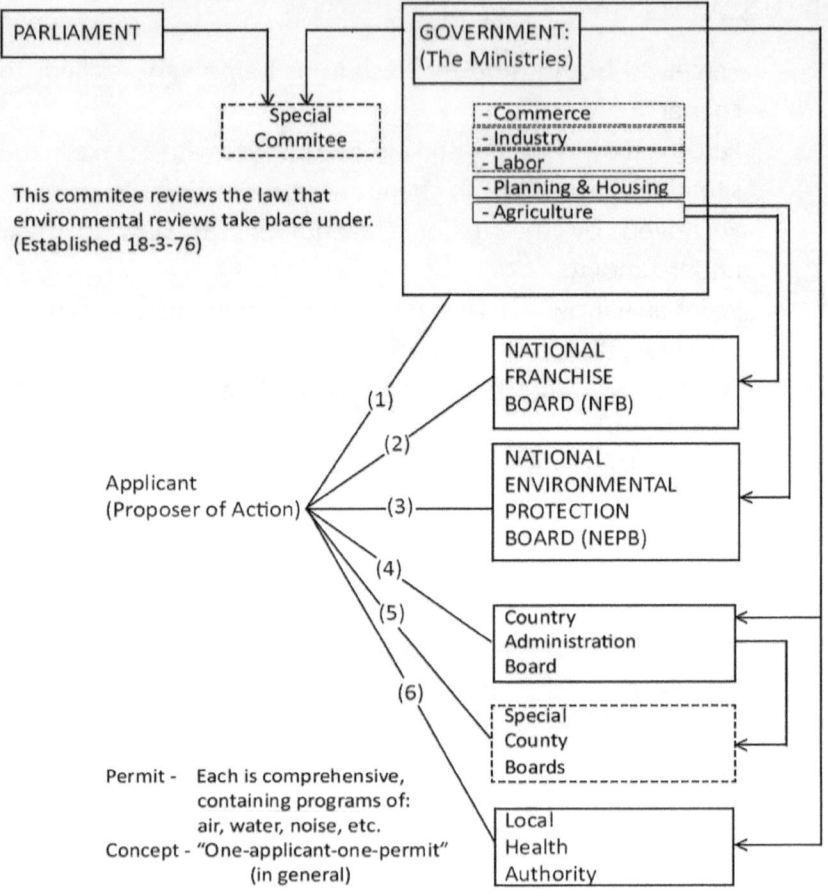

Figure 5.4 Swedish Permitting Process

It is difficult to establish a broad comparison of the results and consequences of the two regulation systems, but information is building up in several areas. The results/consequences are compared in terms of goals/objectives in some of these in the following section.

Too Early, Too Late, now what?

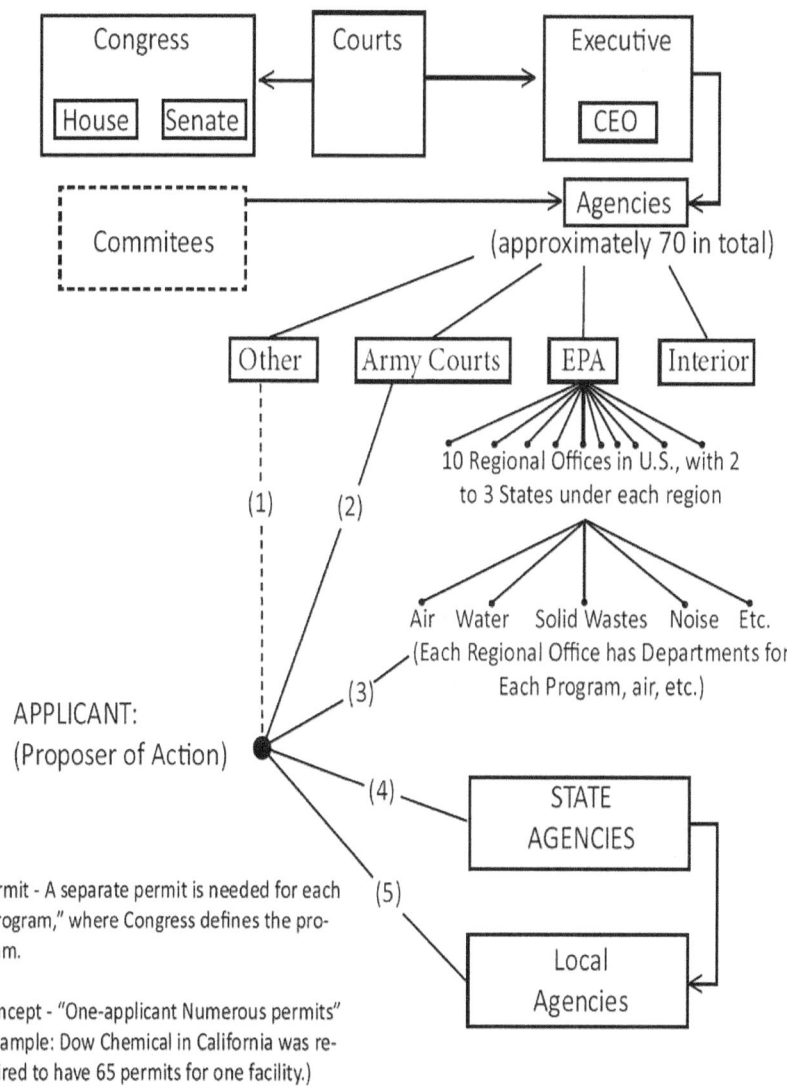

5.5 United States Permitting Process

5.7 Contextual Comparison of Regulation Modes

Goals/Objectives

<u>Sweden</u>

The longer-term objective was to reduce the impact of pollutants on the physical environment and eventually gain control over man's impact on the environment. The shorter-term objectives (the goals) to achieve this were the following.

1. To gain and retain the cooperation of those who were polluting to work with the regulators to jointly design methods of controlling the pollution.[102]
2. To refrain from concentrating on short—term results of pollution reduction, and instead plan towards long—term control of pollution, so as not to create problems in other areas of society through that control.[103]
3. To refrain from dependence on a centralized bureaucracy for regulation implementation.[104]

<u>United States</u>

The longer-term objective was to reduce the dysfunctions in man—environment relations so as to improve the quality of life of man (NEPA, 1969). (The shorter-term objectives (goals) to achieve this were not very explicit, but they can be inferred from many discrete policies and regulatory activities carried out during the past eight years.)

1. To gain explicit control over those who pollute the environment and force them to do what they would not normally do and do it in a manner which is beyond what is possible at the time of the laws. (Taken from interview notes with those responsible for design and implementation of regulations) (Hawk, 1977).

---

[102] Hawk, 1977
[103] Hawk, 1977
[104] Lundqvist, 1974

2. To achieve spectacular short—term results (to set a standard of achievement) by setting up firm guidelines and timetables. If there were long term problems with this, then the law, "could be changed" (Hawk, 1977). "Economic and technical feasibility could not be considerations."[105]
3. To set up a "decentralized" governmental system to administer the regulation.[106]

Results/consequences

Sweden

1. There is close cooperation between the regulators and those regulated. In many cases those regulated set their own requirements, thereby becoming their own regulators. The most noticeable result of this is the reduction of the administrative need for enforcement and policing of regulations; this could also be considered a consequence.
2. The initial requirements of the regulators were lenient in terms of standards and timetables, with limited success in quick reduction of pollutant outfalls as the result. The goal of longer-term improvement now appears to be emerging with substantial reductions now coming about through redesign of the basic industrial technical processes. The consequences of this are the costs (economic) are reasonable, the commitment of those regulated continues and the innovation of pollution reduction methods is high.
3. Although the goal was to avoid the centralized bureaucratic approach, only limited success has been achieved in carrying this out at this point, although efforts are being made to transfer most of the permit negotiating powers to the county level of government. (This would correspond to the regional government in the U.S.) The consequence of not achieving this goal is that there are some interpersonal relations difficulties with government people at the central and local levels. The

---

[105] Water Quality of Amendments of 1972
[106] Hawk, 1977

former views the latter as less than competent, while the latter side doesn't trust the intent of the former. The dominant argument for centralization is that the <u>technical sophistication and complexity requires highly trained experts</u> in many disciplines, a requirement which the local governments cannot afford to meet.

United States

1. The goal to gain control over those who pollute has been achieved in terms of statutes, but its administration is becoming more impossible with time. Of the regional offices sampled, 30% of their resources were spent monitoring 10% of the major sources in their region. To force people to do what a regulator perceives they would not normally do requires considerable monitoring. The consequence of <u>desiring</u> to attain this goal (although the goal has not actually been achieved), has meant that most sources of pollution are not monitored, and those that are, tend to rely on the court system to delay the requirements imposed on them. (This is for existing plants; for new plants, it tends to mean that approval is so difficult to gain that they are not approved or built.)
2. In many respects short term results were achieved in some areas of pollutants, but as the standards become stricter, the pollutants are not further reduced. The reason for this is that to meet the early clean—updates the pollution sources had to add "filters" onto existing equipment, and did not have the time to go back and redesign the production equipment (Hawk, 1977). To meet the stricter standards, equipment redesign is essential, but most resources had already been invested in the "add—on filters." Comparing the Honda automobile with the U.S. automobiles illustrates this consequence clearly. (Honda <u>redesigned</u> the idea of "engine," while the U.S. cars added catalytic converters.)
3. The U.S. has had no more success in decentralizing the regulation system than the Swedes have had. The consequences of not achieving this In the U.S. has been similar to that in Sweden. Technical sophistication, as the argument for central decision

control, appears to be the key variable in the U.S system as well. Although there is evidence in both countries of less sophisticated equipment possibly working better, and longer, in pollution clean—up, little attention is paid to it. The consequence of central decision making is that the same technical solutions tend to be applied regardless of a situation's circumstances. A consequence following this is that the local individuals accept little responsibility for maintenance or monitoring, or, of more importance, further improvements.

5.8 Comparisons of Municipal Treatment of Sewage

As of the Spring of 1976, over 60% of the municipalities in Sweden had connected to third order treatment. (This is very high cleaning with chemical and biochemical treatment. Second order is biological treatment, with first order being only sedimentation.) Similar figures are not available in the U.S., but the Comptroller General's Office undertook a representative sampling in 1976 of 120 municipalities. Their conclusion was that:

- 34 municipalities were at secondary or higher levels of treatment which was operating well enough to meet the national water quality standards,
- 32 had secondary treatment, but did not operate so as to achieve the water quality standards,
- 42 had achieved primary treatment levels,
- 7 had almost no treatment but were soon to hook up with regional waste facilities, and
- 5 had only primary treatment, but due to lack of money were not required to do better.

This begins to introduce the issue of monetary resources required to achieve the legislated requirements in the U.S. In 1976 it was estimated that it would take 107 billion dollars for the municipalities to meet the 1972 water quality laws in sewage control. (This would be by 1983). In 1973 it was discovered that the sewage problem was not the most crucial. Storm water was part of a larger problem with "non—point" sources. To deal with storm water run—off in cities it would require an additional 225 billion dollars. The following chart illustrates the results of a 1975 study by the National Academy of Sciences on <u>sources of pollution</u>.

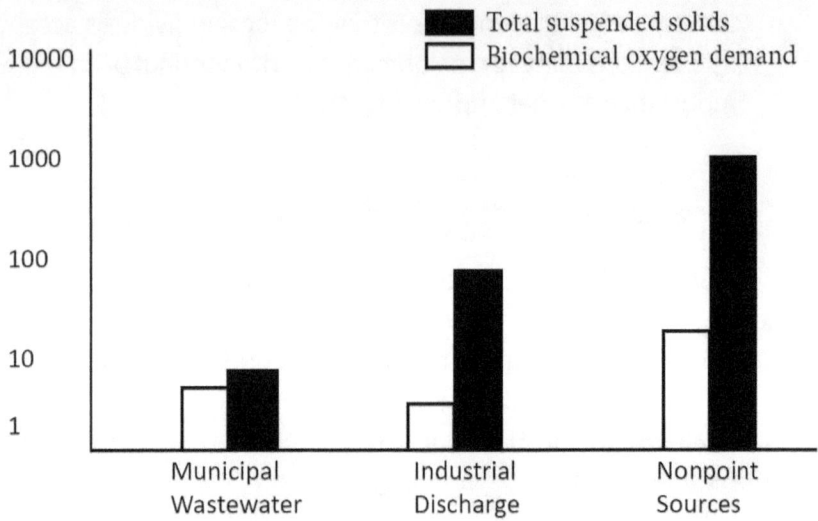

Figure 5.6 Pollution sources in the United States

5.9 Industrial Pollution Sources

The specific comparison data on industrial production facilities in Sweden and the U.S. is presented in the next two chapters.

From the cases investigated in the research, the Swedish facilities tended to have less stringent restrictions, yet were achieving lower levels of emissions in most of the categories of pollution. In addition, the reduction of pollutants in the Swedish context appeared to be at a "take—off" point of success, with further substantial gains beginning to be made. For example, one pulp and paper facility was required to meet a limit of 5.4 kilos of suspended solids in the outflowing water per ton of pulp production. (The U. S. counterpart was required to meet a 5.4 kiloton of production.)

The actual outflow of the Swedish facility during 1976 ranged from 8.8 kilo/ton P. to 2.5 kilo/ton P. with the first six months of 1977 showing substantial reductions below this:

January:	.16 K/ ton P.
February:	.19 K/ton P.
March:	.14 K/ ton P.
April:	.15 K/ ton P.
May:	.11 R/ton P.
June:	.08 K/ton P.

Figure 5.7: Success in Swedish Pollution Control

On the other hand, the U.S. facilities seemed to be reaching a leveling off point to their initial advances gained by adding filtration systems on the end of the production streams. For example, the counterpart of the Swedish pulp and paper plant had been cited in 1976 as being one of the "cleanest facilities of its kind in the world" by the Environmental Protection Agency was due to a biological treatment phase where "bugs" would eat the biological organisms which were using up the oxygen in the water. The difficulty, which was discovered later, was that due to the first law of thermodynamics, the bugs then became suspended solids in the water. Later, a mechanism was developed to "skim" off the bugs, but this has only increased the quantities of solid waste which require disposal. There are some aspects of these same problems within the Swedish context, but somehow, they tend to be resolved in a more desirable manner over the longer term.

The advantages of the cooperation and learning activities of the more appreciative Swedish system of environmental regulation appear to present a more desirable response to the complexities of the environmental deterioration situation. The formalistic logic of the U.S. system seems not to be able to deal with the dilemmas which surface from the ambiguity of "messes." The following two chapters present information on the research which allowed formulation of the two hypotheses Chapters 5 and 6 will develop the thesis more fully.

CHAPTER 6

Researching Environmental Protection Regulation

The area of research interest lies with the regulation and control of interrelationships. In Chapter 1 this interest was discussed in the areas of man attempting to regulate nature, technology, other humans, and his self. It was pointed out that current attempts to regulate man to nature relations have excluded considerations of the man to man and the man-to-self areas. The current mode of regulation is evaluated in a comparative manner against an alternative mode of regulation advanced in the second chapter using concepts of regulation, change and complexity.

Where U.S. regulatory attitudes typify much of the current thinking and practice in the area, the Swedish attitude poses an alternative. The Swedish regulation system does not fit the appreciation mode exactly, but it does allow enough of an approximation to give an idea of the operations of appreciation. The description of the U. S. and Swedish modes of regulating environmental affairs is laid out in detail in the final research report (Hawk, 1977). Parts of that report are outlined in the following two chapters, with special reference to the conclusions and the summation of the results. Chapters 5 and 6 build on these conclusions and link the implications of the conclusions into the theoretical base of Chapters 1 and 2.

The contents of the 1977 Report demonstrate the shortcomings of continuing to apply a fixed repertoire of analytical solutions to complex societal problems. Complex problems were defined in Chapter 2 of this paper, but essentially, they are problems with interdependent parts which combine to exhibit properties beyond those of the parts. Complex problems appear to be increasingly characteristic of modern societies. It is important to note here that complex problems defy analytical dissection and simplistic reduction, methods which have previously been enormously successful for the industrialized world. Perhaps a portion of the complex societal problems we now must deal with can be attributed to some of the historic achievements of traditional analytical thinking.

The single most important point to come out of the 1977 Report is that continued reliance on <u>reductionistic analysis</u> to deal with complex societal problems is, simply not on anymore. Not only are we, as western industrial societies, not dealing with these complex problems at a time when the stakes are reaching a perilous level, but our current preferred mode of problem solving may further complicate the problems.

The environmental deterioration situation was selected as an example of a complex societal problem which was in a stage of its "life cycle" advantageous to research. There is a business phenomenon termed the "product life cycle" where a product is introduced, gains increased acceptance and use, declines from favor, and then passes from public attention which seems to have counterpart in societal issues. Donald Schon (1971) has termed the social phenomenon "ideas in good currency." In September of 1975, when the project was initiated, environmental protection appeared to be the socially acceptable response to environmental deterioration. Due to the stage it was in, it offered a valuable example to study the consequences of current solutions to complex problems.

Environmental protection first emerged as a reaction to environmental deterioration during the 1950s. Numerous divergent interest groups coalesced around the response during the 1960s and strict legislation was used to institute the response in the early seventies. Thus, by 1975 - the initiation of the research - there should have emerged substantial information on the consequences of protection actions. This thesis was generally correct, but the vastness of the environmental protection issue posed serious methodological difficulties.

6.1 The Research Project

In September of 1975 a research project was launched which was titled <u>Environmental Regulation and Organizational Behavior: A Comparative Study of Interaction Processes In Sweden and the U.S.</u>

> The socially mandated meeting ground of the industrialists and environmentalists came to be known as environmental protection. This meeting ground was the domain of the research where the research objective was to describe, and perhaps understand, the dynamics and significance of environmental protection activities. Close cooperation of leading governmental and industrial organizations was essential to this objective.[107]

Ostensibly, the purpose of industrial organizations is to utilize raw materials in the production of consumable goods and services, where many of the raw materials are found in the natural environment. Environmentalists, on the other hand, propose to protect and preserve the natural environment. This poses a possible conflict of interest. Important to the research study was the identification of the consequences of activities which attempted to reconcile, ignore, or expand the conflicts. Considerable data surfaced which would support the position of either side. This posed a dilemma for evaluating past action and suggesting future activities. After the research commenced it was discovered that much of the data in the area was of the strictly quantitative type, as collected from technical, biological, and chemical phenomena in the domain of the research. Later it was discovered that the other major variety of data, the "qualitative," was important to give meaning to the quantitative. This was so because the more qualitative

---

[107] The 1977 Report, p. i

data described the behavioral attributes of the humans who were carrying out the technical, biological, and chemical operations. As such, the qualitative arena allowed access to the normative and goal-directed design behavior which is essential to human activity.

The following introductory comments from the research report outlines some of the dilemmas encountered in the research.

> The results of the project were encouraging in some respects, yet quite discouraging in others. A substantial source of encouragement originated with the ease of the research process. Individuals contacted throughout the research offered active and committed help in describing the aspects of environmental concerns important to them. The individuals appeared genuinely concerned with identification of what "good" environmental protection means, and then implementing it. This was the case even with representatives of organizations with "bad" reputations. For example, one of the companies assisting with the research had been characterized in a 1975 book on large corporations as, "The meanest of the big companies, the loner in the West, refusing to contribute anything for profit... They established a tradition of skinflint management and centralized control." But, based on evidence from government officials, documentation and physical construction, this firm had one of the most successful approaches to environmental improvement.[108]

In general, both industry and government representatives were found to be responsive to concerns in the environmental area and to act responsibly within a definition they had been given. Yet, something seemed to be wrong.

---

[108] Ibid., p. ii

> A surprisingly high proportion of the individuals interviewed felt that something was seriously wrong with the mode of environmental protection they were dealing with, but none felt they held the power to do much to change the situation. This introduced the discouragement found within the research project.[109]

If individuals are acting in a manner responsive to problems encountered, and if the actions are within a framework which defines allowable actions, and yet if the same individuals feel there is something wrong with the actions they are taking, a <u>dilemma</u> exists. Current practices of environmental protection illustrate a clear example of reductionistic analysis utilized to solve complex problems. This form of analysis tends to induce dilemmas. (Pages 175 to 181 of the 1977 Report explain reductionistic analysis.) Essentially it is where the parameters, characteristics, and mechanisms of a problem are presented by reducing a problem to its most obvious components, then solving the components. This rests on the belief that the sum of "solved" components will add up to a total solution of the problem. There is ample evidence of this not being so.

> The results of the research point out that members of Western industrial societies now face a Faustian dilemma where the powers of analysis of ever smaller and more specialized phenomena, are turning against the social order which sponsors it. Indeed, the environmental ethic, which the research concentrated on, may have only been a temporary pause in the growth of the dilemma, where the ethic itself has now been delegated to further reduction.[110]

Within the research, Sweden provided an example of a system that has avoided some aspects of the analytical dilemma. Analysis is relied

---

[109] Ibid., p. ii
[110] Ibid., p. ii

on in the Swedish system, but the results of analysis are held in lower reverence than in the U.S.

> In the Swedish environmental protection system technology takes a lower profile and individuals from differing interest groups appear to have a clearer perception of the validity of competing interests. In the Swedish system there is at least the image - in environmental regulation – that all interests should compose into a larger social interest. In the U.S. it appears that adequate social policy is to allow the "strongest" interest to prevail. This facet of the U.S. system can be studied by plotting a chart of the "attitude path" of individuals as they travel back and forth from industry to government appointments.[111]

Within the realm of environmental protection, it is becoming increasingly popular to seek the solution of returning to the initial industrial processes, to eliminate pollution at the outset. In many cases this policy has been used, in Sweden and has met with some success, but in the U.S., where the policy is most discussed, little action has been taken. One barrier in the U.S. may well have been the overriding emphasis on a political ideal which resist any outside interference in a private facility. Another significant barrier, emerging from the research data, points to the U.S. strategy behind the regulation. Based on documentation and interviews with those most responsible, it was found that the U.S. regulators wanted rapid and ostentatious results. Swedish environmental regulation took a slower and more deliberate approach, where initial advances, made to reduce pollution, were expected to be minimal, but significant changes in industrial process design was expected to commence at the outset. Here we find evidence of the more behavioristic considerations found in the Swedish environmental policies. Individuals were allowed a longer period in Sweden to formulate changes which better matched their

---

[111] Ibid., p. ii

circumstances. This allowed the time to return to initial processes. Americans were adding on filters to "the end of the pipe" instead.

Of great Interest here is how the effort to return to initial process designs has not been enough to meet environmental ethic objectives. The U.S. system faces difficult problems in that the short-term gains have been found counter—productive to long term objectives. Sweden is now faced with other types of dilemmas where the return to initial processes had only limited success for these two reasons: 1) thermodynamic reasons relating to the conservation of matter and energy, and changes in quality due to use of either, and 2) man has now discovered that even if production processes are "clean," the subsequent use of the products produced may present greater pollution dangers to the environment. It is currently calculated that in the U.S. over half the pollution found has resulted from runoff. (Runoff is where the rainwater has washed over the ground surface and picked up particles and pollutants from the normal use of a product, e.g., agricultural pesticides or fertilizers.)

Thus, relying on analysis to reduce a complex problem so that it may become "solvable" will not necessarily result in a solution, it now appears that such an approach also creates dilemmas arising from contradictions between parts that are handled in isolation. For example, much of the initial policy for pollution reduction in the U.S. was directed at reduction of pollutants coming from the air and water streams at the ends of the production processes. This action collected a great deal of solid waste, which then required disposal, which, in turn, added to runoff.

Within the research, other dilemmas were identified which point out contradictions between what a society expresses as a value and what they act to attain. As an example, in both Sweden and the U.S. there is a strongly expressed concern against centralization of power in either government or business. In the U.S., the Small Business Administration is one manifestation of this value. It was interesting to note though, how current regulation policies and practices, especially in the U.S., are biased against smaller organizations. Although there was 11ttle evidence of this having been planned but there was considerable evidence of it occurring. In The 1977 Report an argument is put forward as to how the regulation of environmental protection has been working to the disadvantage against smaller organizations. Not only were larger organizations found to be more adept in dealing with regulation, once it had been instituted, but they were found to be more capable in forecasting regulation and intervening in the processes which designs the regulation.

Regulation in the U.S., and in some ways In Sweden, has explicitly directed control efforts against larger organizations for two reasons: 1) larger organizations tend to control larger facilities which generate greater amounts of pollution, (thus, it is assumable that greater value per expenditure of resource is received by controlling a few large sources), and 2) it was felt, with some justification, that the smaller organizations did not have sufficient resources to comply with the regulation requirements.

There are difficulties associated with each of these reasons. Under the first, it is now known that the total of all pollutants from sources considered "small" amounts to more than the total of those considered "large". Following up this discovery an attempt was made to control small sources, but now they appear to find it very difficult to adapt to regulation. This highlights a major fault with concentrating on large organizations first. When large polluters are the first target of regulation, they are the first to develop a set of competencies to deal with it. Then when the regulation activities reach out to the small organizations severe difficulties emerge. The small firms still do not have the resources to deal with specialized regulation activities and are forced to hire experts and buy technology from those who have already developed it, i.e., the large firms. In many cases this allows the larger organizations to have a market to subsidize their expertise. In some cases, some of the larger companies created a special division which would sell its competence in dealing with environmental regulations. In a later section on general issues raised in the research more specific information is offered about this dilemma of small versus large organizations confronting environmental regulation.

Additional dilemmas are also surfacing in contradictions between competing, societal ideals. Noticeable problems are emerging between ideas on environmental protection and energy conservation.

Contradictions between economic, energy and environmental values abound even for a Swedish system of regulation, although not at such a high level as in the U.S. In part the contradictions stem from the vast array of different specialties attempting to manage different issues, and in most cases even the same issue, and doing it as if the other specialties were unimportant. Presently we see no "specialty" with the ability to manage the collection of specialties. One example of an apparent conflict between values about environment and those on energy comes from the Department of Commerce in the U.S. Their analysis of the iron and steel, pulp and paper, and aluminum industries illustrated how these industries were expending 3.8 to 7.2% more energy to operate pollution control equipment for one pollutant, while at the same time the industries were being asked to conserve 10 to 15% of their energy use.[112]

6.2 Research Method

The method was <u>comparative</u>, with the comparison being between two sets of social systems. One set from Sweden, the other from the United States. The specific components within each set were selected in terms of their importance to the pollution control aspect of environmental protection activities. These components were identified through sample interviewing and a literature search. Approximately 20% of the initial fields were dropped from the research due to the low level of involvement they had in pollution control. The "grounding" for the research was finally set with specific industrial production <u>facilities</u> that were operated, and/or controlled, by the corporate systems selected for the research.

    A methodological difficulty with comparative research was faced at the outset of the investigation. In any research comparison

---

[112] Ibid., p. v

of dissimilar social unit sets there must be assumptions common to both which allow the research data to be comparable. Three such assumptions were arrived at for the research which this dissertation is based on.

1. The classification of sets of social systems — in this case Sweden and the U.S. - assumes that the two sets are sufficiently like each other with respect to specifically defined criteria that they may be compared analytically. This assumption allows the researcher to hold some criteria constant to rule them out as sources of variation.
2. Using specific variables to describe both sets assumes that these variables are present in all cases and are not specific to only some cases.
3. Using specific variables to measure processes taking place in the sets assumes that the causal processes furnishing these measures are sufficiently similar in both sets so that the variables indeed are similar enough to allow study.

This accepts that there will of course be differences between the compared sets, but that there must be enough commonality of criteria to allow measurement of differences. To study processes taking place in two countries like Sweden and the U.S., which are reported to have substantial differences in socio—political structuring and value—systems, climate, and size, etc., appears to make any such research difficult. If traditional comparative research would have been used these differences could still have been compared due to many similarities between Sweden and the U. S. There is more commonality between the two societies and their contexts than the news media and some scientific journals would imply. The socio—political structuring is less different than some literature might imply in that they both have an approximation of a democratic government. They both rely on legislation and governmental bureaucracy to implement their policies. The types of products which members of each society consume are remarkably similar, even though there is considerable variation in the quantities of certain products, e.g. in energy consumption per capita, Sweden uses about 60% as much as the U. S. There does tend to be more homogeneity in culture within Swedish society than in U.S. society, but even this social science idea has been questioned. A considerable number of people from other countries and cultures has immigrated to Sweden during the past ten years under the classification "political prisoners". During the Spring of 1977 racial conflicts like those of the U.S. emerged South of Stockholm, in a town called Sodertalje, inter—racial differences boiled over into open conflict. Traditional comparative analysis would probably have been possible, although difficult, between Swedish and American regulatory systems. One successful example is research published in a book entitled, <u>Size and Democracy</u>, by R. A. Dahl and E. Tufte (1973). Many potential difficulties of comparative analysis were avoided in this research through the addition of one more dimension. Difficulties with the three assumptions previously listed were reduced by adding an additional layer of social systems to the investigation. Thus, this means that there was a set of regulators within the Swedish context, a set of regulators within the U.S. context, and a third set of social systems common to and regulated by both countries.

Figure 5.1 illustrates the advantage of adding the third social system set to the research.

Traditional comparative analysis:

Comparative analysis as used in this research:

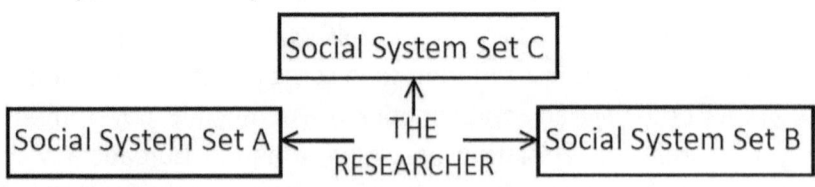

<u>Figure 6.1 Two alternatives to comparative analysis</u>

6.3 Data Collection and Major Participants

Data through interviewing and from documents obtained from interviewed individuals and general literature is presented in the 1977 Report (Hawk, 1977, pp. 113—115 offers a list of the interviewees). The interviews were carried out with individuals from the organizations listed on pages 18—20, where the individuals were chosen because of their level of contact in managing environmental protection issues for their organization. The individuals were identified through informal discussions with top management people in the organizations and through document search. Various points of each organization's hierarchy were sampled during the interviewing in order to allow a broader base for the information on strategies and practices of environmental protection. This layering of interviews made possible a study of attitudinal differences within each organization to discover the change in approach of a change in attitude. The collected information was then organized around twenty case studies to form a comparative base, from this base varying responses to regulation systems could then be identified.

The interviews were structured around a question set ranging from strategic, to organizational, to equipment design issues. During each interview considerable flexibility could the interviewee so that he, or she, could elaborate on items felt to be most important to him or her. The compilation of these items later was found to be a very important inquiry aspect of the research information. The interview times ranged from one and a half to eight hours, with variation depending on the depth of involvement of the individual in the issues being covered. In each case the initial questions centered on the interviewee's definition of "environment." In some cases, it included socio—behavioral components; in others it was limited to strict physical—technical areas. The second domain of questioning centered on how their organization was initially structured, how its structure had been modified to meet environmental protection regulation activities, and how it was being further modified to adapt to emerging regulation. The next three questions dealt with the actual policies and opera— t Ions in the environmental protection area. Five issue areas were:

1. Organizational structure and how it has been affected by environmental issues.
2. Strategies for dealing with environmental issues.
3. Dilemmas encountered in dealing with environmental issues with current policies. What changes would you like to make in these policies?
4. Relations with government people, or for government their relations with industry people in the environmental protection realm.
5. Relations between different sectors of the same organization over environmental protection issues.

This structure was followed by a more extemporaneous discussion of issues of importance to the person being interviewed. Various, quite specific questions were laced throughout the five areas mentioned above, to always offer a context to the question. Some of the information obtained, such as the capital expenditure for pollution control equipment plotted against total capital expenditure, was highly confidential.

The interviewees were also used as a basis for later implementation of the research results where individuals interviewed were relied on to distribute information about the research to their organization. Considerable effort was expended to make the interviewees an active part of the research, in some instances the interviewees wrote small subject papers to describe their recent roles in the environmental regulation process, and their desires for future roles. Papers were commonly sent back and forth between the interviewees and the researcher, to assure the interviewees of the seriousness of the project and to help the researcher to acquire a better understanding of the concepts and accepted terminology in the area of research for each organization.

The participants were drawn from three major sets of organization: 1) governmental, 2) industrial, and 3) environmental activists who monitor government and industry. The following is a list of the major governmental organizations from Sweden and the United States used in the research:

Sweden

- Swedish Environmental Protection Board (Naturvardsverket)
- National Franchise Board (Koncessionsnamden)
- Ministry of Physical Planning (Bostads Departementet)
- Ministry of Agriculture (Jordbruks Departmentet)
- Ministry of Industry and Energy (Industry Departementet)
- County Governments (Lansstyrelsen)
- Local Governments (Kommunes)

United States

- President's Council on Environmental Quality (CEQ)
- Central Environmental Protection Agency (EPA, Washington)
- Regional Environmental Protection Agency (REPA)
- State Environmental Protection Departments
- Local Councils
- Related Agencies and Washington Departments (Commerce, etc.)

Ten industrial production companies were involved in the research. The companies were selected in part by the types of facility they operated, where the facilities were selected in terms of similarities of inputs, outputs and technologies involved in production. The ten companies spanned eight major industrial sectors:

- steel
- petroleum
- Petro—chemical
- chemical
- heavy metals
- pulp and paper
- ferro—alloys
- carbon products

This selection allowed for a wide cross section of pollution types and regulation difficulties. Also, there was a wide variation in technological sophistication between these sectors, as well as differences in characteristics of raw materials — two important factors in pollution control difficulties.

All ten companies in the research were wholly owned, with two of the twenty cases being joint ventures. A "case" represents a facility. The joint venture examples allowed an examination of differences which joint Swedish—U.S. company ownership might make in pollution control.

In addition, numerous secondary organizations were relied on to help fill information gaps at the national and international level. Some of these organizations were:

- The Organization for Economic Cooperation and Development
- The European Economic Commission
- Center for Education of International Management
- and various central government ministries in France, Great Britain, Germany and the Netherlands

In all cases, the secondary organizations had some direct contact with the industries included in the study. Also, various industry groups aided with the research. One example at the national level was MCA (The Manufacturing Chemists Association of 140 U.S. Chemical Companies) and its counterpart in Europe. These organizations were either in part, or in total, established to deal with environmental protection issues and had put together a skilled multi-disciplinary staff on the issues.

6.4 The Research Domain

The history of environmental deterioration being delimited as a problem of environmental pollution has been discussed in other parts of this dissertation. Of more importance here is how the participants in the research project match the research domain. For this purpose, it is enough to know that the environment which is being polluted physically has been legislatively broken down into three areas. (Evidence for this categorization comes from the study of legislation and operations in several countries.)

Figure 6.2: Research Domain

These three domains have resulted from the idea of <u>protecting</u> environments from pollutants, where pollutants are those substances entering the human environment considered harmful to life. Within the <u>working environment</u> pollutants are generated by the production process itself as well as from the materials directly used for production. In the <u>community environment</u> pollutants come from production processes and travel beyond the perimeter of the production facility to impact humans not directly engaged in the production and pose some danger to other life systems beyond the human that compose the phenomena called biological life. The <u>consuming environment</u> is the most recent domain to enter the environmental pollution area. It is perhaps the most difficult to deal with. Pollution to the consuming environment comes not as a by—product of production, but directly from the desired products themselves. In the U.S. the Food and Drug Administration regulates many of the products used by society. The Environmental Protection Agency is now expanding into this area as well (Hawk, 1977).

The community environment is the major emphasis of the research for various reasons: 1) it contains the widest array of social interest groups, 2) it has a longer history of legislation, and 3) it appears as a wider, more general category containing many elements of the other two domains. The definition of community is somewhat of a problem for regulatory agencies. This is due mainly to their administrative reliance on highly formalizable methods which must be equally applicable to all cases. One recommendation resulting from the research suggests that efforts be made to reduce reliance on methods which level the uniqueness of each situation, and instead rely on greater use of "locally—based" practices. To simplify the research initially the generally accepted sense of community environment was used, where community is the surrounding area immediately and directly impacted by pollutants from specific production facilities which are a part of the community. (This disregards the pollution carried by major air and water sheds, where they are a source which the research discovered as being quite significant thus making the actual community "global".) This introduced a major dilemma underlying the operation of current environmental deterioration activities. Even though the complexity of the situation of environmental deterioration (in large part due to differences between locations) points towards a regulation approach which allows more control at the <u>local</u> level, the transportation range of the pollution demands a more <u>central</u> approach. It should be possible to account for both, but current approaches tend to control neither.

Thus, with the community delimited as the pollution target for the research it is important to identify the <u>source</u> of pollution to be researched. As discussed previously, the subject area of environmental deterioration is very complex. One viable method for researching complexity is to concentrate on "leading systems" (Emery and Trist, 1973), thereby reducing the area of study to something more manageable.

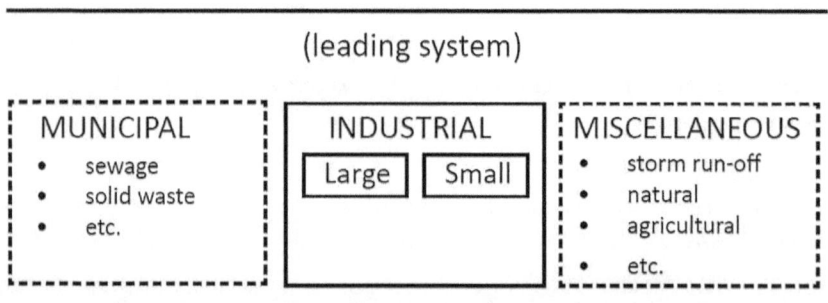

Figure 6.3 Industry as a leading system for research

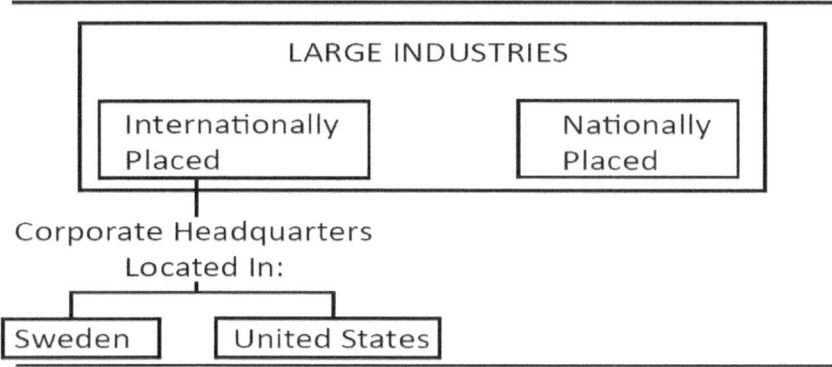

Figure 6. 4 Selection of Specific Large Industries

Within the research, a comparative check was made of how the municipal aspect of pollution compares with the miscellaneous, and how both combine to relate to the industrial. Due to the previously discussed factors related to the comparative research method, industrial sources were selected for study. With large industrial facilities as the pollution source it was important to delimit which industries would be of most help in researching the environmental protection area. Aside from being "large" the industries had to be engaged in primary industrial production, where the dominant pollution difficulties would lie.

Then, within the researched companies, the limits of the research were drawn around the parts of the companies which had direct interrelations with the Swedish and the United States environmental protection regulation systems. In the case of some companies this area was expanded to include those parts of the companies interfacing with the French, German, British and Dutch regulation systems.

Out of this research design process ten multinational companies were selected for extensive involvement in the research. Four of the companies were based in Sweden and six of them in the United States. All ten operated production facilities in the two nations and in some cases they operated facilities in the other European countries mentioned previously. The production facilities operated by these companies outside the Swedish—U.S. comparative system were not integral to the research. As such they were used only to provide additional clarification of certain points highlighted by the Swedish-U.S. comparison.

6.5 The Research Sponsor

The first half of the research was sponsored by the resources of the Stockholm School of Economics and the Institute of International Business within that school. The greater part of the resources for the second half came from governmental sources.

The research questions, concerns, and models were established in the Fall of 1975. In March of 1976 a Parliamentary Committee was up in Sweden to investigate the 1969 Environmental Protection Act. Since some of the members of that Committee had been contacted prior to its establishment there was a natural inter-relation between this research and the objectives of the Committee. During the Spring of 1976 aspects of the research were modified to match better the objectives of the Committee and the major issues they wanted covered. During September of 1977 the tentative conclusions were presented to the Committee during a formal meeting. Thereafter, the 1977 Report underwent modification, so as to account for suggestions by the research participants.

CHAPTER 7

The Research Report

The 1977 Report (Hawk, 1977), was formulated in three volumes:

Part I — Environmental Review: Analysis

Part II — Environmental Review in Operation: The Need for Synthesis

Part III — Learning from Environmental Review: The Search for Synthesis

"Environmental review" was a term specifically defined for the research to serve as an ideal and a focus for the research interviews. It was used as a generic concept for a process of raising questions for social debate about the possible impacts of man's actions on the environment of that action. A concept in common use at the time of the beginning of the research - environmental assessment — served as a basis for development of the ideal concept before an ideal was found necessary. One objective important to environmental review was social debate, where the research discovered that environmental assessment tended to reduce social debate. The importance of social debate for the issues involved in environmental review is seen by looking at the broad spectrum of human activity involved. Utilitarian activities of building highways and factories were found to normally conflict with qualitative domains of beautiful scenery, low noise levels, and interpersonal relations. Past, present, and prospective social value systems as well, are normally brought into such debate. Allowing such a wide spectrum into a review process poses serious problems for the use of strict reductionistic analysis of environmental assessment.

Comparing environmental review with the traditional practice of environmental assessment pointed out these and other difficulties with current social mechanisms of problem control, i.e., regulation.

The environmental assessment concept was linguistically initiated with the passage of the 1969 National Environmental Policy Act in the United States.

> This Act was the basic mandate to institutionalize environmental considerations into the governmental decision—making process. One of the most noticed aspects of this Act was the process resulting in the documents titled "Environmental Impact Statements," or EISs. This Act is important simple due to its existence. It represents the first attempt by a government to <u>formally</u> declare measures for putting environmental concerns into normal decision—making systems.[113]

An argument is posed in the 1977 Report (see pages 8 to 12), that environmental assessment is not conceptually different from the technology assessment of the previous decade but that institutionally they have become very different things. One concern initiating the research, and motivating its continuation was information that most members of the Western industrialized world were looking to the U.S. version of environmental assessment to duplicate versions of it in their own nation's regulatory systems. Members of the OECD (Organization for Economic Cooperation and Development) exemplified this.

Part I of The 1977 Report presented the argument behind environmental review, dominant concepts and practices in current accepted use, and an outline of the major regulatory components required for its operation in Sweden and the United States. Also, Part I examines the role of government as the main initiator of the review activity. As the research was based on comparing Swedish and U.S. regulation systems, relevant statutes and agencies of the respective nations were listed In Part I. A portion of the considerable descriptive complexity involved in environmental assessment, as it is

---

[113] The 1977 Report, p. 39

now practiced, is exposed in Part I. This helps in the later discussion of the contradictions resulting from complexity.

In Part II the focus shifts from components of environmental review of the operations and their consequences of environmental review. While government was the major actor in Part I, industrial production facilities are the emphasis in Part 11. Characteristics of each industrial type represented in the research are presented as well as specifics of cases researched. Basic to the examination of the cases are the "legal permits" required to operate the facilities within allowable levels of pollution. The models, methods, and basic concepts relied on to gain and structure information were presented in Part II. This provided a basis for discussing some of the dilemmas of current environmental assessment operations.

Combining the governmental social system sets described in Part I with the industrial sets described in Part 11 allows a view of the complexity involved in the regulation of environmental affairs and offers a base to examine the failures of current regulatory systems attempting to control the complexity. (This was especially so within the U.S. context.)

In Part III the theoretical development for an alternative to the existing modes of environmental protection regulation is begun. In this part an idea of Hasan Ozbekhan (1974) was espoused (that complex problems which society is faced with are not problems in the traditional sense of the word). A "problem" cannot be assumed to be something which has a "solution." Instead we can think in terms of situations. Ozbekhan's ideas give additional support to the thesis repeatedly put forward here, that we cannot treat the complex situations we are faced with as if they are problems merely waiting for the proper solution to arrive after rigorous analysis. Some of the systems logic of Emery (1969) and Ackoff (1974) is presented in Part III to serve as a basis for an alternative paradigm for dealing with complex societal situations; where the environmental protection situation is one example. This alternative logic is coming to be known as "Systems Thinking" (Emery, 1969).

Following is a summary of current attempts to "improve" the environment by protecting it.

This research concludes that the environmental protection effort will not satisfy the needs behind the concern for an individual's environment and its quality. Although the need to question the trend of technical manifestations of current social thinking was legitimate, we have only furthered specialization and have lost the composite social understanding of current efforts to question technology. Lack of composite understanding in a society manifests itself in fear of the unknown. Through an elaborate analytically technical approach we have advanced two wrongs : 1) Through the use of the word "protection" we have introduced a negative connotation, which adds to fear, 2) And by turning the environmental issue over to the experts we have seen it dissected and parceled out in a manner that further obscures whatever holistic meaning it may have once had.[114]

7.1 Summary of the Research

Chapter 5 contains information with significance for long—range environmental protection activities, while the information in this chapter was directed at shorter—term circumstantial evidence relating to immediately discernable results. In this summary an attempt is made to link these two varieties of data together. Even the more circumstantial evidence implies longer range consequences when structured.

The discussion in Chapter 2 on two modes of regulation, <u>formal legislative</u> and <u>informally negotiated</u>, specified the characteristics of the two modes. Some of this information clarifies the research data. One means of comparing the alternative modes is to weight the research data against the modes by following the role of <u>facts</u>, in each of the cases.   (Facts relate to those things "known to be true.") Within the framework of the "legal order" approach deliberated actions are

---

[114] Hawk, 1977, p. 193

generally taken by a group of experts competent at getting into the "facts of the case"; at least such is an ideal as expressed by those hiring the experts. There also is an assumption here that facts have a relatively long lifespan. Also, they generally are oriented towards the technical domains of the situation. Factors associated with human variables, like interpersonal relations, are not included, whenever possible. The "negotiated order" mode, on the other hand, is based on development the appreciation systems which underlie the ordering of facts. Here the facts of the case take on a role of reduced consequence, due to the considerable uncertainty present in the situation allowing facts to fluctuate with perceptions of the situation. When the facts become ambiguous, even contradictory, the behavioral factors can explicitly play a larger role in decisions. Interpersonal relations can then be openly relied on to mutually define an ambiguous situation, or to redefine a mutually objectionable situation. Under a legal order system this is implicit; with negotiated order it becomes explicit. Under legal order, facts become an end in themselves; with negotiated order facts and values are part of a larger process giving normative direction to both. The information in the cases is now related to the two alternatives of regulation.

Summary of case material

Case I-s

Interpersonal relations between company management and community residents remain as key to more complete control of environmental problems. Relations have improved, but a more comprehensive solution remains difficult due to large amounts of solid waste residue piled up and left from successes in cleaning up air and water streams. Suspending legal order and experimenting with negotiated order appears appropriate as a response to this case to improve community-industry relations and identify a collective means to resolve the remaining and growing solid waste problems.

Case I—A

In this case, no community was immediately identifiable in the surrounding area, but substantial difficulties were emerging with a nearby metropolitan area. Numerous industrial pollution sources were combining to form a larger problem. The facts of this case once appeared rather stable, but recently these facts have acquired a life of their own and are overpowering the situation. One set of facts points out that much of the industry in the area should shut down for health reasons; another set of facts (unemployment), finds this distasteful. Five years ago, the facts about capital expenditures implied that after initial high expenditure, the amounts would decline. Recent evidence on the costs of maintenance has disrupted this belief and further upset the facility management. Negotiation appears desirable in this case.

Case 2-S

This company had put their facts together in a superbly rational manner, but their case approval was delayed a year due to one aspect of their initial behavior during negotiations. The company exhibits a lack of trust for others, which appears to instill a similar response in those they must deal with. This comes from the distrust the company has of the facts of others, as this company feels they have the "smartest" experts in the world. The legislation mode of legal order seemed workable here up until three years ago, but the events have shown that hiring the "smartest" experts is not enough.

Case 2-A

This company is very concerned about secrecy at this facility. They are so worried that they have a policy of giving the surrounding community little idea of their production. The pollution characteristics of the plant are well under control, but the facility will have difficulty in ever gaining permission to expand. Again, the company has ignored the humanistic variables involved in dealing with their plant's environment.

Case 2-G

The plant management are much less secretive here, but, on the other hand, appear less willing to relate to any new "ideals" in environmental protection. Part of this is due to past problems with contradictions in ideals behind regulation activities, thus the management team now prefers to wait until they are told to carry out a process for pollution reduction. Management is particularly concerned that a communist conspiracy lies behind environmental ideals. It appears that a more interpersonal system of regulation would help enlighten both sides involved in regulating this facility.

Note on Company 2: In general, the company which manages these three facilities has been a real leader in environmental control technology. One reason for this is so they could simply avoid much of the regulation process of dealing with government officials by being so far advanced that no discussions would be called for. This may not have been to their long—term benefit (keeping contact and credibility with the larger society they are part of), because much of their management exhibits anti—social behavior and many of the communities they are located in exhibit anti—company behavior, both sides tended to lose opportunities.

Case 3—S and Case 3-A

In each country the same company was operating a production facility which lay in the same major classification category of environmental regulation (e.g., Petro—chemicals). After reviewing the operating characteristics of each facility, it was found that no legitimate comparison could take place within the research framework. The facilities differed substantially in terms of technology, products, pollutants, and process layout. This discovery was of value to the research at a level higher than the monitoring of emission streams. When the difficulty of comparing the plants of this type was pursued, it was discovered that most industrialized countries had encountered problems regulating the pollution of these plants with their existing regulation modes. The OECD (Organization for Economic Cooperation and Development) has been given the responsibility of defining this industrial category so that generalization regulation is workable. Many governmental agencies had encountered the same problems as the researcher — that although legislation to regulate this group was in place, a definition to delimit the group could not be found thus the legislation was unworkable. It appears that a more flexible negotiation system of arriving at consensus is in order to at least arrive at a definition of the limits of this industrial category.

Case 4-S

There are interpersonal relation difficulties here, with the American half of the joint venture having good relations with the local government but the Swedish half in conflict. This in turn has deteriorated intra—industry relations. It appears that the main difference here is that the American managers are advocating a more "geocentric" attitude (Perlmutter, 1965), while the Swedish managers pursue a more provincial attitude. It would be difficult to generalize from this, but the geocentric attitude tends to be based (in this case) on uncertainty of the facts available; thus, large—scale cooperation is needed. The locally based people tend to rely more on the facts present in the plant and see no need of "dragging in more information". This poses a serious dilemma for any research conclusion that gives a blank check to decentralization. Perhaps the conclusions this would lead us to is that <u>small actions may be beautiful but small perspectives are not</u>. Negotiation might help combine these differing views of the world.

Case 4-A

To better determine the facts surrounding the Swedish plant, some Swedish authority had visited this facility; part of the problems in Case 4—S resulted from this visit. Due to that visit and the behavioral phenomena surrounding it, several technical experiments were held up by the management in Case 4—S "stonewalling".

Case 5-S

In this case the government officials secured data on quantities of raw material entering the facility and compared this with quantities of product leaving the facility. With this information they had a good idea of the amounts of highly toxic material being put into the environment beyond the controlled product. These "facts" did not improve the situation until the people involved on both sides had resigned, and their replacements took over.

Case 5-A

In this case contradictory modes of rationality were pointed out in the environmental review process. The company people had proposed a facility with very low levels of pollutants and the government officials accepted and applauded their plans. Two community groups intervened in the approval process with a rational that, "No new facilities should ever be allowed to open in the community". This was in spite of the community having around 10% unemployment at the time, where the proposed facility would add 300 jobs to the area. Court cases are still pending. The facts of the case do not point to a clear solution and there is little sign that the litigation process will add any clarity. Broad based renegotiation of the facts is needed here to reorganize the situation at a higher level.

Case 6—S

This was found to be the most successful case in the research in terms of meeting the objectives of reduction of pollutants being emitted from the plant. This also included reduction of solid waste collected from air and water pollution streams. In this case the local plant management insisted on taking a new approach to process design, with local government officials helping in negotiations with central government. Here a "zero—sum game" was redefined to bring about a "non—zero sum game" which ended in a plus. If it had ended in a minus, the plant management had agreed to rebuild the facility along the lines of a more traditional approach to pollution control.

Case 7-A

Very advanced technology was in use here to clean up the pollution stream from the plant. At one point in time the Federal Environmental

Protection Agency was applauding this case, until it was found that the technology was only pushing the initial problem into another area, from air pollution to solid waste. This case also pointed out the basic limitations in relying on others to exhibit "economic rationality" in their decision making.

Case 8-S

Here the company would agree to almost nothing which the central officials wanted and the central officials of the government would not negotiate. The officials' argument was that five years prior the same situation had presented itself and the company had put in some inappropriate technology, which did not function; thus, the government had the responsibility to keep that from occurring again. Relations improved significantly when the local government officials took over negotiations and agreed with part of what the company had suggested. It is too early to see if this will result in better pollution control but early indications are that it will be an improvement.

Case 8-A

In this case the company pursued the attitude that, "Little contact with government people is good contact" and that "When the inspectors come, we will plead ignorance." In part due to administrative problems in the U.S. regulatory system, this approach has been successful until now. This case also exhibited some of the problems encountered in relying extensively on expert consultants to take care of a company's "environmental variables." The consultants had pretended to do things they were not able to do, and now the company finds it is responsible regardless. This case also pointed out the growing dilemma of industrial expansion in the industrialized countries. Although companies have not been found to run away from environmental regulation, they are finding it increasingly difficult to open new facilities in a timely fashion under current modes. There needs to be broad based social negotiation to see if indeed further industrial expansion is desirable. If it is, then we must <u>modify</u> existing regulation modes. If it is not, <u>we still need to modify</u> the modes because they are not being used in a purposeful manner. We find neither planning, nor anti—planning, present in the regulation system; simply mindless stimulus—response activities.

Case 9-S

This facility is located on the most controversial site in the study. Very extensive "negotiations" took place over several years, but they were not the type which were to redefine the situation into a non—zero sum game. Instead, they were based on an eventual yes—no response to construction of the facility. Eventually, the "Yes" response emerged, but neither side is particularly happy, nor feeling they gave up too much for what they got.

Case 9-A

This was considered the most strictly controlled plant in the study, where the severity of restrictions has not proven to be to anyone's benefit. This case presents an example of the "drive them to the wall" approach of regulating industry. One official had ordered the facility to meet an unusually low effluent level, and although it was technically unfeasible to meet it, the company management had agreed for public relation reasons. Later, another firm proved in court that the reason behind the standard was to make the calculations of a government official easier. He had simply, "Preferred the number one". This plant illustrates the contradictions which arise when three separate agencies control the same facility, the difficulties of inter—industrial cooperation due to U.S. anti—trust laws, and the underlying dilemma of solid waste problems with current regulation modes.

Case 9-B

This case illustrates the difficulties of a double standard between public and private sources of pollution control and how that initiates stonewalling of regulation.

Case 10-S

Even though pollution requirements did not exist at this site, the plant management did initiate discussions with community representatives to see how improvement could be achieved. This went a long way towards establishing credibility which was later needed for unforeseen problems.

Case 10-A

This facility is located next to the facility in Case 1—A, but there is an added difficulty to the regulation procedures for this case. The headquarters for the company prefers to centralize responsibility for negotiations with government officials. Their purpose is to have a few very highly experienced employees to deal with all industry—government relations. The problem with this objective occurs when the government officials realize this — they then institute a whole new series of behavioral responses to the company. One government official stated that the company representatives were, "Just a bit too slick."

Case 10-F

This case is of a very clean facility that was under no governmental restrictions in its design. In fact, the government would have gone to considerable trouble to offer incentives to any kind of plant which would open in this underdeveloped region of the country. There were no strictly rational facts behind the expense invested in the facility to make it the cleanest of its kind, except the stylistic objective of "Wanting to try this."

Case 10-E

In this case the complexities of older plants show up very clearly, complexity which any successful environmental regulation program must understand. Part of this complexity originates with dominant social values which exhibit themselves in technical design. In this plant there was a general problem at the outset for any environmental regulation mode, in that the plant had been sited under the value set of the World War II concern for bombing. Following this there were major problems with the process layout of the plant that resulted from three successive additions — where each had been laid out with different approaches to the design of a <u>rational</u> industrial process.

Summary of issues in the chapter

In addition to the case information, four general issues emerged from looking at the cases collectively:

1. Location of Responsibility (in terms of a center—periphery model of control)
2. Regulation Modes Impacting on Large versus Small Organizations
3. Growing Interdependencies of Industry and Industrial Process and Growing Fragmentation of the Regulation Processes
4. Trust versus Surveillance as an Attitude

Here it has been seen that most of the issues intertwined with the environmental objectives of material pollution control are highly social—behavioristic concerns. Even in the few cases where the "facts of the case" are relatively clear, very little occurs in a positive direction until human behavior allows it. It is important that there be a joint recognition that changes need to be instituted and then joint design of those changes. An appreciation of each other's point of departure and point of view in a situation is helpful to resolution of problems in a situation.

Although many of the results of the case studies appeared rather diverse, they did tend to settle into the interpersonal realm, at least indirectly. For all individuals attitude was, one attribute that tended to dominate the problems discovered and the resolutions offered. Three basic attitudes were found in those interviewed: 1) cooperation, 2) confrontation, or 3) a mixture of 1 and 2. These could also be considered strategies, but they seemed to cover more than consciously planned activities; in fact, they tended to permeate the individual's personality. Besides cooperation and confrontation, the mixed area formed a vast gray area where individuals appeared uncommitted to either. Instead, they appeared to be trying to get hold of the situation they were in by slowing it down so they could understand it. Perhaps the concept of Donald Schon (1971) called "dynamic conservatism" best labels this group. For purposes of classifying the interviewees, this group was termed "the baffled." The dominant characteristic of those who tended to rely on cooperation was that they tended to "compose" the elements of a situation, while those relying on confrontation "analyzed" a situation for resolution.

Thus, we have the following three types:

Type I Confrontational: "The Analyzer"	Relies on expert analysis
	Trust is not relevant; if there is a problem there must be a solution to it.
Type II Committee Member: "The Baffled"	The silent watchers
	Lack of trust for others; Committees are set up to Keep an eye on each other. Passive acceptance of complex Technologies.
Type III Cooperation: "The Composer"	Tries to synthesize all elements of a situation.
	Trust is essential, even of the Untrustworthy, to teach them.
	Cooperation is a means to learn.
	Technology is a service function.

TABLE 7.1: ATTITUDE TYPOLOGIES IN THE STUDY

Since cooperation, or the lack of it, appeared throughout the research evidence, seventeen of the cases were classified in terms of the level of cooperation found in those most involved in the negotiations over facility permits. The results are:

	Very Cooperative	Cooperative	Limited Cooperation	None
SWEDEN	5	2	3	0
US	1	1	5	0

Industry Attitude of Government's Willingness to Cooperate

	Very Cooperative	Cooperative	Limited Cooperation	None
SWEDEN	5	4	0	0
US	0	0	4	4

Government Attitude to Industry Willingness to Cooperate

TABLE 7.2: PERCEPTION OF COOPERATION FROM OTHERS

The apparent difference in attitude which exist in Sweden versus the U.S. was illustrated through a seminar offered at the Stockholm School of Economics in October of 1976. The purpose of the seminar was for participants of the main organizations in the research to discuss issues raised in the research to that date and advise on future directions of the research. There were twenty—two participants at the seminar, with all but two of the organizations in the research represented. In most cases the representative was the chief executive of the organization, or from top management if not the top executive. It was very interesting to find that such a meeting was possible in Sweden, especially when compared with interview information of similar people in the U.S., which concluded that such a meeting would not be allowed in the U.S. for anti—trust and other legal—behavioral reasons.

MODEL FOR EVALUATION OF THE PROCESS

ATTITUDE:	STRATEGY:	INDICATORS FOR EVALUATION: "TOOLS"
TYPE A-ANALYZER Key-characteristic - "Bring in the facts to hit the bastards over the head with."	CONFRONTATION	1. Redundancy of parts in the review system, with many "specialists" on the standby to be called in to "replace" non-functioning ones. 2. There will always be "technical" solutions. 3. Construction of a computerized "prediction" model.
TYPE B-BAFFLED Key-characteristic - "Doesn't know the facts but comes to the meetings to undermine facts of others."	COMMITTEES	1. Redundancy through "multiple" committees with overlapping and preferably "contradictory" objectives and goals. 2. Delay, until the dilemma can be "redifined" and sent to anothe committee for study. 3. Consequences are not considered, results pose enough problems without adding more to the pile.
TYPE C-COMPOSER Key-characteristic - "Unsure of all facts, but combines his best ones with the best ones of others."	COOPERATION	1. Redundancy of function in the review system with fewer specialists, but each having several specialties to draw from during the review. 2. Makes a choice, accepting that is in the very difficult situations, and accepts responsibility. 3. Considers far ranging effects, although it complicates his life, and at the same time tries to ease the lives of others by giving them flexibility through forecasting models.

Evaluation Indicator Code:
1. Redundancy - Means for taking care of the majority of "Dilemmas," "Contradictions" or "Dialectical Relations" in the system. (insulation, slack, etc.)
2. Dilemmas - Contradictions between parts in the system that must be taken to a higher level in the system of resolution. (sending a law back to Congress or Parliament)
3. Consequences - Relationship between "results" of parts of the system, providing an ideal base for the generation of dilemmas, contraditions, etc.

Figure 7.1 Process Evaluation

CASES	Government Decision Point Central	Government Decision Point Local	Company Decision Point Central	Company Decision Point Local	Industry Attitude to Government	Government Attitude To Industry	Limits Strictness	Success	Redundancy	Dilemmas	Consequences
1-S	X		X		V. C.	V. C.	Medium	Good	C	B	B
1-A	X		X		L. C.	L.C.	Strict	Not-Good	A	B	B
2-S	X		X		L. C.	C.	Medium	Good	B	A	C
2-A		X		X	L. C.	N. C.			C	A	C
3-S	X			X	V. C.	V. C.	Medium	Good	C	C	C
3-A	X			X	C.	N. C.			B	A	A
4-S	X			X	L. C.	C.	Medium	Good	A	A	B
4-A											
5-S	X		X		C.	C.	Strict	Good	A	B	B
5-A	X		X		C.	L. C.	Strict	Good	A	B	B
6-S		X		X	V. C.	V. C.	Strict	Very-Good	C	C	C
7-A	X			X	L. C.	L. C.	Strict	Medium	B	A	A
8-S	X		X		L. C.	C.	Medium	Medium	A	B	A
8-A		X		X	L. C.	N. C.	Medium	Medium	B	A	B
9-S		X		X	V. C.	V. C.	Strict	Good	C	B	C
9-A		X	X		L. C.	N. C.	Strict	Good	B	B	C
10-S	X			X	V. C.	V. C.	Medium	Good	C	C	B
10-A		X	X		V. C.	L. C.	Medium	Good	B	A	A

U. S. Central: EPA
U.S. Local : State takes responsibility
Swedish Central: Stockholm
Swedish Local : County takes responsibility

V. C. - Very Cooperative
C. - Cooperative
L. C. - Limited Cooperation
N. C. - No Cooperation

Redundancy: Type A: Narrow Based
Type B: Contradictory
Type C: Broad Based

Dilemmas: Tech.Solut.
Delay
Planning

Consequences: Prediction
Not Consider
Forecast, Flex

Government Environmental Decision:
Sweden - 7 central, 3 local
U.S. - 4 central, 3 local

Company Environmental Decision:
Sweden - 4 central, 5 plant
U.S. - 4 central, 4 plant

Attitudes:
Sweden-Industry towards government
(5 V.C., 2 C., & 3 L.C.)
U.S.-Industry towards government
(1 V.C., 1 C., & 5 L.C)
Sweden-Governmental towards industry
(5 V.C., 4 C.)
U.S.-Government towards industry
(4 L.C., 4 N.C.)

Indicators:
Sweden: 6 As, 9 Bs, & 12 Cs
U.S.: 10 As, 11 Bs, & 3 Cs
  Red.   Dilem.   Con.
Sweden: 3-1-5   2-4-3   1-4-4
U.S.:   2-5-1   5-3-0   3-3-2

Figure 7.2 Composite Case Information

All the information previously mentioned has been placed in a composite chart to compare the cooperation/confrontation characteristics with the location of decision—making responsibility and with the results of the permit for each case in the study.

7.2 Conclusions from the Report

The research conclusions were directed at <u>six general areas</u> found important to the operation of environmental protection operations.

<u>A theory of regulation</u>

Since this dissertation itself is directed at the development of a theory of regulation there is little value to concentrating on the theory within the 1977 Report. The tenuous theory found there was mainly concerned with the location of regulatory responsibility, where the report bias was towards a decentralized system of regulation which could accommodate the considerable variety in modern society. This dissertation develops a theory of regulation in terms of the holistic operation of a regulation system where the location of the responsibility for control is only one component of the whole.

The concept of the expert

Centralization of control tends to correlate well with increased reliance on experts, at least within the environmental protection area. As such any viable theory of regulation must address questions concerning the location and role of the expert in that regulation. The extensive role of the expert throughout the enforcement of regulation has come to be accepted and even expected. Some of the dangers of this phenomenon were pointed out in the 1977 Report, where one example in the U.S. comes out of the Environmental Protection Agency. The regulation of the environment was legislatively divided up into eight major parcels (see Part I of the 1977 Report), but once the enforcement of these parcels began, they were further divided along expert discipline lines. The problem with this is that each discipline developed its own practices and policies. In too many cases there was substantial conflict between any two practices and/or policies, where all seemed to be removed from local reality.

In addition, it was discovered within the research that expert decisions were the justification for much of the statute design itself. If there is value in retaining the political processes which Americans feel they have, then this reliance on expert decision—making seems to deny much of that value. In the U.S. Congress there are 435 Representatives, 100 Senators, and 11,000 aides to advise them. As United States society has become more complex the reliance on expert aides to supply decision—making information has greatly increased.

> The problems confronting Congress have become so technical and the problems so complicated that they demand the attention of specialists. A Congressman simultaneously faced with proposals concerning

> automobile safety, deregulation of natural gas pricing, Federal funds for abortion and the revision of the Panama Canal Treaty would crumble in confusion unless he could rely on expert advisors or committee staff directors...[115]

This does not sound so worrisome, but this trend has generated a power shift that does cause concern; especially so if experts live up to their definition of only having specialized knowledge of a very limited part of a situation. It appears that the trend of increased reliance on experts in regulation complements the trend of fractionalization of industrial societies.

> With Congress currently more fragmented than it has ever been, the power of legislative aides has soared. Today, Senators and Representatives, function more and more independently rather than in concert with the Congress as a whole, and are virtually autonomous barons and hence more dependent than ever on their professional staffs. As a result, much of the consequential legislation passed by Congress in recent years has been the work of individual Congressmen and their assistants rather than the result of committee or joint efforts.[116]

The dilemma underlying this is that as the society becomes more interdependent and complex, the mode of regulation is becoming more fractionalized. As well as the legislative branch of the U.S. regulatory system basing its operations on the overreliance on experts, the court system is now having to retain to its own extensive collection of experts. In the research a very workable alternative to expert fractionalization was uncovered in Sweden in what is called the National Franchise Board. (See page 25 of the 1977 Report for further explanation of the design and composition of the Board.) The work

---

[115] Newsweek, August 15, 1977, p. 27
[116] Ibid.

of this Board compares well with the principles of "negotiated order" presented in Chapter 2 of this paper.

Redefinition of environmental issues

The issues of environmental deterioration and environmental protection are overlaid with negative overtones. Environmental deterioration appears linguistically as a very nasty phenomenon. Environmental protection, as a response, implies creating a stand-off, where although the environment may not be improved, at least it will not be allowed to worsen. At the outset of environmental concern in the late 1950s to early 1960s the negative aspects were not such a noticeable issue. Much of this was due to the vague character of the environment where the vagueness allowed flexibility of meaning and direction. (In line with this the vagueness allowed
traditionally divergent interests to fit under the same umbrella and work collectively for what was felt to be a common cause.) When environmental issues started to be defined in narrower terms of pollution, and what constituted pollution, the negative connotation began to overpower the initial general environmental ethic. This has serious repercussions for the mechanisms of enforcement of any specific system of regulation. For example,

> If a central authority must play a role in environment — and under current conditions, it cannot withdraw due to the attitudes and dependencies it has built up — the least the authority can do is to coordinate regulation activities in a positive and creative manner. A positive tone to regulation allows for more desirable and voluntary participation of the regulated with the regulators; where the ideal is for the two to merge into one group. Unless society is able and willing to furnish one "policeman" per pollution source, a Teutonic, or totalitarian, system cannot be successful. A system designed to force actions out of one set of people, by another set, which the first are not in logical support of, will only have limited successes. Research shows that

"actions" will result from such a system of regulation, but they will not be the most desirable for either party, or the larger society which both parties are a part of.[117]

In many instances' "environment" has been used as a weapon to force individuals to do something they would not want to do. The difficulty is that force instills fear at best and encourage hate at worst towards the target and the enforcer. Several dimensions of the phenomenon called <u>threats</u> has been presented in a book entitled, <u>The Effects of Threats</u> by George Kent (1967). Even if the concept of force could be handled effectively - which it appears in democratic societies that it should not or cannot be - another dilemma awaits a forceful regulation of major social issues. Having the power to force an action does not guarantee one the knowledge of how best to carry it out, or, in essence, "omnipotence does not insure access to omniscience." (Perhaps too great of a concentration on the first may actually restrict the second.)

<u>Utilizing environmental review for "learning"</u>

It Is important to notice the sense of learning used in the 1977 Report, as it underlies the logic of the alternative mode of regulation called negotiated order. The capacity to generate alternatives to deal with a confronted situation is essential to learning. The 1977 Report defined a "non—learning" situation as one where there were no alternatives to deal with it beyond a simple yes or no response to a stimulus. Four types of learning were listed in a hierarchical fashion, from "zero—base" to "learning type III." These were an elaboration of Gregory Bateson's (1973) "learning types." For him "zero base" is simply a "response to a stimulus" and no real choice is available. Learning III on the other hand involves such a wide latitude of possible choices that, if an individual takes this route, he questions the most basic assumptions. This model of learning was used In The 1977 Report to analyze some of the limitations of current environmental review and, illustrate why environmental review choices are so severely limited.

---

[117] The 1977 Report, p. 198

The two arguments for environmental review, or environmental impact assessment, are: 1) it enhances public participation and 2) it generates alternatives. With traditional environmental impact assessment, the research found little evidence of the process enhancing public participation and no evidence that viable alternatives were generated by the process. In fact there was more evidence that the process reduced participation by inducing greater use of experts and specialists. The public is discouraged from taking a "positive" part in the process. Most of the actions they are asked to review are designed in such a manner that the only alternative is between yes or no. This researcher hypothesizes that due to the increasing technical sophistication of future proposed actions, there will be an increasing use of the <u>no alternative</u> as more public participation is elicited. Reasons for this are varied, but two possibilities may be that if you don't understand a proposal you tend to say no for the sake of safety and the chance for this is increased if you can't directly see how the proposal will benefit you and can see how it may harm you.[118]

If learning were an integral part of environmental review, as illustrated in the diagram on page 12 of the 1977 Report, then the review process would be vastly more complex and intellectually difficult. On the other hand, it would have been publicly more credible and have elicited more interest, thereby making it more meaningful and socially desirable. As environmental review is now developing steps are taken to cut back on participation in order that "socially necessary" projects can be approved in a timely fashion. This, of course, further erodes the democratic ideals of the larger society, of which environmental review is only a part.

---

[118] Ibid., p. 199

The role of attitude

Throughout the research the role of <u>attitude</u> was emphasized as it appeared to be more important than technology in explaining environmental activities in industry and government. Many of the industrial personnel who worked in both Sweden and the U.S. felt that, "The technical innovativeness for environmental protection in the U.S. system is quite high, but the application of the innovation seems to be more successful outside the U.S. Continuing with this feeling

> Our system requires tremendous monitoring. Our office investigates 10% of the major pollution sources in our area each year. This takes 30% of our total manpower resources. It is difficult when you don't trust them.[119]

A redirection of attitudes towards environment

The Swedish regulation system is openly more cooperative in its basic attitude towards solving environmental problems than the U.S. system, but a satisfactory resolution of environmental dilemmas will require more than cooperation. This is not to detract from the fact that cooperation as a basis for resolution is essential; but basic knowledge is critical also.

> The difficulty of fighting in all ill—defined complex situation, like environmental deterioration, is that two opponents may well miss each other completely in the darkness, or go down the wrong road in parallel.[120]

Beyond the basic value of a cooperative attitude it is generally important to begin to identify attitudes towards a subject of interest in a problem resolution effort. In the environmental protection area specifically, it is important to identify the dominant attitudes towards the area. This point was alluded

---

[119] Ibid., p. 203
[120] Ibid., p. 204

to in the section on Redefinition of Environmental Issues[121] where the dominant attitude in the environmental area tends to be, as stated by Rene Dubos:

> It is a sad commentary on our civilization that when we speak of the environment it is usually in reference to its undesirable effects. The very word environment now evokes the nightmares of industrial and urban life, depletion of natural resources, accumulation of wastes, pollution in all its forms, noise, crowding, regimentation, the thousand devils of the ecological crisis… As a result, we are chiefly concerned with the avoidance of dangers and maintenance of a tolerable state, rather than with the creation of new, positive values through the development of environmental and human potentials.[122]

Dubos has also pointed out the implications of this attitude towards environment, which in 1978 we can now see realized.

> If we limit our efforts to the correction of environmental defects, we shall increasingly behave like hunted beasts taking shelter behind an endless succession of protective devices, each more complex and costly, less dependable and less comfortable than its predecessors… Although technological fixes have transient usefulness, they complicate life and eventually decrease its quality.[123]

Along with the more positive attitude which believes in human potentialities, there should be a healthy pessimism of outside limitations facing man's endeavors. This is not to restrict man's creativity but to give it an informed direction. In the case of environmental issues, it

---

[121] Hawk, 1977, p. 3
[122] Rene Dubos, 1972, p. 192, as quoted on page 2 of the 1977 Report
[123] Ibid., p. 1973

is important to weight the available creativity for new solutions to pollution problems with knowledge of the first and second law of thermodynamics.

The first law has great validity in stating that matter can neither be created nor destroyed but this has lured too many with an industrialist interest in mind into believing that there is no material cost associated with using natural resources. These people might well enhance their perception through respect for the second law which notes that although matter may not be created nor destroyed, it does go through qualitative changes through use. When a barrel of oil is "burned" it is no longer available for further "burning".

On the other hand, too many with an environmental interest in mind seem to rely on the second law to the exclusion of the limits of the first. They seem to feel that any current use of a material necessarily reduces its quality while at the same time they ask for a "pollution less plant" which means that a great deal of by—product must vanish. Officials in the State of New Jersey typify part of this attitude. The officials noted that there was a significant problem with toxic wastes leeching into groundwater in the state from solid waste disposal sites. They resolved the problem by simply outlawing the disposal of toxic solid waste, with no alternative method of getting rid of it offered. It was then disposed of in less legal ways.

7.3 Evidence from the Research: Specific Cases

Using the method of research presented previously, the following information was generated. Some of the information relates only to the specific cases being studied, while other parts relate to larger regulatory concerns. Although this distinction is difficult to maintain, an attempt is made to do so.

Most of the following information comes from individuals formally interviewed in the companies and other organizations. There were 229 of these individuals; a breakdown of what organizations they come from is presented on page 114 of the 1977 Report. An outline of each of the companies follows.

Outline of companies

Company 1

Company 1 uses special ores of metallic substances combined with oxygen to produce ferro—alloys which give steels their properties. The company is headquartered in the U.S. with the parent company employing 13,000 people and having a gross revenue of one billion dollars. (Dollar figures for all ten companies are in 1976 dollars.)

Company 2

Company 2 uses Petro—chemical and other hydrocarbon materials to produce insulation, paint bases and a wide variety of other chemicals for many uses. The company is headquartered in the U.S. with the parent company employing 50,000 people and having a gross revenue of five and one—half billion dollars.

Company 3

Company 3 uses petroleum and natural gas as raw materials to produce Petro—chemicals for the chemical industry. The company is headquartered in the U.S. with the parent company employing 30,000 people and having a gross revenue of over twenty—five billion dollars.

Company 4

Company 4 uses Petro—chemicals to produce high- and low-density plastics for wide use in the construction and manufacturing industries. The company is headquartered in Sweden with the parent company employing 7,000 people and having a gross revenue of half a billion dollars.

Company 5

Company 5 uses heavy metals and chemicals as raw materials to produce energy storage equipment for use throughout the service industry. The parent company employs 2,500 people, is based in Sweden, and has an annual gross revenue of a tenth of a billion dollars.

Company 6

Company 6 uses forests as a raw material to produce pulp and paper for the manufacturing, packaging and construction industries. It is headquartered in Sweden and employs 16,000 people and has a gross revenue of one billion dollars.

Company 7

Company 7 uses forests as a raw material to produce pulp and paper for the manufacturing, packaging and construction industries. It is headquartered in the U.S. and employs 28,000 people and has a gross revenue of one and a half billion dollars.

Company 8

Company 8 uses iron ores and coke as raw materials to produce specialty steels for the manufacturing and power generation industries and consumer goods. The company is headquartered In Sweden, employs 28,000 people and has a gross revenue of one billion dollars.

Company 9

Company 9 uses petroleum and additives as raw materials to produce gasoline, fuels, heavy oils and light oils for transportation, power generation, manufacturing, etc. The company is headquartered in the U S., employs 75,000 people and has a gross income of over twenty—five billion dollars.

Company 10

Company 10 uses coke, pitch and oils as raw materials to produce goods for steel production and manufacturing use. The company is headquartered in the U.S., employs 55,000 people, and has a gross income of six and a half billion dollars.

In Table 4.1 the ten companies are related to the specific cases investigated in the research, where in turn the cases are related to the national context. The twenty facilities of the ten companies are in six countries.

Following is an outline of the major points raised during the interviews and drawn from documents which relate directly to the specific cases. More general information will follow this outline.

Company 1	1 – S	1 – A		
Company 2	2 – S	2 – A	2 – G	
Company 3	3 – S	3 – A		
Company 4	4 – S	4 – A		
Company 5	5 – S	5 – A		
Company 6	6 – S	6 – A		
Company 7	7 – S	7 – A		
Company 8	8 – S	8 – A		
Company 9	9 – S	9 – A	9 – B	
Company 10	10 – S	10 – A	10 – E	10 – F
Nation:				
A = America				
B = Belgium				
E = English				
G = Germany				
S = Sweden				

<u>TABLE 7.3 INTERNATIONAL COMPANIES</u>

Summary of cases

Case 1-S

This case illustrated some very difficult community relations problems where 3,000 of the communities' 5,000 residents had signed a petition to close the facility. Prior to this incident considerable "technical" activities had been carried out by the plant management to fit into the community context. After the incident, more "social" activities were initiated to fit into the community context. <u>Results</u> were more of an emphasis than "rules" during the negotiations with government representatives. Good results were achieved in redesigning old equipment during a five-year period.

Case 1—A

The "community" in this case is a large industrial park but significant problems are emerging with a neighboring city which has an unusually high incidence of certain types of cancers in humans. In this case the government representatives have concentrated on standards during permit negotiations. The clean-up results are a bit questionable. Although the production equipment is about as clean as the Swedish plant, it is in some cases more recently acquired.

For both Case 1-S and 1—A plants capital expenditures over the past six years have been about 30% of gross. The maintenance costs have run about 10 to 15% and energy consumption for abatement equipment has been 7 to 8% of the total. In both locations there is a significant solid waste disposal dilemma.

Case 2-S

The parent company has been having difficulty in opening new production facilities in several Western industrialized countries. Although the 2-S facility was finally approved, its approval process points out some of the attitude problems of this organization. It is important to note that in the early sixties this firm exposed what is now considered the "proper" environmental attitude but has since come to take a very hard line against negotiation with government representatives. The company continues to carry out pollution abatement, which is technically more than required, but that abatement appears to be secondary in many instances. The central company management allowed this facility considerable autonomy in negotiation.

Case 2-A

This facility is in an area of the U.S. with a slightly different approach to pollution abatement, called "economic law enforcement." The difficulty with this approach is two—fold: it still retains the non—negotiable attitude of other U.S. enforcement modes and depends on an economic logic which may well not work. Page 115 of the 1977 Report points out the weakness of the cost—benefit approach as it now works.

Case 2-G

This facility is in a country which is passing through a major transition in environmental regulation modes from a legislative approach to pollution purchase rights system. The facility is continuing to make abatement improvements which are mandated by the corporate headquarters group but is postponing extensive technical changes until the new law has been in existence for a while.

As this company tends to construct more new facilities than other companies it faces more of the dilemmas of new site construction under environmental protection legislation. This means that it is almost impossible currently for the company to gain approval for new sites. The company does appear to do very well with environmental legislation covering existing facilities. Extensive records are kept on the payback of pollution control equipment in terms of either the reuse of normally lost raw material, or sales of process designs to other companies, where both appear profitable. The firm has a unique and quite successful organizational management system which allows it to deal effectively with concerns such as environmental protection legislation.

Case 3-S with Case 3-A

For purposes of the research the only noteworthy discovery made in comparing facilities of this company was that they cannot effectively be compared. Facilities of this type are of such a nature that no two are similar, as far as environmental pollution abatement is concerned. Each facility is unique and specialized, where the single greatest determinant of the mix of processes found in any one of these plants is the consumption patterns of the society which uses its products. This causes some problems for environmental protection officials, who insist on generalizations between facilities.

Case 4-S

This is a joint venture between a major Swedish and a major U.S. company where the U.S. partner supplied the technology and part of the capital. The Swedish partner supplied the rest of the capital and now supplies the management and the personal. The U.S. partner has better relations with the government officials than the Swedish partner. This case illustrates the complexity of some of the industrial processes and their substances. For example, one substance was leaking from the process at various stages; it was dangerous, but it simply disappeared into the environment. No measurable amount could be detected outside the plant.

Case 4-A

This is an American facility located in Puerto Rico and owned and operated by the American partner of Case 4—S. The Swedish officials controlling Case 4—S visited this facility, as it was a very advanced example of its industrial type and found that the management of the 4—S plant appeared to be hedging on what they could and couldn't do. Hard feelings began to develop on both sides for a period of a year or so.

Comparing Case 4—S and 4—A exemplifies the importance of the more "behavioristic" variables in a regulation process and demonstrates how, although technology is usually the discussion point, it is at most only a part of any successful regulation process where the social aspects must also be accounted for in some way.

Case 5—S

This case illustrated how initial distrust by industry people of government people lead to eventual distrust by the government people as well. Greater mutual trust eventually developed but not until there was a turn—over of the dominant individuals in each case with new people entering the negotiations. This case also pointed out the dilemmas of government funding assistance to help in the development of new technology for pollution abatement. Neither government nor industry people considered the subsidiary process to be beneficial. The main disadvantages were that companies tended to "wait" for financial help if they thought there was a chance of receiving it before launching research, and that the administrative aspect of receiving assistance was far too cumbersome.

Case 5—A

As Case 2-S exemplified the dilemmas of a U.S. company entering the Swedish regulatory context, Case 5—A exemplifies the dilemmas of a Swedish company entering the U.S. regulatory context. The Swedish businessmen were regarded as being too "naïve" in their expectations about the ultimate rationality of the U.S. (On the other hand, the U.S. businessmen had been regarded in Case 2—S, as being too "pushy.") The Swedish businessmen demonstrated an attitude that if they simply did the proper thing as far as the laws were concerned, they would have no problems. Serious problems did develop, however; although the facility eventually opened, many of the problems have persisted. The major difficulties centered on community groups which did not want the production plant to open no matter how clean it might be.

Due to similarities of production technology and process design this company provided a viable example of Swedish versus U.S. regulatory effectiveness in pollution reduction. Most people would judge the Swedish case to be more successful from the viewpoint of regulation due to pollution reductions achieved with existing technology. One major socio—contextual issue to emerge from this set of cases was how Swedish society tends to place greater trust in their governmental processes, while in the U.S. the lack of trust is apparent. Of special interest was how the community groups felt government to be more of an enemy than the industry representatives.

Case 6—S

This is the second example of a joint Swedish American venture to build a production facility. In this case the Swedish partner supplied the site, the raw materials and the management; while the American partner supplied some of the technology, the capital and the market for the product. This facility was the most successful at pollution control in the research. A unique process design was implemented here, against the wishes of the central regulatory agency, which incorporated some ideas from industrial democracy to make each worker more responsible for his role in the larger process. The outcome was remarkable. Also, of interest is how the local government officials intervened, in initial permit negotiations, to support the company's "experiment." The company finally received permission to build, on the condition that if the new design did not function properly the company would rebuild the plant along more traditional lines.

Case 7-A

This is a plant owned and operated by the American partner in Case 6—S. The raw material, product and relative age of the main processing equipment is similar; thus, it gives another good opportunity for comparison of pollution control results. Some of the most advanced "technical" thinking was implemented at the facility, but the results point out the dilemma of the law of conservation of matter. Although biological pollution was reduced, the facility eventually had a solid waste problem with the "dead bugs" which had eaten up the biological material.

Case 6-S illustrated some of the advantages of company headquarters allowing considerable plant autonomy. Case 7-A illustrated some of the disadvantages of plant autonomy. Since it appears difficult, indeed dangerous, to generalize in the complex problem area of environmental deterioration, it seems that a regulation method is needed which does not require so much generalization between cases.

Case 8-S

This case pointed out some of the impasses which develop between certain people and how the socio—behavioral characteristics can block technology development. In this case the impasse developed between the company people and the central government environmental protection people. The negotiation problems were resolved after local government people took over the regulation responsibilities. The evidence pointed out that one factor behind improved relations between company and local government people was increased frequency of meetings which appeared to build greater trust. With greater trust each side appeared to be more amiable and more willing to achieve desirable objectives.

Case 8-A

In this case the company pursued an attitude of "little contact with government people is good contact." It appears to have been moderately successful, due to the administrative problems in the U.S. regulatory system. Mistakes were made in issuing the pollution permit which were not discovered until the research project raised questions about the permit. This case also illustrated the problems surrounding the reliance on expert consultants for environmental affairs. The company had purposely allowed consultants to take the major responsibility for identifying needs and actions in the environmental area without first checking the competence of the consultants.

The review of many of the production facilities which this company has in forty countries gave an opportunity to study the rapidly growing impact which the environmental review decision making process is having on the location of new industrial plants. Others had expressed a concern that international companies were going to certain countries as pollution havens due to those countries lack legislation in the environmental area. No evidence was found of this being true, but there was considerable evidence that a major criterion for deciding on a new production facility investment was the length of time needed for going through the permitting process. The time it takes to "bring a plant on stream" is crucial and recent pollution control permitting procedures are becoming the major element in the total time required.

Case 9-S

This new facility was involved in national and international controversy. It is in the middle of a prime Swedish recreational area. New environmental review legislation was enacted as a result of this case where the legislation called for extensive and comprehensive examination of the future location of environmentally threatening industrial facilities. The specifics of this facility and its environmental permits point out the very close relationships between environmental and energy issues for a society. This case also demonstrates an example where the current plant management felt they were too "negotiable" during negotiations with government people. Next time, they claim, they would take a much harder line.

Case 9—A

This case is reported to be the most strictly controlled plant of its kind in the world. There are severe problems at the facility about what the state government expects and what is feasible; the area of solid waste highlights this dilemma. The operations of this plant point out some of the difficulties in the U.S. regulatory system due to the "Anti—Trust Laws," which make inter—industrial cooperation very precarious. At one point, a mechanism was initiated where the different companies in the industry, in this region, would always hold joint discussions with an environmental regulation official present. When the regulation agency attempted to modify this arrangement so that instead of having a meeting the various companies would simply send the agency their information, the process was abandoned. Due to slightly older equipment at the facility it was hard to compare effectively Case 9-A and 9-S, because to preserve the older technology a substance was added to the cooling water. It was then very difficult to remove this substance from the wastewater.

Case 9-B

This facility was regulated very loosely; thus, it did not face the dilemmas of the Swedish—U.S. contexts. One dilemma which was of growing concern was the "double—standard" between the legal expectations of facilities operated by a government versus those operated by private industry. Where private industry was expected to do things which public industry was not expected to do serious attitude problems developed.

The joint comparison of these three facilities pointed out that each regulatory context emphasized different pollutants and different ways of detecting them. Overall, the Swedish facility had the greatest pollution reduction, but, due to their final product mix, they did not have as difficult a job as the U.S. facility. Case 9—A was regulated by three different agencies and each agency had legislated different expectations; thus, it provided an interesting case of the extensions of legalistic regulation.

Case 10-S

This case exemplified a management attitude which confronted community environmental problems before they were statutorily mandated. The case also illustrates how an old production facility was brought up to cleaner standards with some innovative thinking, this case also illustrated how the environmental improvement process was threatened by a government official who appeared at the plant one day and threatened the management with legal action. After a complaint by management a different official was sent, thereby reducing the tensions and continuing the technical improvement.

Case 10-A

This facility was located next to the plant in Case 1—A and thus faced similar community relations problems of unusually high incidences of cancer in a neighboring city. In this case the headquarters' engineering staff preferred to take over the negotiation with the government officials. This has the advantage of creating some considerable expertise at headquarters, but it has distinct disadvantages as well. For example, the people most responsible for the plant operation, and in turn pollution side effects, are not as responsive to problems. Also, they tend not to be as responsive to needed changes which are found. In addition, the local government people tend to prefer to deal with plant management as they feel that headquarters' people are a "bit too polished in their behavior."

Case 10—F

This is a new facility in France, a country without the strictness of the U.S. or Swedish regulation for environmental protection. This facility is the cleanest in its industry which provides a strong argument that at least this company did not select a new plant location in terms of ease of pollution regulations.

Case 10-E

This is an older facility located in England, which illustrates how design criteria tend to reflect social values at the time facilities are built. The problem is that these changes may not complement each other. This case points out that the social values of World War II, which called for industries to be decentralized throughout the countryside for protection from German bombing, do not match well with the values of the 1960s, which called for the separation of industrial impacts from residential areas. This case contains considerable data on policies and practices tried by plant management over a two-year period which did and did not improve industry—community relations.

7.4 Issues that can be Generalized

The previous information tended to be unique to the cases in the research. Although much of the material was case specific, the collective information body does imply certain things about current modes and manners of regulation. The collective information is presented in terms of general issues, which at a later point are combined to aid in the design of an alternative system of regulation for complex problems.

Location of plant management responsibility

Based on the research information it was difficult to ascertain the "best" location of management responsibility for a production facility with major pollution characteristics. In some cases, it was advantageous for major responsibilities to be left with personnel at the facility. In other cases, this proved to be dangerous and counterproductive to environmental goals. In most of the cases it did seem that greater plant autonomy, which means greater responsibilities for decision making at the plant personnel level, was the more desirable approach, especially in terms of technology design and negotiation with government officials. A qualification needs to be made here concerning negotiation; negotiations were considered more successful, in terms of desirable solutions, when both industry and governmental people came from the more "local" level. When central government people were negotiating with plant people, or vice—versa, the outcomes and process were less desirable. As far as the industry aspect was concerned there were two disadvantages to too much involvement in pollution control by headquarters: 1) plant personnel, who were the most involved with day to day operation where most pollution is initiated, felt less responsible or committed to the ideals involved if others took care of negotiations and equipment design, and 2) by depending on a small group of headquarters' staff people for innovation, the opportunities for different approaches were greatly reduced. When a "fixed" solution was applied throughout a company, regardless of contextual factors at the facility, the results were not encouraging.

The dilemma in this issue is that, although more local autonomy may be desirable, the statutes and regulatory agencies are set up in a manner necessitating the use of highly specialized experts during the negotiation process. Since few organizations can afford to have the wide variety of expertise at each facility, the plants rely on headquarters to supply it, or hire consultants through headquarters. This introduces the second major item to emerge from the research data.

Difficulties of small businesses dealing with regulations

Closely associated with the issue of current legislative modes necessitating extensive expert assistance in dealing with regulation activities is the problem of small organizations not having the capacity for this. This problem was initially detected during the research into the smaller firms in the study; and even the "smaller" firms were in the order of one—half billion-dollar gross sales. Based on this initial indication, specific questions were directed at key government officials to see what evidence they had as to how successful small business organizations were in environmental regulation affairs. In addition, some individuals within some small firms (with less than one—hundred million gross sales), were interviewed informally to gain their perceptions on the subject. Many of those interviewed felt their future greatly threatened by increasing levels of regulation; others were not even aware of current legislation which they were obligated to comply with.

A report has been compiled by the Small Business Administration in Washington D.C. which results from a research project into "The Impact on Small Business Concerns of Government Regulations that Force Technological Change." The research investigated regulation in the areas of environmental protection, worker health and safety, and product safety. The report concluded that,

> The impacts of environmental regulations appear greatest on small companies where economies of scale suggest that compliance expenditures per unit of output would be inversely proportional to size, but the surveys reported the smallest companies facing lesser impacts than larger small companies, no doubt a reflection of regulatory exceptions applicable to very small firms... There were also indications that the ratio of compliance spending to total assets is inversely proportional to company size.[124]

Based on evidence gained through interviewing and the SBA Report, the "larger" small industries were spending 20 to 50% of their assets to finance technical modifications. Although the regulation tended to affect smaller industries later than larger industries, this was distinctly not to the small firm's benefit. One reason why a large corporation encountered the regulation sooner was that it had specially trained people working in Washington full time to identify

---

[124] SBA Report, 1975

what statutes and policies were emerging before they were finalized. The large corporations could "plan" for potential regulation impacts. The small firms not only could not plan, they could not even afford personnel to deal with the regulation activities once regulations began to affect them.

A way of expressing this dilemma which fits into the theme of the development of an alternative mode of regulation follows. Essentially, the governmental regulation system and the large corporations are creating a highly formalized system of planning - not too unlike a long—range comprehensive plan. The small businesses and the more "local" government officials are operating within a more "incremental" planning system that is highly informal and extemporaneous. The formal approach relies on generalizable scientific truths which present the "factos-of-the-case," while behavioral factors are considered secondary. "Facts" are felt to remain the same, regardless of who expressed them; thus, interpersonal relations are not crucial to success. On the other hand, the informal approach relies on inter—personal relations between the main actors to make sense of the facts available. In our situation the first approach — the more formal one - would allow easier regulation. The only argument in favor of the more extemporaneous approach is where there is considerable uncertainty about the facts—of—the—case. The disconcerting feature about environmental protection issues is that the facts are very uncertain, and indeed seem to become more uncertain with time. For example, in the early sixty's government experts felt we could identify the facts involved in environmental quality. A 1975 report by the President's Council for Environmental Quality points out how difficult it now is to determine even the facts of water quality.

> Just as there is no single measure of human health, there is no single measure of water quality. Rather there are dozens of specific physical, chemical, and biological characteristics of the nation's waters.[125]

---

[125] CEQ Report, 1975, p. 348

Currently, there are about sixty quantitative criteria covering forty—three water quality variables for the U.S. Environmental Protection Agency, and the list is growing. In addition, what is considered a "good" measure of one of these variables for one particular use may in fact be a "bad" measure for another use. See pages 67 to 69 of the 1977 Report for a further discussion of these issues.

If we place social value on retaining smaller social organizations in both public and private sectors — and we do seem to value such — we need an alternative regulation mode for societal problem areas which have considerable uncertainties in them. Even the large social organizations within the research are now finding it increasingly difficult to continue with the highly formalistic approach to regulation which demands high predictability. Perhaps part of the reason why large organizations found the formal method viable at first was due to their initiating costs having gone to smaller organizations, who traditionally were competitors. It now seems that even the competitive ethic has run sour in this type of problem area, the hypothesis being that, under conditions of great uncertainty, competition is harmful to most actors involved and that a more cooperative regulation method is desirable.

Production interrelations and regulation separations

Many of the specific issues raised in the cases began to merge, but, considered against a context of regulation activities, the issues become separated. Of more immediate significance is a comparison of how interrelated the production aspects of the companies are and how segregated the regulation aspects are. A point which emerged very strongly from the research project was how closely interwoven the companies in the research were. Each production process, each facility, each company, fit into a larger network where the composite formed the industrial system which our current lifestyle depends upon. Even traditional competitors were drawing closer together to deal with the uncertainties of the increasingly complex systems with which they were interacting. Some of the interdependencies were pointed out in the proceedings from a seminar of the major participants in the research held in October of 1976. But, in addition, a chart was put together, with the assistance of individuals from the companies, to illustrate the path which the raw materials pass through on the way to become consumable products. Many firms which were traditionally considered quite separated now have at least a secondary relationship with each other, if not a primary relationship. For example, a paper production company was beginning to merge with a chemical production company as it was discovered that they were dealing with similar materials and processes but did not have to compete for consumers. They had discovered that their longer—range objectives were quite similar, as were their long—range concerns.

The figure on the following page illustrates one dimension of the researched companies' interrelations.

It is especially interesting, from a research standpoint, to note how the differing aspects of the societal industrial process are becoming more complexly interlocked, while at the same time the regulative systems of the same societies are becoming increasingly fragmented, yet also complex. Using Company 9 as an example, the overall company is faced with a wide variety of governmental regulative attempts, in addition to the corporate ones, where Case 9—S was the most holistically regulated facility of the three in the research which this company operates. Two conditions did exist at the Case 9, which stem from characteristics of the plant and its management. One, due to the sensitivity of the plant location, various technical changes were introduced which looked good politically, but which did not match the larger industrial process, nor have they been effective against pollution; and two, where two companies operate the facility, the company from the host country does not add lead to the product while the company from outside the country does. Case 9-A on the other hand presents almost a worst—case example of fragmented regulation activities. This facility is regulated by three different governmental authorities each with its own standards and policies. And Case 9—B exemplifies the dilemma building up in many countries between governmental regulation of the private versus the public sector. In this case the facility, which is private, is required to meet a standard of no more than 3% Sulphur content of its final product. A public power plant on a neighboring site is also governed by the 3% rule. The difficulty arises because the plant in the study was the supplier of the product to the public power plant where the power plant continues to ask for 5% Sulphur content, saying, that they did not have to comply with the law.

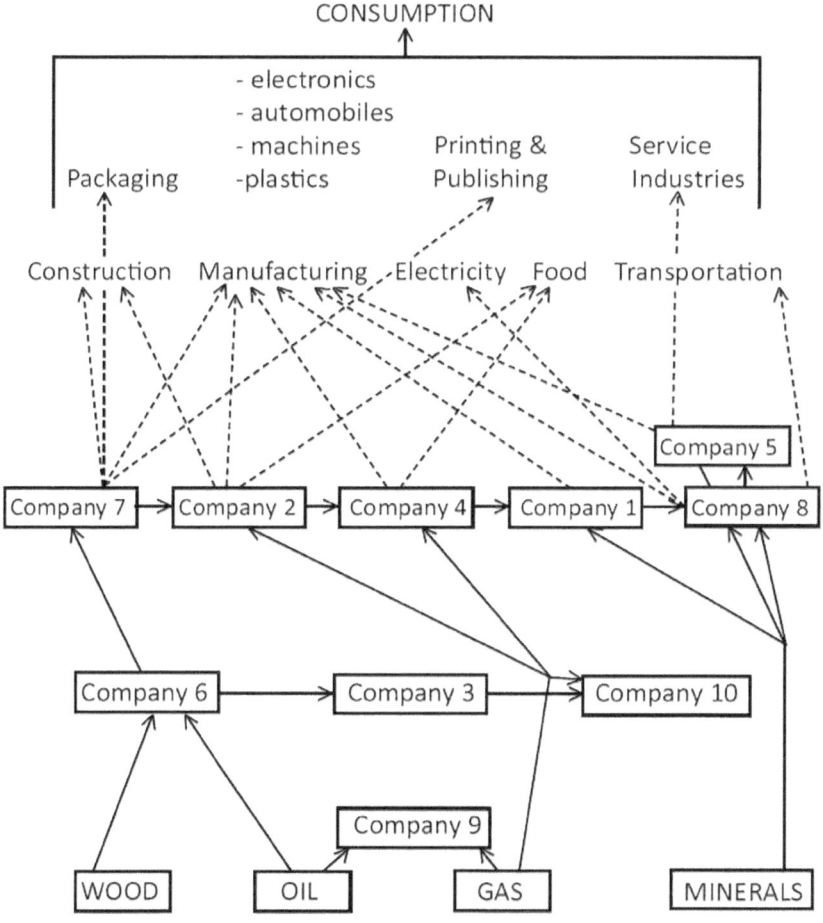

Figure 7.3 Interdependence of the Production Industry

Connections between components of the total industrial process are closely interwoven. Anyone attempting to regulate any part, or collection of parts, of the process must become more familiar with and respect the interdependencies. At present, in all the countries studied, there is a rather fragmented approach to regulation of production facilities.

Interpersonal cooperation (trust) vs. surveillance

A comparison of the actual permits resulting from the regulation activities in Sweden and the U.S. illustrates the consequences of a variation in approaches to policing the targets of a regulation activity and exemplifies how the "trusting" approach becomes more desirable in achieving the objectives of the regulation. Various indications are available within the research of the differences between the more cooperative mode of Sweden and the surveillance mode of the U.S. The basis of the cooperative approach appears to lie in a faith that the members of a given society will, in general, behave in accordance with the best interests of the society of which they are part. This, of course, moves some of the problem focus into the definition of the "best" interests of a society. An advantage of such a move is that if there is agreement that there should be cooperation in identifying "best," at least one element of the "best" is identified. The basis of the close surveillance approach to regulation rests on an assumption that there exist irreconcilable differences of interest between members of a society and that the society, and the members of it must be forced to act in ways that they normally would not. Associated with this is an assumption that the most efficient method of forcing is governmental action from as central as possible.

Based on the research, the Swedish environmental regulation system typifies a more trusting approach while the U.S. regulation attitude relies more on the forcing approach. The following chapter on some of the consequences of different approaches to regulation offers more evidence about the Swedish and U.S. approach to environmental regulation. This information is of a greater degree of generality than that presented in this chapter.

CHAPTER 8

Regulation as Integrative

The last chapter brought out the considerable importance which <u>attitude</u> takes on in regulation processes, where in the cases presented attitude was the only variable which correlated with the qualitative differences between cases. Temporarily let us assume that attitude serves as a control, or <u>correctional</u> feature in the process of carrying out an array of acts (called a process) by an individual or a social system. The question then arises as to what determines the <u>end-state</u> which the array of acts moves towards? Although attitude is a crucial consideration, questions concerning end-states seem even more fundamental. As such, they are addressed in this chapter.

Accepting man's considerable potentials for designing future environments before the environments arrive. What types of end-states are worthy of man? Some call this design, others call it planning. I will not be too concerned with terms for the process; it is concern for the end-state which is most important for regulation theory as it is here developed. Of all the possible terms for end-state conditions, I will rely on <u>integration</u> and <u>disintegration</u>.

Not only are these possible end-states in terms of both physiology and psychology, but they signify general processes which can accommodate design and planning. Integration is also important for discussing the physical dimensions of the world beyond life forms, in that it implies the opposite of entropy. Entropy refers to "an index of bound energy," where, in social sciences, organization is a possible form of neg-entropy where the potential for acts is bound together, or integrated. Following this logic, disorganization of social systems is like the thermodynamic sense of "reduction of bound energy," or simply disintegration.

Using this base, it is then assumed that integration is more desirable to life-systems (in that "life" is another name for the potential to carry out acts) than disintegration. Additional support for this thesis comes from the notion that entropic processes are an inherent tendency in the total physical universe, and the most that any life—system can do is reduced its contribution to entropic tendencies, in that they are counter to life systems. (See Nicholas Georgescu—Roegen, 1971, for a discussion of this.)

Integration will be assumed as the most desirable end—state for life-systems to work towards. At this point attitude reemerges as important where we want an attitude which allows life—systems to take actions towards integration. Prescribing an attitude which carries us towards a desired end—state is difficult. At this point the concept of regulation, as it was presented in Chapter 2, converges on the concept of integration and they become closely linked.

In the remainder of the chapter, integration, its appropriateness for evaluation, and how it relates to social regulation modes is discussed and developed with special reference to its appropriateness as an end—state for life systems.

8.1 Integration and Disintegration Processes

The Oxford Dictionary defines <u>integration</u> as a process of, "making up or composing of a whole by adding together or combining the separate parts or elements; combining into an integral whole; a making whole or entire." <u>Disintegration</u> is defined as, "The action or process of separating a whole into its component parts or particles, to re— duce to fragments, break up, destroy the cohesion or integrity.

Each represents a <u>discernably discrete process</u>, but neither appears obviously important to social regulation. Integration, disintegration and regulation are collectively discussed within this chapter to determine if integration has any relevance for the regulation of life systems; where society is one type of life system. <u>Attitudes</u> allow access to the significance of integration, disintegration and regulation, where involvement tends to sponsor integration while beneath disintegration there lies individuation. When actions are guided by involvement, the objective is identification of common characteristics of different elements, and where feasible, achievement, of commonality in desired ends or objectives. When actions are guided by individuation, the search is for difference of characteristics, or objectives, between elements which are already of a common group.

From this discussion it would logically seem that the appropriate means to encourage more involvement of elements, in order to secure greater integration, is science. On the other hand, the means to encourage greater individuation, in order to have greater disintegration, is humanism. Or in other words,

> According to interactivists science is the search for similarities among things that are apparently different, and the humanities are the search for differences among things that are apparently similar. Scientists seek the general and humanists seek the unique.[126]

The logic of relying on either science or humanism to induce a process seems quite attractive to anyone attempting to control a social process, but as Ackoff also points out, the situation is not that simplistic. Neither science nor humanism can alone be relied on to induce either integration or disintegration. Following are three examples to illustrate this.

In the "quality of working life" domain, Frederick Taylor designed social regulation systems with "principles of scientific management according to scientific laws" (Taylor, 1911, p. 9). Evidence now exists as to how this base has led to the differentiation, segregation and disintegration of the quality of life of the humans involved. The human components did become "involved" to such a degree of integration that the production almost resembled a physically connected organism, but during the process of that "involvement" the human life space became more disintegrated with major distinctions between home life, working life, entertainment life, education life, etc. An

---

[126] Ackoff, 1974, p. 27

approach to counter this was to introduce more "individuation" into the production process but doing so could also reduce the integration of the total production process. (At this point the difficulties of the concepts with which social regulation must deal become apparent.)

In the domain of "quality of educational life" we now see the impact of the decision, following the 1957 Russian Satellite launching, to heighten the "scientific" content of schools.

> Educators have reduced education to many discrete and disconnected parts. They have dissected education into schools, curricula, grades, subjects, courses, lectures, lessons and exercises. A system of quantification and qualification has been developed to reflect this atomistic concept of education: ... Formal education is never treated as a whole, nor is it appropriately conceptualized as a part of a process, much of which takes place out of school.[127]

The more holistic perspectives generally lie in the area of the humanities. Through art, poetry, literature, music, history, religion, and other means, mankind tries to illustrate what man is, or has been, or wants to become. But even here we have difficulties deciding if the humanistic means lead either to integration or disintegration of personal life space, society, or nature. Religion has been used as successfully for emphasizing differences between peoples so that religious wars could take place, as it has been used to draw people together with common ideals.

Despite these dilemmas of integration or disintegration inducing processes, the importance of them for mankind and the life systems he is a component of remains undiminished. If an objective of social regulation is provision of enough stability in social settings to allow individual actions to have a commonality of meaning (Vickers 1970), then the potential of integration for stabilizing processes becomes important.

---

[127] Ackoff, 1974, p. 75

Although individual action provides the raw material of social integration, this does not help with evaluation. One viable means does exist to evaluate an act, and that is in terms of its adaptiveness for the stream of actions it is part of, and the life systems impacted by the actions. An important question within this dissertation is whether taking actions that are tending towards integration is always adaptive? There is a dilemma in this question, centering on the definition of integration. In other words, is the concept of integration a title for a specific process, which is distinctly separate from its converse, disintegration, or is it a dialectical concept? First, we must look at dialectical concepts.

8.2 Dialectical Concepts

The major distinction beneath dialectics is between the <u>One</u> and the <u>Many</u> things which a concept means, where dialectics deal with the Many. We humans who have developed systems of organization which rely on discrete boundaries between things have considerable difficulty with dialectics. Plato had considerable difficulty managing such concepts. For example, he tried to locate the "discrete" and "distinct" concepts of justice and injustice in his system of social organization, but said, with reference to his ideal city state:

> Then, where in it shall we find justice or Injustice? If they have come in with one of the elements we have been considering, can you say with which one?
>
> I have no idea, Socrates; unless it be somewhere in their dealings with one another.
>
> You may be right, I answered. Anyhow, it is a question which we shall have to face.[128]

That which is not a dialectical concept is a concept which is the One and which refers to "discretely distinct" items. A dialectical concept

---
[128] Plato's Republic, pp. 58, 59

is a concept which is the Many, and, although it is distinct, it is not discretely distinct. (One difficulty here is that we are using dialectics to help define what dialectical concepts are.) Aristotle did little better than Plato when he confronted concepts which deal with the Many. In fact, Aristotelian logic is based on only dealing with propositions that are of the One (see Georgescu-Roegen, 1971, p. 45). The difficulty for human beings in so doing, is that most of the vital concepts with which they conduct their decision—making belong to the class of the Many. With regard to the Many,

> A vast number of concepts belong to this very category; among them are the most vital concepts for human judgements, like "good," "justice," "likelihood," "want," etc. They have no arithmomorphic boundaries; instead, <u>they are surrounded by a penumbra within which they overlap with their opposites.</u>[129]

Several authors have linked biological life processes with dialectical concepts and also social life processes.

> At a particular historical moment, a nation may be both a "democracy" and a "nondemocracy," just as there is an age when a man is both "young" and "old". Biologists have lately realized that even "life" has no arithmomorphic boundary: there are some crystal—viruses that constitute a penumbra between living and dead matter.[130]

*****

> Most biological processes are, in fact, dialectical; that is to say, they go forward as an interplay of opposed but mutually determined phases. The essential forms

---

[129] Georgescu—Roegen, 1971, p. 45
[130] Ibid., p. 45

of vitality repeat themselves on all levels of life, from metabolism to ratiocination.[131]

Dialectical rhythms, like rhythms per se, are not limited to the actions of vital systems… but they play such a major role in vital functions that their importance in the activity and even the physical existence of organisms makes them an essential mark of living form in nature, as their virtual image is of "living form" in art.[132]

Langer attributes the initiation of the concept of dialectics to Plato, as a pattern of philosophical thought, but she goes beyond Plato to believe that, "It is also the basic biophysical pattern, the principle of cyclic concatenation of acts, whereby the cadence of each consummated act is the preparatory phase of the repetition of the act" (Langer, 1972, p. 17). Langer goes on to call this the dynamic form known as "rhythm," and basic to the <u>inductor</u> and <u>inhibitor</u> processes for sustaining biological "steady states" through <u>homeostasis</u>.

Langer confronts issues beyond biological dialectics in the realm of the dialectical attributes of most of what man does or is, or - the domain of most interest in this paper - <u>what man wants to become</u>.

> The unity of a work of art stems primarily from the interdependence of its elements and is further secured by this dialectical pattern of their relations. The principle of dialectic is a phase principle; the consummation of one phase is the preparation for another, which in its own consummation prepares its successor, often a replica of the predecessor. Dialectic is the basis of rhythm, which consequently is more than sheer periodicity, or even spaced repetition of any occurrence. A rhythmic phenomenon may even involve no exact repetition but is always a dialectical

---

[131] Langer, 1972, pp. 16, 17
[132] Langer, 1967, p. 324

pattern in which the resolution of tensions set up new tensions.[133]

Langer then addresses the crucial issue of the dialectical structure of a <u>virtual object</u> giving it its source of unity. Since a virtual object is one that is so in essence or effect but not so formally or, this dissertation assumes that social systems are "virtual objects" which, although they have substantive character, its main properties are illusory. Recognition of this gives considerable power to the designers of social systems, or at least offers the opportunity to make use of primary and secondary illusion forces:

> The most essential force to induce "unity" is the interaction of the primary illusion with the highly variable secondary illusions that arise and dissolve again, while it remains steady, complete and all but imperceptible because of its ubiquity. The fact that secondary illusions never present completely developed realms of virtual time, space, etc.… gives [them] an air of indefinite potentially.
>
> In nature, such indefinite potentiality is the essence of bodily existence, which feeds the continuous burgeoning of life. Life is the progressive realization of potential acts; and as every realized act changes the pattern and range of what is possible, the living body is an ever—new constellation of possibilities.[134]

At this point it is important to digress into the apparent similarities between the primary and secondary illusions in social ideals and the environmental protection subject matter of the paper. Don Schon (1971) has talked about the concept of "ideals in good currency" and how they come into being, have widespread significance, then pass from the scene. Langer, in the prior quotations seems to be describing

---

[133] Ibid., pp. 204—205
[134] Ibid., pp. 205—206

the same process, except in her terms the life span of the idea, in its last two stages, goes from secondary illusion, with all its indefinite potentiality, into primary Illusion, which is much more definite and static.

The same process tends to describe the life span of environmental deterioration, environmental enhancement, environmental protection and environmental disinterest. The qualitative ideas involved in the deterioration—towards—enhancement attitude were powerful secondary illusions which <u>mobilized</u> a great number of individuals behind "indefinite potentiality." As the regulation systems of societies began to bring the illusions into the "primary" realm, their potentiality was encased. One objective of the mode of regulation developed in Chapter 6, is to make better use of the substantial power of retaining the secondary illusion quality in a more continuous manner. Our present modes of regulation do not seem to value illusory qualities.

Returning to the realms of logic, Georgescu—Roegen points out how dialectics are in open and continual violation of logic.

> It goes without saying that to the category of concepts just illustrated we cannot apply the fundamental law of Logic, the Principle of Contradiction: "B cannot be both A and non—A. On the contrary, we must accept that, in <u>certain instances</u> at least, "B is both A and non—A" is the case. Since the latter principle is one cornerstone of Hegel's Dialectics, I propose to refer to the concepts that may violate the Principle of Contradiction as <u>dialectical</u>.[135]

The following are four major characteristics of dialectical concepts.

1. Dialectical concepts are such that we do not have a perfect sense of them; or the extensions of our senses, measuring instruments, are imperfect for the concepts. If we had a perfect sense, or measure of environmental quality, we would need only to follow logical steps to bring it about.

---

[135] Georgescu—Roegen, 1971, p. 46

2. Dialectical concepts are <u>not purely distinct but they are distinct</u> because, "A dialectical concept does not overlap with its opposite throughout the entire range of denotations."[136]
   Even though the concepts of life and non-life are not separated at a pure line, the "distinction" between life and non—life is critical even to dialectics.[137]
3. Dialectical concepts are rhythmic, where the resolution of one set of "tensions" lays the stage for a new set. Resolution of the forces which involved a group of individuals in a process of integration sets the conditions for individuation and disintegration of the group (e.g., diminishing Importance of Earth Day).
4. Dialectical concepts have tremendous utility for social and individual activities due to the characteristic of implying "indefinite potentiality." 'Life is the progressive realization of potential acts; and as every realized act changes the pattern of range of what is possible, the living body is an ever—new constellation of possibilities."[138] (The term "constellation" will reappear in a later section on adaptation.)

8.3 Integration as a Dialectical Concept

If, as I believe it to be, integration is a dialectical concept, this means that we cannot design any modes of social regulation to induce an integration process without respecting the power of the alternative "phase" of disintegration. To disregard the characteristics which integration would have as a dialectical concept would be dysfunctional to the social systems impacted by the regulation mode; and, it would be dangerous to assume, categorically, that integration would not be followed by the converse in society. Since we are now beginning to concentrate our thoughts on the integration of human activities, we require a definition of integration more in line with human

---

[136] Ibid., pe 47
[137] Langer, 1967, p. 259
[138] Langer, 1972, p . 205

potentialities. Integration of human activities implies a sequence of activities where,

> The concept of an integrated sequence of activities, therefore, stands for a relation between these activities which enables us to attribute an individual goal to each, and at the same time a goal to the whole sequence.[139]

Even Sommerhoff illustrates the dialectical principle at work - in his definition of integration we see that the definition depends on the "differentiation" of activities so that each might have an individual goal. Integration and disintegration, "go forward as an interplay of opposed but mutually determined phases."[140]

But still we have not quite made the connection between biological integration of <u>physical characteristics</u> and social Integration of <u>psychological characteristics</u>. Sonmerhoff helps us by stating that,

> A living organism is a physical unit by virtue of the stable physical substrate that unite its parts into a single compact body; it is a biological unit by virtue of the hierarchies of integrated directive correlations of the type described in the last section. A social aggregate such as an insect colony is not a physical unit in the above sense, but it can still be a biological unit in the same sense as above. Provided there is communication between its members, the physical prerequisites are satisfied that enable the activities of one member to become functions of the activities of others.[141]

Thus, Sommerhoff has equated "biological" directive correlations with "social-communication" directive correlations to define an

---

[139] Sommerhoff, in Emery (Ed.) <u>Systems Thinking,</u> 1969, p. 188
[140] Langer, 1972, p. 16
[141] Sommerhoff, in Emery (Ed.) <u>Systems Thinking,</u> 1969, p. 191

"integrated unit. Is this appropriate, or for purposes of social regulation, is it helpful to our understanding of social processes? Although Langer points out the difficulty of going from a "biologically related" unit to a "socially related" unit with the concept of integration (see p. 349 of Langer, 1967), and expecting it to mean the same thing, I shall proceed to tentatively follow Sommerhoff but add one additional concept. The "bridging concept" will be that of the more discernable elements of a process, the <u>acts</u>. The directive correlations of the directives of both biological and social processes are directed at the <u>act</u>. In both instances, acts occur and give support to, or detract from, a continuum. Acts are considered the elements of processes, where in the case of integration and disintegration processes tend toward a different idea of progress. The idea of progress is different in integration than it is in disintegration. Specifically,

1. Integration: Acts of progressive involvement of previously separated elements.
2. Disintegration: Acts of progressive individuation of previously integrated elements.

In one instance the acts lead towards the joining of relations towards a larger whole. In the other instance the acts lead toward the more autonomous being of "smaller wholes". Their appropriateness would seem to depend on the situation within which an entity was going to act. Under some circumstances a larger combined entity is desirable, while in some cases numerous autonomous entitles are more desirable. To further complicate matters, and return us to dialectics, one cannot be sure if acting to induce integration will better serve integration processes.

Following Langer, acts are not "material parts of a living thing, but elements in the continuum of a life" (Langer, 1967, p. 261). Acts apply to natural events and, although they are special, they take place throughout the world. Although they are not characteristic of only living things, they nonetheless do characterize life forms. Assuming a constant activity pattern, acts show,

> ...a phase of acceleration, or intensification of a distinguishable dynamic pattern, then reach a point at which the pattern changes, whereupon the movement subsidies. That point of general change is the consummation of the act. The subsequent phase, the conclusion or cadence, is the most variable aspect of the total process. It may be gradual or abrupt, run a clearly identifiable course or merge almost at once into other acts, or sink smoothly, imperceptibly, back into the minutely structures general flow of events from which the act took rise.[142]

Through the remainder of the paper <u>the act will be considered as the basic phenomenon which social regulation will be directed toward</u>, and thereby useful for evaluation of varying modes of it. Looking at the act may seem like an escape from the problems of dealing with whole systems. As Paul Weiss has stated,

> As soon as one raises the eye from the unit to the whole system, the subject becomes fuzzy, the problems ill—descript and the prospect of fruitful attack discouraging in its indefiniteness... the "whole" gets a large share of one's thought and talk, but the elements get all the benefit of one's actual work; here the problems seem to be so infinitely more tangible.[143]

Using "acts" as an avenue towards evaluation of a mode of social regulation provides the advantages of an "element" yet gives a perspective toward the whole. To locate such elements is difficult, to say the least, but as Langer says,

> Acts are such elements; for their functional subunits, separately considered, close in on themselves to present in miniature the typical act form, and in

---

[142] Ibid., p. 261
[143] Weiss, 1941, p. 4

contrary perspective acts merge and grow into whole lives, still maintaining that same essential structure.[144]

And, as she continues describing the fundamental characteristic which gives an act its indivisible wholeness, is where its initial phase is the building up of a tension, "a store of energy which has to be spent; all subsequent phases are modes of meting out that charge, and the end of the act is the complete resolution of the tension" (Ibid., p. 268).

As stated before, the modes of social regulation in this paper will be evaluated in terms of acts, where in turn acts are to be evaluated in terms of consequences in Ozbekhan's terms,

> In the case of purposeful systems, acts are directed toward prefigured results which are called goals. The consequences of attaining goals should rationally be envisioned as the objectives of the action. If, as it often happens, they are not, it means that the thought processes underlying and motivating the action were exclusively directed toward results and that consequences.[145]

---

[144] Langer, 1967, p. 264
[145] Ozbekhan, 1974, p. 8

Summarizing these concepts gives the following figure:

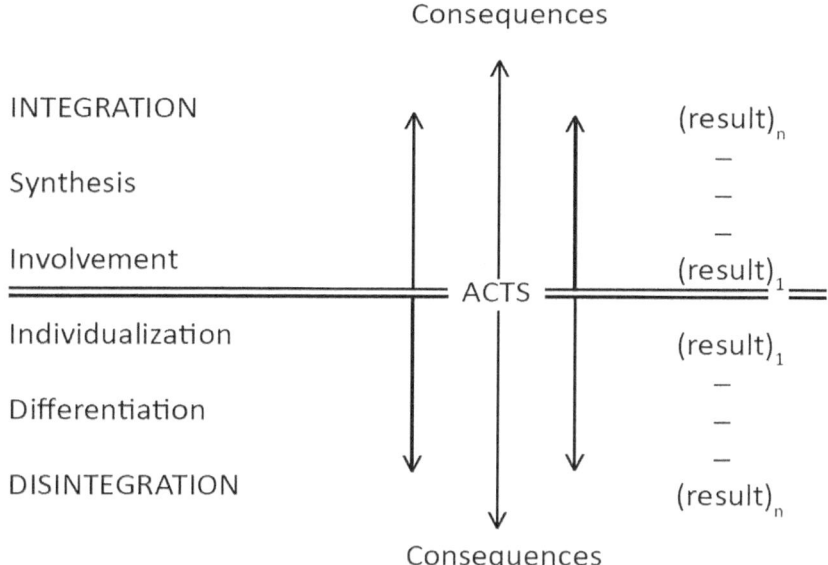

Figure 8.1 Acts into the Becoming and the Unexpected

The consequences of acts are evaluated in terms of their adaptiveness to the situation they are part of, where,

> Every act arises from a situation. The situation is a constellation of other acts in progress, often including some which develop with the acute initial phase of peripherally originating acts, such as we feel as impact if they are intense enough to develop a physical phase. But the substance of a situation is always the stream of advancing acts which have already arisen from previous situations punctuated by previous impacts.[146]

Social Regulation is established to provide stability for interpersonal relations so that collective actions may be taken to enhance the well—being of the society. With the consequences of the

---

[146] Langer, 1967, p. 281

acts being the emphasis of evaluation of varying modes of regulation, the consequences are valued in terms of their adaptiveness.

8.4 Adaptation

Adaptation lies at the heart of any attempt to evaluate consequences, with the central question surrounding an act being is it adaptive. In order to answer this, we need conceptual links between acts and adaptation.

> Why does a purposeful system act? The classical answer was that it acts in order to adapt itself to the changes that are occurring in its situation. This is the long—recognized stimulus—response pattern of behavior, and some action is definitely of this kind.[147]

But this sense of acting is directed to passive adaptation, and fails to take advantage of human potentialities, or in other words it is not active enough. Using Ackoff's definition of an act helps us in the active realm. "An act of a system is a system event for the occurrence of which no change in the system's environment is either necessary or sufficient" (Ackoff 1971). From this definition Ozbekhan finds three forms of adaptation through acts; the first passive, with two and three being active.

1. Stimulus—response behavior
2. In response to internal teleological and functional characteristics
3. "Behaves in such a way that the relationship that exists between it and the environment is constantly altered in its favor."[148]

Still, we do not have a very clear idea of adaptation, be it passive or active. Angyal tries to clarify adaptation by defining it in terms of subject and object poles in a constellation and how they rearrange themselves, and each other, due to changes in the constellation.

---

[147] Ozbekhan, 1974, p. 8
[148] Ozbekhan, 1974, p. 8

> Subject is that factor which governs, <u>subjects</u> the raw environment. Object means that which is thrown before the subject, but also that which opposes, offers resistance, i.e., <u>objects</u> to the subject's influences.[149]

This distinction is then relied on for adaptation,

> In the rearrangement of a constellation the response may take place either by positional shifts close to the object pole of the biospheric occurrence or by positional shifts close to the subject pole. In the latter case, which is sort of "change of attack", one speaks of adaptation.[150]

The following figure illustrates the subject—object distinction of Angyal, and how it relates to adaptive and non—adaptive acts.

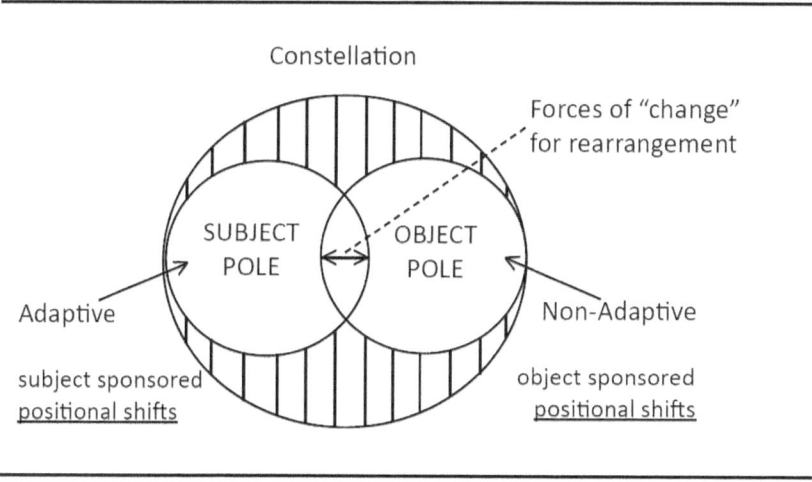

Figure 8.2 Angyal's Definition of Adaptation

Emery and Trist rely on Angyal's sense of adaptation, but they add another dimension of adaptation, which they term, <u>active</u>.

---

[149] Angyal 1941, p. 102
[150] Ibid., p. 285

Men are not limited simply to adapting to the environment as given. Insofar as they understand the laws governing their environment, they can modify the conditions producing their subsequent environments and hence radically change the definition of "an adaptive response."[151]

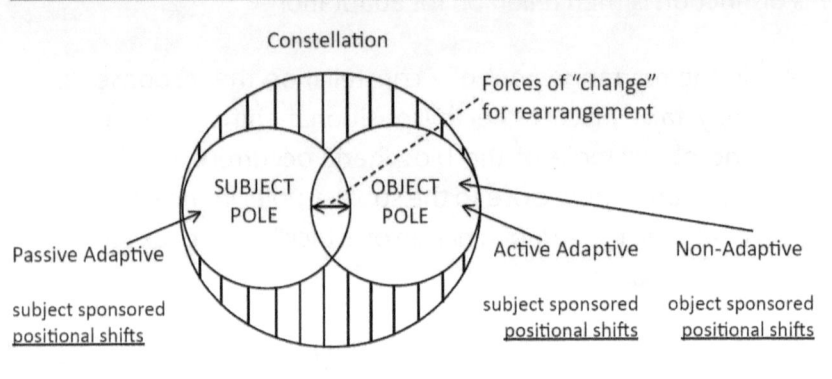

Figure 8.3 Emery & Trist Model of Adaptation

If the subject pole consisted of a human being, and the object pole referred to the environment of the subject, a passive adaptive act (leading to a positional shift in the subject) would appear like a "stimulus—response situation." Does this mean that a human would simply readjust his position to accommodate the stimulus? For example, if a man is operating a production facility which is emitting excessive pollution into the environment and other men in his environment order him to, "Cease pollution production activities," what would happen? If the man simply shut down all facility activities, would he have taken a passive adaptive response? If, on the other hand, he would have shut down the pollution, but not the production, would he be in the active adaptive mode? Or, if the same man contacted the men who sent him the initial message and arranged things so that no more messages would be sent, so he would not have to change his operation, would he still be within the active adaptive mode of behavior? Finally, if the man simply took no action and the environment continued to absorb the effects of his production, would this be considered non—adaptive behavior?

---

[151] Emery and Trist 1973, p. 68

These are very serious questions which need to be addressed in designing an effective mode of social regulation. One method of beginning to reframe the questions is to return to the type of behavior we are most sure of in life systems - the biological stimulus - response (S—R) situation. For biological life systems, the stimulus comes from the environment of the life system, and the response is critical so that the system may adjust so as to remain within the limits of requirements of life. This adjustment is what is meant by adaptation. As Ashby states the situation,

> We can now recognize that "adaptive" behavior is equivalent to the behavior of a stable system, the region of the stability being the region of the phase—space in which all the essential variables lie within their normal limits.[152]

The essential characteristic of such responses is that, "They are triggered off by the environment."[153] Emery and Trist have referred to this type response as <u>passive</u>, where their emphasis was to encourage man to make use of his potentials and become <u>active</u> in his responses and adaptation by altering the conditions for future environments in ways that are to his advantage. This encouragement has been based on the belief that the life systems of man can go beyond the biological into the social-psychological realms. Man can thereby go beyond "stimulus response" into "responses before stimulus" (R—S). Of course, there still remained the option of "stimulus without response. The shorthand symbols I rely on to describe these three alternatives are:

Non-Adaptive	Passive Adaptive	Active Adaptive
S	S-R	R-S
Stimulus-No Response	Stimulus-Response	Response-Stimulus

---

[152] Ashby 1960, p. 6
[153] Emery and Trist 1973, p. 58

At least as far as the regulation theory developed here is concerned, the S— of non—adaptive behavior is associated with non—living systems. If they were living systems, then by not responding to environmental changes some of the life characteristics would be lost. The S—R of passive behavior is associated with biological life systems where a response is triggered by the environment. And the R—S of active behavior is associated with human life systems which have social—psychological properties to draw responses from. I relied on the stimulus—response set of terms because they imply <u>acts</u>. The systems of regulation discussed in this paper will be categorized in terms of these three types of behavior through acts, which are meant to control future acts. Following is an outline of this categorization.

Responses to stimuli

<u>S-</u>

As this is non—response to stimulus, this is also <u>non—regulation</u>, meaning instability goes unaddressed.

<u>S-R</u>

As this is simply response to a stimulus it is like regulation which induces stability simply through modification of those components which were stimulated, as based on the best information available near the time of stimulation. (Much of our social regulation which enacts a statute in terms of "reaction" to a stimulus," as based on information collected from the time of the stimulus, is of this nature.)

<u>R-S</u>

This is different than responding to a stimulus; it is responding before a stimulus, towards the environmental conditions which generate stimuli. Knowledge and learning are critical here in that men can do more than simply adapt to environmental changes, "Insofar as they understand the laws governing their environment, they can modify the conditions producing their subsequent environment..."[154]

---

[154] Emery and Trist 1973, p. 68

Regulation under this mode of action would be directed at inducing the conditions for future stability before destabilizing stimuli occurred. This type of regulation is like the mode of planning advanced by Ackoff, Ozbekhan and Trist.

It appears that active adaptive behavior, the R—S pattern of acts, encourages the regulation of future environments in the manner which is most desirable to human life systems. If this is so, then an active adaptive mode of social regulation would seem most appropriate to social life systems. Is this so?

Restating the situation, we can say that the S— pattern of acts is not conducive to life systems because life systems require that certain variables be maintained within narrow limits, which requires some response to stimuli, which requires adaptation. Thus, any social regulation systems with the S— pattern of acts will be considered inappropriate at the outset.

Although the S—R pattern of acts are indeed necessary to life systems, they seem to not take advantage of human potential. Thus, regulation systems utilizing S—R behavior will be considered adaptive to life systems in general, but very limiting for social-human life systems. In other words, basing social regulation activities on S—R behavior negates much of human potential, although in instances it may be highly adaptive. R-S patterns of acting represent the highest form of life potential, where the life form itself can affect its future environments. Where a life form can act in this domain, it seems desirable that the social regulation of that form also make use of this domain. If humans can affect their future environments through responses based on perceived stimuli, then social regulation must include the R—S approach to in turn organize the separate acts and actors.

The difficulty with R—S behavior is that it involves more risk. Just because a human life system sets out to modify the conditions producing their subsequent environments, this does not guarantee that the knowledge is present to do the modification effectively. We now have arrived at a new interpretation of the grounding conditions for environmental deterioration. Although mankind has shown considerable success in the modification of future environments, he has not always done so in a manner desirable to physiological or psychological life systems.

And, although integration and disintegration processes are dialectical, they are discrete and under most conditions, the integrative mode is more to the favor of life systems, including social systems. As was discussed, there are biological reasons for the importance of integration for life. Perhaps another term for entropic processes is disintegrative processes. Through the combination and organization of elements into an integrated whole, that whole is capable of phenomena which none of the elements is capable of. This is especially true for social phenomena, where integration of individuals and social action appear as two terms for the same phenomenon.

Considering the importance of integration processes for life systems, especially social systems, it seems strange to note the large number of human, even social, activities which tend to induce disintegration processes. In Chapter 6 I will assume that disintegration is not generally a product of willful choice, even when a human activity does induce disintegration, but instead results from lack of knowledge on the part of mankind in the R—S domain of activities. We initiate actions aimed at specific results but are not aware of the consequences of achieving those results.[155] This means that "active adaptive" behavior is not always adaptive but may also be maladaptive. Human attempts to change the dimensions of the pie of life we depend on may well shrink the pie and not expand it. In the realm of the individual personality we are gaining a clearer picture of the importance of integration.

> The problem of the integration of part processes in the total organism is the most important and at the same time the most difficult problem for a science of personality.[156]

Angyal's statement of 1941 appears to have special relevance for social regulation in 1978. The problem of integrating individual acts in

---

[155] Ozbekhan 1974
[156] Angyal 1941, p. 243

society into complementing that society is one of the most important and most difficult problems for designing an alternative mode of social regulation. The assumption is that the current modes seem not to integrate individual acts, and in fact may tend towards disintegration. The only cases where it seems appropriate for individual acts to not complement a society is where that society is conducting itself in terms of a value set dysfunctional to total life systems survival. The western industrialized world may well exemplify such a case of dysfunction, but as stated previously there is an assumption in all this R—S that when the behavior is dysfunctional to life systems environments it is so due to lack of knowledge, not maliciousness. If this assumption is legitimate, then social integration is essential to help build a more appropriate knowledge base for future behavior.

Angyal has given us some clues toward a better understanding of the social integration process along three dimensional coordinates, with the act forming the locus. Since integration is a dialectical concept, integrating dimensions may also turn into pathways for social systems' disintegration. Angyal has identified three possible dimensions of systems' integration:

- The vertical dimension. The items are so arranged along this dimension that one of them (the more superficial) is a concretization of the other (the deeper one)
- The dimension of progression. The arrangement of items in this dimension forms a means-ends organization
- The transverse dimension. The items of this dimension form a synergetic organization or coordination.[157]

These three dimensions are helpful to begin understanding the nature of integration processes, but still a dilemma persists in that the entire constellation of coordinates (X, Y, and Z), may be moving in a disintegration direction for life systems. If we add one additional coordinate, for a fourth dimension, we can see that even where man—kind has emphasized - 1) the underlying human processes, and reduced the use of human resources for superficial acts, 2) the

---

[157] Angyal 1941, p. 271

creation and attainment of ends, and not concentrated on the means to reach the ends, and 3) the coordination of individual efforts, while de— emphasizing individual actions - the entire constellation may be moving toward disintegration of larger sets of systems. A great deal of the industrial revolution and its consequences may be explained in terms of such constellation movement. This may seem to be one of the eternal dilemmas of mankind, and as such have no discrete answer, but that does not mean that the dilemma is beyond discussion. Much of our social activity in current societies appears to avoid discussion of this constellation of movement of man's activities through time, but this should not mean that mankind does not need such discussion. Another name for this constellation of activities moving through time may well be progress, and what is involved in the definition of progress by a society. Perhaps a society may be defined by its definition of progress. The following figure attempts to synthesize the previous discussion.

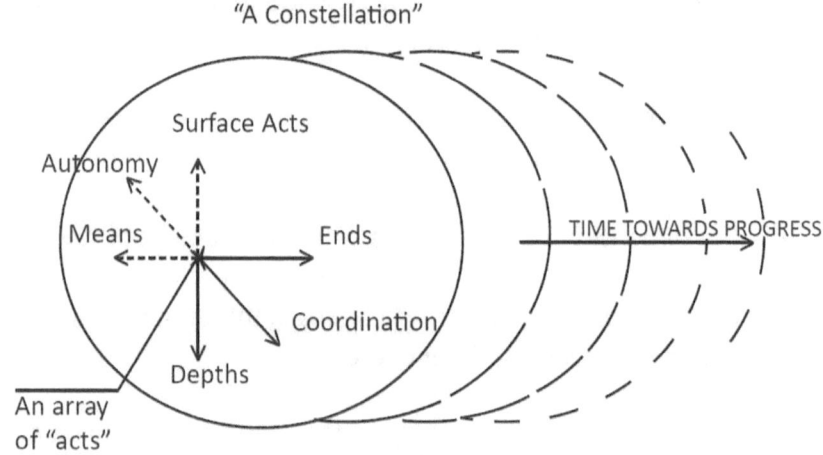

Figure 8.4: A constellation OVER TIME

From this figure we can see that the major questions center around the definition of progress, or the "ends". For the remainder of the paper I will assume that integration is a means to an end, and that integration may also be suitable to become an end—state.

Relating this assumption to S—R and R—S patterns of acts and to biological and social forms of regulation allows us to re-approach the dilemmas in integration, as well as regulation. The S—R pattern of activities is indeed basic to biological life, and since man's physiological aspects are indeed biological, we should not disregard this type of activity in designing modes of social regulation completely. There may well be some instances where social regulation should accommodate S—R acts, but social regulation should not be <u>based on</u> S—R. R-S acts better represent the indefinite potential of the psychological aspects of man. Any mode of social regulation which means to enhance the conditions of life systems, in general, and human life, specifically, must enhance the R—S pattern of activities; but we must be capable of evaluating R—S activities.

8.5 Social Regulation Towards Integration

Returning to the dialectical concept of integration we see that it now begins to enter into our systems for adaptive responses. At the outset of this chapter I was willing to advocate that regulation modes should be designed to always encourage integration for two reasons: 1) there are sufficient forces inducing disintegration processes so that it is critical for social regulation to be an instrument for inducing integration processes, and 2) even in instances where disintegration of a society is critical to the re-evaluation of their value—set (such as Nazi Germany during the four ties), there must still be integration of the individual personalities making up that society. (This is called individuation.)

These two reasons are based only on circumstantial evidence and some amount of speculation, and more importantly, they are no longer necessary. Through the development of this chapter we have uncovered a much stronger logic for the critical need to design social regulation modes in terms of, and in order to, enhance integrated systems.

The R—S pattern of activities for controlling future environments depends for its success on knowledge about the nature and direction of future environmental conditions. In order to affect any control over those environments such knowledge is crucial, at least for planned control. The knowledge in question is within the systemic, or holistic, properties of the environments; in other words, within the realm of integrated systems. There are some patterns of activities which are not based on knowledge of the systemic properties of future environments, but instead on piecemeal information about isolated components of the environment, i.e., disintegration of the environments.

Thus, for a social regulation system to be desirable for total life systems in general and human life systems it must encourage:

1. Integration of life systems, and
2. Understanding of properties of integrated system

Applying this to the problem area of environmental deterioration we can see that most of the forces behind the problem were based on an undesirable form of activities; a form which was based on <u>disintegrated information</u> about life systems, so that the acts which were initiated were disintegrative to those life systems. Another way to look at this is in terms of S—R behavior relating to "zero—sum—game" thinking. In Angyal's (1941) terms, his "constellation" relates to a "pie." There is a fixed dimension in a "zero—sum situation"; or a fixed—size pie, with the decisions being in terms of how to cut it. Behavior, on the other hand, relates to "non—zero—sum—game" thinking. In Emery and Trist's (1973) terms, man can completely rearrange future environments, and thereby greatly affect the dimensions of future "pies". There now becomes possible a far greater range of available options, with the major decisions being in terms of <u>changing the pie's dimensions</u>. The problem, of course, is that the pie could become <u>smaller</u> by these R-S actions. (The environmental deterioration issues are such.)

These characteristics begin to sound like the properties of the two modes of regulation presented in Chapter 2, where S—R relates to "Legislation," while R—S relates to "Appreciation."

Characteristics of S—R and R-S pattern

Following are the dominant characteristics of S—R and R-S patterns of activities:

S-R
- allows greater predictability
- relates to a smaller time frame constant values fixed situation

R-S
- dynamic
- involves greater change
- greater risk/greater possible reward
- involves more of the environment

TABLE 8.1: THE TAKING OF RISK

Although we can see where S—R activities can readily lead to maladaptive behavior, R—S activities can also become maladaptive. I hypothesize that most of the components of the environmental deterioration problem can be explained in terms of inappropriate activities. Much of the environmental disruptions we are faced with has come about through active adaptive efforts to rearrange the potentials of the environment for mankind, but the rearrangement was conducted in terms of <u>disintegrated information</u>, which placed severe limits on knowledge for acts. Perhaps we could best rename the problem of environmental deterioration as <u>environmental disintegration</u>. Too much attention has been paid to analysis and differentiation of environmental factors, with too little thought toward eventual synthesis. Although integration—disintegration is dialectical, man can value one or the other tendency, and mankind can make choices about his future in terms of information that is either integrated or disintegrated.

Out of this logic the phenomenon of "environmental deterioration" becomes redefined as a problem of "environmental disintegration," where the disintegration is in terms of both man's current action tendencies and the information on which acts are taken. An assumption herein is that the disintegration of information is basic to the disintegration of the environmental field and the objects within it.

Relating this to the cases in the empirical section of this dissertation we see how the U.S. system of environmental regulation tends toward increasing disintegration of information and control. The Swedish system tends somewhat more towards reliance on integrated information, but still has difficulties with achieving such integration. There are numerous ways to gain a sense of the integration qualities of the two national systems. In terms of actual pollution permits, which form the legal basis of the information and control systems for both countries, it took the researcher two days to secure the permits for the Swedish cases, and seven months to secure permits for the U.S. cases in the study. In terms of the actual permit characteristics we gain another sense of the integration differences between the two countries. For a similar facility in both contexts, the permit for the Swedish plant was one composite report of about twenty pages describing the guidelines for plant operation. For the U.S. plant there were assorted sets of permits from three different government levels (Federal, Regional, and State) dealing with various types of air, water and solid waste pollutants and where over time the types were increasing. For example, each storage tank had been recently determined to be a source of environmental pollution and each of the several hundred tanks then required a "permit." In addition, the regulation required that any changes in emission required a new permit; the difficulty was that each temperature change in a day resulted in emission changes.

Both the private and public sector representatives are expected to take actions with respect to the facilities mentioned above. Assuming there were equally as ethical people involved in both cases (meaning they would make choices in the interest of larger life systems), which case would allow greater chance for adaptive actions? To underline the Swedish example and point out a difference of attitude as well between the two regulation systems, several important decisions—makers in Sweden were advocating the American environmental regulation system as a potential model for Sweden to follow. Their argument was based on the agreement that the U.S. system for environmental regulation was so complex (with almost total lack of integration of information about it) that it was beyond understanding, but that it was to the advantage of the social systems administering the laws to have a complex regulation system. Their rational was, "If you are trying to regulate a complex system which is beyond understanding, you need a complex system of regulation which is also beyond understanding." This note set the stage for what I believe to be maladaptive regulation behavior through acts which will lead increasingly to disintegration of the systems involved.

In Chapter 6, a basis for social regulation will be developed which enhances the conditions for integration of activities in a way which is informal enough to deal with continually changing circumstances, but formal enough to allow a reference structure for activity integration. Identifying the minimum conditions necessary for a system of regulation based on appreciation (of self and others) and which will result in negotiated order will be the difficult task of the last chapter in this dissertation. Utilizing the human potentials of R—S activities but doing so in an adaptive manner that tends toward integration, is the objective.

Bertrand Russell accents the dilemma posed to mankind in having the ability to modify future environments (R—S behavior) but not possessing the integrated knowledge needed for adaptive modification:

> The conclusion is that we know so very little, and yet it is astonishing that we know so much, and still more astonishing that so little knowledge can give us so much power (Russell 1958, p. 144).

The objective of the system of regulation discussed in Chapter 7 is to allow a <u>sense of direction</u> to that power, while encouraging the <u>growth of the knowledge</u> directing the power.

CHAPTER 9

Towards Business as Unusual

9.1 A New Idea(l) of Regulation

The mode of social regulation presented here is to satisfy two objectives: 1) encouraging greater use of human potentiality, and 2) using that potential in support of systems of life, i.e., encourage an integrative respect of life. not act to disintegrate via acts leading to deterioration. The dilemmas of self-centered human expressions of negative potentiality were raised in Chapters 3, 4, and 5. The ideal of directing human activity towards integration, in a manner allowing individualistic activity, was introduced in Chapter 5. Both objectives are and need to be mutually achievable. More humans see how they are part of a larger systems of life, including nature. They begin to see that the human interest is enhanced in this realization. It helps to see how including more of the larger conditions of life, then just seeing humans walking around in it, enhances that life.

Seeing humans as a member of a larger set of living systems begins to allow a more extensive and fluid sense of life, and its characteristics. Regulation needs to be seen in that same sense. A metaphor for this could be to regulate as if we are in Einstein's universe, not Newton's England; from fixed to fluid. This will help humans adapt to change, much like nature as continuance. Herein, adaptation refers to activities that are in the survival interests of the acting subject. Regulation should be designed in a manner which enhances the conditions for adaptive responses by providing a structure for stability. The nature of that structure and how it deals with difference over time is an important issue for discussion in this chapter. The connecting tissue between the concept of regulation and the concept of adaption is stability. (Stability in the sense of "homeostasis", not changelessness.) Adaptation provides requisite stability for the essential variables of life systems, while regulation enhances the conditions for adaptation, or at least it is meant to.

> Stability is not the enemy of change. It is the condition of any change which can hope to be welcome and enduring. The inertia of institutions and of concepts does indeed resist change, sometimes usefully, sometimes mischievously. But stability, in the sense which I am giving it, is a condition of future development, as well as of conservation. It is intimately connected with rates of change. It may require that they be slowed or that they be speeded. Both are functions of regulation, which is concerned with creating and maintaining order in the dimension of time.[158]

A mode of social regulation can feasibly accomplish several activities: enhance interpersonal relations and communications, encourage adaptive behavior, discourage maladaptive behavior, etc., but unless it provides a requisite sense of stability, the other activities cannot occur with meaning. Instability may make regulation itself impossible.

> I shall describe as unstable any state of affairs in which the nature and the rate of change makes regulation impossible and thus defeats the creation of any order. I shall also include as unstable that state of affairs in which any order generates its own negation so quickly that none of them can be effectively realized. I shall further include as unstable those orders which

---
[158] Vickers 1970, p. 127

are realized only at the cost of leaving the physical, the institutional or the cultural environment unfit to support a worthy successor.[159]

But this should not lead one to believe that a mode of regulation must be rigid and inflexible for stability. It must be fluid and conducive to the extemporaneous flow of life processes. The mode of social regulation advanced here, which attempts to provide for "fluid stability," is called <u>appreciative</u>. The stabilizing structure of appreciative regulation is provided by human interests and habits. The flow is inherent in the variation of interests which interrelate over time and at certain points combine (integrate) to define larger interests and then separate (disintegrate) to redefine individual interests. Through accommodating this flow, appreciative regulation allows adaptability of life systems and active adaption of human life systems within the regulation mode. Adaptability was defined earlier as a process in the direction of integration, where integration was a dialectical process like an "extemporaneous flow."

Although this discussion gives a sense of appreciation and what it is, it does not allow us to distinguish what it is not. A brief review of some historic trends of regulation modes sets the stage for delineation of where appreciation lies in the range of the regulatory responses possible for a society.

Many variations on the theme of social regulation have been implemented during man's history, but two of importance for appreciation are <u>Legalism</u> and <u>Anarchism</u>. These two regulation modes help illustrate what appreciation is not, as well as what it needs to be.

9.2 Legalism

The legalistic tradition is exemplified by the Legalistic School of ancient China where the school reached its peak of implementation under the dictatorship of Ch'in from 221 to 206 B.C. Under this rein China was unified into a single nation, but it was in terms of "the

---

[159] Ibid. 9 p. 127

tightest regimentation of life and thought in Chinese history" (Chan 1963, p. 251). The ruthlessness of the Legalists, as exhibited by their brutality and violence, appears to be in opposition to the Chinese tradition. "There has been no Legalist School in China in the last two thousand years, or even any Legalist scholar of any prominence" (Ibid., p. 251). The authoritarian methods of the Legalists have been used from time to time during the past two thousand years, but there has been no continuous tradition like that of the Confucianists and Taoists Schools. The characteristics of the Legalistic School were, (as described in some detail by Chan), and outlined here:

- It was consistently and vigorously anti—ancient. It looked to the present rather than the past; to changing circumstances rather than any prescribed condition.
- It denounced moral platitudes and vain talks.
- It demanded actual accomplishments and concrete results.
- It was strongly objective and realistic; instead of moral doctrines it advocated the concept of law as written, uniform, and publicly proclaimed to the people.
- It insisted that the laws must be applicable to all regardless of position and rank.

These characteristics assumed about man; the model was man as an entity in need of correction and "straightening." "The theory of the originally evil nature of man is a basic assumption of the Legalists" (Fung, History of Chinese Philosophy, Vol. 1, p. 320). This viewpoint is found in other Chinese schools of thought, but the others relied on education, ceremonies, music, etc. to "straighten human character." The Legalists relied on a system of reward and punishment. The Legalists viewed laws as a tool for the rule, where the alternative to laws was stagecraft. Laws were items enacted into statute books where their success depended on having been widely proclaimed to the people. Stagecraft (such as ceremonies, music, education, etc.), in turn, relied on secrecy for success, according to the Legalists.

The Legalists used two "handles" for straightening man:

> The two handles are punishment and kindness. What do we mean by punishment and kindness? To execute is called punishment and to offer congratulations or rewards is called kindness.[160]

The Legalists made a precise distinction between government and humanity, they found the two incompatible.

> Furthermore, if the ruler sheds tears when punishment is carried out according to the law, that is a way to show humanity but not the way to conduct a government. For it is humanity that causes one to shed tears and wish for no punishment, but it is law that punishments cannot be avoided. Ancient kings relied on laws and paid no heed to tears. It is clear that humanity is not adequate for a government.[161]

The Legalistic School generated the conditions which led to its necessary downfall. Legalistic tradition could not accommodate changes in circumstances or situation in decisions of right or wrong; which led to a build—up of dilemmas that could not be reconciled within the system. The system could not deal with mutually incompatible actions existing together. This is another way of saying that the strictness which reliance of laws demands cannot deal with dialectical situations where an action is both right and wrong, under the law. For example,

> To reward those who kill their enemies in battle and at the same time to exalt acts of kindness and benevolence, to bestow honors and offices to those who capture cities and at the same time to believe in the doctrine of universal laws, to sharpen weapons and strengthen troops as preparation for emergency and at the same time to praise the style of flowing robes...

---

[160] Chan 1963, p. 256
[161] Ibid., p. 258

how can an orderly and strong state result from such self—contradictory acts? Thus, those who have been benefited by the government cannot be used by it and those used by it have not been benefited.[162]

The Legalistic came to feel that the success of their government led to its downfall, in that as the government became successful in bringing stability those who serve would take their work lightly and the number of traveling scholars would increase. Due to this phenomenon, "the world has become disorderly" (Ibid., p. 260). The Legalists returned to the refuge of "strict laws" to combat human tendencies by allowing no literature or books and records, but only laws to act as teachers. This, of course, led them back to dilemmas of not being able to deal with changing circumstances and environments and then a negation of cumulative knowledge. It was quite difficult to find a rationale for changing the laws, thus in 206 B.S. the entire system was overthrown. Prior to and after the Legalistic period, individuals and their humanistic approaches were relied on for regulation. Much less attention was given to law as the prime source of regulation.

In the western tradition similar difficulties with modes of regulation were encountered. The role of the law and the role of social phenomena for the regulation of society and individuals was still in dispute. During Aristotle's period, 384—322 B.C., there was concern about what issues were appropriate for law to deal with, and which ones required other means.

> These considerations lead us to conclude that the one best man must be a lawgiver, and there must be a body of laws, but these laws must not be sovereign where they fail to hit the mark — though they must be so in all other cases. There is, however, a whole class of matters which cannot be decided at all, or cannot be decided properly, by rules of law.[163]

---

[162] Ibid., p. 259
[163] Barker, 1906

Aristotle goes on to explain that the class of matters beyond the law can be dealt with through unwritten custom,

> To seek for justice is to seek for a neutral authority; and law is a neutral authority. But laws resting on unwritten custom are even more sovereign and concerned with issues of still more sovereign importance, than written laws; and thus suggests that, even if the rule of a man be safer than the rule of written law, it need not therefore be safer than the rule of unwritten law.[164]

This idea of the "unwritten law" begins to describe the appreciative mode of regulation, except that Aristotle gives the illusion that in most instances the rule of law is adequate. The research which this paper is based on begins to illustrate that perhaps most problems now facing our complex societies cannot be dealt with through the rule of law. Thus, the problems which the rule of law can effectively deal with may be the exception and not the rule.

Continuing with the Western tradition of regulation, the Stoics under Zeno (about 300 B.C.) furnished another advancement of the cause of regulation beyond the rule of law. In many respects their version of man being part of a "divine order" (that was the name for the natural order of the universe), which he could understand through reason, was similar to much of the Eastern thought on regulation. According to the Stoics, "The golden rule was 'follow nature', live consistently with nature, obey the universal law of nature" (Curtis 1961, p. 97). The Stoic approach to regulation was adapted by the Romans, where from the basis of universal law they developed concepts of a "law of nations" to live alongside the Stoic law of nature; and to overcome the provincial problems of the civil law of Rome. At first it was felt that this "common law" of man would complement the natural law since the common practice of all nations was likely to be the same as the natural law. Later the discrepancies between laws of man, even common ones, and laws of nature emerged. In addition to formulation of common law between nations, the Romans were

---

[164] Ibid.

concerned with a distinction between public law and private law. Public law was primarily concerned with constitutional law, while private law was concerned with individuals, with special reference to their property. The final authority for the Romans in these matters was called "right reason," although some, like Lactantius, argued that reason came only from self—interest.

> Men have established laws to serve their own advantages. These laws, of course, were different to suit the different characters of peoples, and even in the same people they were often modified to accord with changing conditions. On the other hand, there is no natural law. All human beings as well as all other living creatures are led by nature to consult their own self-interest. Hence, either there is no such thing as justice, or, if there is, it is the height of folly, since a person would do injury to himself by consulting the interests of others.[165]

From this we begin to see ideas like modes of regulation modeled after Darwin's concept of natural selection driven by self—interest.

Beyond the political and legal systems offered by the Greeks and Romans, the early Christians laid religious and ethical values; values which are well documented in the Laws of the Bible. During the next twelve hundred years a great deal more happened to fill in the development of what we currently consider as our appropriate mode of regulation in societies. There is not space here to dwell on that development, except to briefly outline the concept of anarchy as it developed during the nineteenth century. Anarchy is especially important to our understanding of regulation; in that it poses a radical alternative to the mode of legalism which initiated this discussion.

---

[165] Cowell, 1948

9.3 Anarchism

One of the most difficult political concepts to gain a clear sense of is anarchy but it does pose the most radical alternative to the Legalists.

> Historically, anarchism is a doctrine which poses a criticism of existing society; a view of a desirable future society; and a means of passing from one to the other. Mere unthinking revolt does not make an anarchist, nor does a philosophical or religious rejection of earthly power. Mystics and stoics seek not anarchy, but another kingdom. Anarchism, historically speaking is concerned mainly with man in his relation to society.[166]

The terms "anarchy" and "anarchist" began to be used widely during the French Revolution, where they were mainly negative criticism of opponents. The French Directory in 1797 declared,

> By "anarchists" the Directory means these men covered with crimes, stained with blood, and fattened by rapine, enemies of laws they do not make and of all governments in which they do not govern, who preach liberty and practice despotism, speak of fraternity and slaughter their brothers...; tyrants, slaves, servile adulators of the clever dominator who can subjugate them, capable in a word of all excesses, all baseness's, and all crimes.[167]

The term "anarchy" originated with the Greek word <u>Anarchos</u>, meaning "without a ruler." From this base definition we can see how anarchy has been able to reference both the positive potential for mankind being without a ruler due to innate characteristics for <u>self—governance</u>, and the negative aspect of the unruliness of man. In popular parlance during the past one hundred and eighty years,

---

[166] Woodcock, 1962, p. 9
167   Ibid., p. 11

anarchy has come to represent the maligned chaos aspect of social affairs, especially by governments and rulers. But the most notable anarchists represented social order rising out of the most basic precepts, thereby representing anything but maligned chaos. Some of the most noted anarchists were Tolstoy, Thoreau, Godwin, Kropotkin, Proudhon and Gandhi; where each relied on the sense of man having capabilities for self—governance as their point of departure. According to these men, anarchy had the following characteristics.

1. <u>A libertarian attitude</u>, including a rejection of dogma, a conscientious avoidance of any rigidly systematic theory, emphasis on freedom of choice and the primary importance of individual judgment. (Here we begin to see why there is so much difficulty with definitions of anarchy. It almost becomes defined as purposeful resistance to rigid definitions.)
2. It is an <u>adaptive mode</u> of regulation in that it takes on various forms in a wide range of societies and cultures; from Bakunin in Spain, to Gandhi in India, to King in the U.S. Woodcock (1962) has characterized it as a movement which is capable of "... disappearing from sight, and then re-emerging where the cracks in the social structure may offer it a source to run."[168]
3. <u>Organization is desirable</u>, but not organization which develops artificial continuity.
4. Individuals must be allowed <u>freedom of interpretation and a variety of approaches</u> to situations.
5. That society must be based on the idea of "Contract," where the contract between individuals is based on <u>economic interdependencies</u>, not governmental laws.
6. <u>Ideals are not to be compromised</u> through the use of negative means. (This is the non—violent attitude to social change.)
7. <u>Anti—utopian attitude</u>. Most anarchists were worried about utopian approaches to situations in society.
   In fact, the very idea of Utopia repels most anarchists, because it is a rigid mental construction which, successfully imposed, would prove as stultifying as any existing state to the free

---

[168] Ibid., p. 17

development of those subjected to it. Moreover, Utopia is conceived as a perfect society, and anything perfect has automatically ceased growing.[169]

8. A deeply <u>moralistic</u> element against wealth itself and in favor of materialistically simple lives.
9. A strong desire to dissolve central authority and government and to decentralize responsibility so that sovereignty lies with the primary units of society.
10. <u>That no specific event in society is inevitable</u>.

In summary, with the anarchistic approach we see where it returns to the notion of Zeno (about 300 B.C.) where regulation, in its truest sense for mankind, emerges from an understanding of the natural order of the universe, which in turn relates to the Chinese approaches which reacted against the Legalists. As Kropotkin describes the anarchists view of social regulation,

The anarchists conceive a society in which all the mutual relations of its members are regulated, not by laws, not by authorities, whether self—imposed or elected, but by mutual agreements between the members of that society, and by a sum of social customs and habits — not petrified by law, routine, or superstition, but continually developing and continually readjusted, in accordance with the ever— growing requirements of a free life, stimulated by the progress of science, invention, and the steady growth of higher ideals. No ruling authorities then. No government of man by man; no crystallization and immobility, but a continual evolution—— such as we see in Nature.[170]

Comparing the Legalists and the Anarchists we begin to see for regulation, regardless of the mode. Strict rationality does not appear to resolve the dilemmas inherent in either approach. The reasoning behind this is that regulation itself is a dialectical process, thus, any mode of regulation must be prepared to deal with oppositions turning into each other. For example, anarchy appears to represent a viable mode of human conduct, at least in terms of the characteristics listed

---

[169] Ibid., P. 24
[170] Kropotkin 1911

previously, yet it also appears as a <u>negation of formal regulation</u>; thus, for those who require formal regulation, it becomes a total negation. Legalism, on the other hand, illustrates a considerable concentration on the formal aspects of a regulatory system, yet it negates much of the complexity of the informal aspects. For those who relate the informal to the variety contained by the individuals regulated, <u>formalism negates the regulated</u>.

Another way to describe the dilemmas between anarchistic and legalistic modes of regulation is to think of the anarchist trusting in the self—regulative abilities of all, while the legalist trusts none to be self—regulative. Anarchy appears susceptible to abuse by those who cannot regulate themselves to enhance their society; while legalism ensures a certain level of abuse to all members of a society, whether they are self—regulative or not. (Anarchy allows some members of a society to maximize their potential for abuse to the society, while legalism insures a minimum level of abuse to all members of the society.

Much of mankind's history of political thought and action shows attempted trade—offs between anarchy and legalism, with recent history appearing to lean towards the legalistic mode

9.4 Seeking a Better Way Forward

The limitations of the legalistic mode of social regulation are described in the prior six chapters based on the three volume 1977 research report. The limitations of legalism became clear in the 1975-77 research done with several major oil and chemical companies that operate production facilities in several countries and compiled in the 1977 report. The need for and potentials of another mode of social regulation emerged from comparing the cases. Due to the complexities and contradictions in the subject matter a model emerged that we called "appreciative regulation." It was based on the idea that one needs to appreciate the difficulty of what you are doing, as well as appreciate the cost of failure as one moves forward in "problem solving" in a world of systemic connections. One potential cost of failure with environmental deterioration becoming environmental desecration is to end much of life as the earth has come to know it. To appreciate this is fundamental to the change as needed.

Concepts such as "problem-solving," "social regulation," "environmental protection," etc. were all found limiting in the research. An entirely new vocabulary seems in order to confront what seems to be emerging in our world. When we set out to solve the problems that matter most, we soon find they are not discrete, systemically woven into a networked fabric that is continually changing, and not susceptible to analysis. Any idea of integration of reality and viable human responses to it is ambiguous at best. The dilemma from this is not new. It has been with humans for centuries. It furnishes us with a world based on what doesn't inform, analysis, where signs are used for further conceptualization, not symbols, and simply leads to further frustration and builds towards simple-minded anger:

> In my dreams I heard a voice:
> -Habib, would you like this onion
> Or just slice of it?
> At this I fell into great disquiet
> This enigmatic question
> Was the question of my life!
> Did I prefer the part to the whole
> Or the whole to the part
> No, I wanted both
> The part of the whole as well as this whole
> And that this choice would involve no contradiction[171]

Finding success in collecting and removing pollution from one source, only to form it into another source seems cynical at best. The system of which this is a part comes to compound the dangers from the consequences. As was cataloged in the research study there are many looming issues from current models of industrialization. These include changing soils and vegetation from industrial farming, polluting water systems in irreversible and untreatable ways, air pollution that disrupts larger systems on which life depends, including

---

[171] Ekelof, Gunnar, *Selected Poems*, Penguin Books: Middlesex, England, 1971, p. 21

the destabilization of climate and the biology of existence, and many other dimensions of life as we know it. The extent of these issues was outlined in prior chapters. The potentials offered by appreciation are still ambiguous, but the appropriateness of a direction for appreciation is clearer, where the direction was described as a quest for integration of life systems into a process of individuation of components, and in a manner which enhanced the conditions for involvement of the components in a meaningful whole.

That there currently are contradictions in the way in which mankind deals with part processes and whole processes lies at the basis of the notion of environmental deterioration, which I have renamed as the processes of environmental disintegration. The threat which the continuation of these contradictions pose for life systems is not trivial. The central question then comes down to what action can humans take to deal with the threat?

The approach followed in this dissertation has been to center the discussion on man-to-man relations through social regulation, based on a view that great potential lies with interpersonal inter-action and mutual goal achievement activities. Based on the discussion in the previous six chapters, we are faced with a choice in approaches to modes of social regulation. The choice is open to a wide array of regulation alternatives, but the two dominant ones emerging from the discussion are: Can mankind enhance his chances for survival by either:

1. Working to restrict and <u>limit the opportunities</u> for abuse in individual and social action, or
2. Working to enhance and provide human potentiality for <u>achievement of the desirable</u> for living systems?

Distinctions made between formal and informal communication avenues, legalistic and appreciative styles of social regulation, and legal and negotiated ordering systems are indicators of a difference of opinion as to what constitutes reality and thereby which means are most appropriate for <u>reality management</u>. (Reality is used in the Platonic sense of the "ideal.")

That an infinite variety of interpretations of reality are possible is indicated by many phenomena and a great deal of analysis of phenomena. Goffman's (1974) Frame Analysis is one indication, but of more assistance here is Plato's logic that "reality is singular, and interpretations are man." In Chapter 5 the mode of dialectics for dealing with the "many" was outlined as an alternative to formal logic which requires the "one". Here it is felt that any regulation system which hopes to include multiple interpretations must be dialectical. The term relied on in this dissertation for operation confrontation with multiple interpretations of reality is "negotiation". That the legalistic mode (of imposing one interpretation on all through legal order) is not dialectical is certain. The evidence for this was presented in Chapters 2, 3 and 4. Whitehead and Russell's (1910) "theory of logical types" also emphasizes that multiple interpretations of reality are possible with the rule that, "the name of the thing is not one thing itself." Once we accept that an infinite range of interpretations will be acceptable in a mode of social regulation, we find several advantages to the appreciative mode.

Although an interpretation of reality is not reality, it does not follow that interpretations have no role in the design of a reality which is to come. The 1977 Research Reports pointed out that the attitudes involved in an interpretation of what is have a great deal to say about what future situations will be like. The link between an individual's interpretations and the actions he will take is of considerable importance for success in the negotiation activity for appreciative regulation. Identifying an individual's interpretation of a situation was found to be easier than identifying his underlying value system, with the interpretation then implying a set of values. For example, the management of one of the industrial facilities used as a research case study firmly believed that the entire environmental ethic was a communist conspiracy designed to overthrow capitalism. With this interpretation as a guideline, they had invested considerable resources to defeat the ethic and "save" capitalism, except where the principles of the ethic were in line with the ends of capitalism (e.g., where resource recovery increased profits as well as decreased pollution). Negotiation makes use of multiple interpretations, even conflicting ones. Where successful, negotiation results in a joint interpretation of reality which transcends viewpoints entering the process. It is here hypothesized that the greater the variety of interpretations, the greater the potential for a joint interpretation which adequately approximates reality, with the ideal being the reality itself.

The objective which the appreciative mode of social regulation should then satisfy is the design of a mode of social regulation which requires multiple interpretations of reality for bringing stability into reality. (Stability in the sense used by Vickers, 1970.) Qualitative differences of opinion about reality then become a potential for desired action and not a shortcoming as they are within the legalistic mode. The legalistic mode, as presented in Chapter's 2, 3 and 4, was a process of selection of one "best interpretation" in terms of the dominating criteria of a situation, and then the imposition of a legal order on all those with differing interpretations.

The desirability of the appreciative mode's properties for social regulation was tested only for situations with the properties of the environmental deterioration situation. These properties are summarized as "rich, large, and richly connected" (Ashby, 1960). At this time is seems probably that some affairs of social systems can be handled more efficiently with a modified legalistic approach, as based on single interpretation, but other research inquiries would be necessary to ascertain the location of the most appropriate boundary line. The line between appreciative and legalistic would vary between social systems, although the appreciative mode might be viable for all systems.

A basic, although non-rigorous, distinction made throughout this dissertation was between formal and informal approaches to situations and the understanding of the situations. If the approach to a situation (as built on potential modification of interpretations) can be likened to the process of gaining knowledge, then the formal-informal distinction becomes like a philosophical distinction between rationalism and empiricism. Both are modes to knowledge. The characteristics of each mode are well-documented in <u>Methods of Inquiry</u> (Churchman and Ackoff, 1950). Rationalism is based on the faculty of reason, which has two fundamental aspects:

> It provides us with information concerning the essences of things, and it shows us how to go from these essences to other characteristics of the world. Put otherwise, reason provides us with "clear and distinct" ideas and guides us to the conclusions we must draw from such ideas. But the history of science and philosophy seems to show that it is no easy matter to identify the clear and distinct ideas; in geometry, for example, there has been a gradual change in man's attitude as to what is obvious and what is not. Leibniz attempted to overcome this difficulty by making analytic statements the beginning points of rational inquiry. These are statements which cannot be denied without violating the Law of Contradiction. But Leibniz never seems to have been able to connect _his_ rational method with reality, though he tried to do so in his proof of the existence of God.[172]

The empiricists, on the other hand, replaced the primacy of reason with sensation as the source of knowledge.

> If all knowledge comes from sensation (and reflection) then we must show how the complex ideas, we actually have, are built up from the simple ideas. Locke made the first comprehensive and systematic attempt to do this. Starting from simple ideas, and with the aid of the mental operations of compounding, relating, and abstracting, he sought to show how other facts (ideas) could be derived. He tried to show how knowledge of general propositions could be derived by the process of comparing ideas. But the theory he developed was seriously challenged by the later philosophers who accepted his general program....

---

[172] Churchman and Ackoff, 1950, pp. 44-45

What we have found in this part of the history of empiricism, then, is a gradual depletion of the number of things we can be said to know with certainty. Knowledge is replaced in most quarters by belief. All that can be known with certainty are our impressions. This knowledge cannot be articulated since it is immediate and irreducible. Except for this type of knowledge, we are committed to skepticism – if we accept the empirical analysis of scientific method.[173]

Thus, the properties of rationalism, which require obedience to the law of contradiction (which states that it is impossible for a thing to be both A and not-A at the same time, as was described in Chapter 5, are similar to the properties of formalism laid out in Chapter 2. Empiricism, which relies on beliefs gained through impressions for immediate and irreducible knowledge, is like the sense of information relied on in this dissertation. Churchman and Ackoff (1950) have described the pragmatists' attempt to form a synthesis of the potentials of both approaches to knowledge, as well as arguing for a synthesis; although they do note that, "to characterized a school as synthetic does not give it an a priori right to claim superiority to the position it synthesizes."[174]

The mode of social regulation called appreciation again attempts a synthesis of aspects of reason and experience, but in the manner, which lessens the concentration on formalization of rules and instead encourages the potentials of the more informal characteristics of human actions. Since both reason and experience contain formal and informal aspects, appreciation does not tend toward either reason of experience but searches for the informal properties of both. Knowledge becomes more of an ongoing dialectical process which draws from many realms, both factual and value laden, to construct a system of organization which changes with the circumstances. It is not based on a static utopian version of the truth.

---

[173] Ibid., p. 94
[174] Ibid., p. 193

> Above all, the appreciated world is both a composite and an inexhaustible world. It is composite because it is composed of views seen from different viewpoints, which cannot be simply added together. It is inexhaustible because these viewpoints may change and multiply without and obvious limits.[175]

The idea of appreciation lends itself well to the concept of reality interpretation and management. A culturally preferred mode of interpreting reality is a given period of history has probably always been important to how man behaved during that period. An argument has been advanced by many authors during the past twenty years, as well as outlined in this dissertation, that it is perhaps more urgent than ever to be aware of our current interpretation of reality and how adequately is matches the actual. The main argument for this lies with recent technical developments of mankind and the awesome potential they contain if used inappropriately. Linked with this danger is the increasingly narrow tolerances for mistakes which these technical developments require for human's associated with them. The potentials of these developments can completely alter life systems as we now know them, in ways we do not yet know.

The discussion in Chapter 1, on plastic tree planting in California satisfying the objective of current U.S. environmental policy as legislated, points out that we continue to be faced with dilemmas in man to nature relations. We have not checked our homocentric value system, which many believe to have been a primary contributor to the problem which the environmental polity attempts to deal with. Perhaps it is not possible to have other than a homocentric interpretation of our situation, but several are attempting to define what it might include. Trist's idea of the "surrender of power" (Emery and Trist, 1973) is one indication.

That our current interpretations of reality are in trouble has been repeatedly pointed out. Some effort had been spent to show the limits of relying on strict rationality for decision making in complex societies. To further emphasize this point while concluding it, I draw

---

[175] Vickers, 1970, p. 99

from a scenario by Anatol Rapoport written in a book addressing man's conflict in his man-made environment. He had written the scenario about the events leading up to a global nuclear war to point out that relying on rationality, to ensure that whatever action a society takes is reasonable, will not prevent actions which are in no one's interest in that society (or world).

> The events that destroyed most of the urban population of Neptunia and Plutonia and of eight other countries had been pre-arranged. They needed only a triggering mechanism to set into implacable motion.... The war occurred not because something went wrong but, on the contrary, because everything went according to prearranged plans, all of which were perfectly executed. Everyone knew exactly what he had to do in specified circumstances and did it.[176]

Throughout the research evidence, similar circumstances were found, although, of course, on a very much smaller scale, of all participants doing what was considered "rational" in term of the rules of the regulation system, but with the results being in no one's interest – either government, industry, or citizen action groups. That this was becoming a characteristic trait in several aspects of the environmental deterioration are was further supported by other evidence from an extensive study into the guiding model for water pollution control within the U.S. The evidence surrounded the actions of the Delaware River Basin Commission (DRBC) in the Eastern United States in establishing a clean-up program for Delaware River. The considerable importance of DRBC case is that it set a model which the remainder of the country followed and continues to follow.

> It should be no surprise, then, that the DRBC has been hailed as a high point in the recent American experience in institutional construction: it blended a sophisticated fact-finding apparatus, an expert

---

[176] Rapoport 1974, p. 105

assessment of the cost and benefits of a wide range of control strategies, a responsible political decision by those intimately concerned with the fate of the region, and a mature use of the legal system to effectuate the goals adopted for the region. It is rare indeed for an institution of government to conform so closely to society's ideals; here Scientific Enlightenment and Democracy, Policy and Law, all seemed harmoniously combined.[177]

Based on an extensive research inquiry into the DRBC and the models and methods which were relied no to rationally determine the best approach, as based on numerous expert's rationales, the research concludes that,

It is easy to imagine that when society decides to spend almost three quarters of a billion dollars to clean up a 40-mile stretch of river, something significant will come of it. The mind rebels at the thought that such vast sums are spent in vain. Yet in 1978, or 1980, or 1984, when the DRBC announces that it has "succeeded" in achieving its DO (dissolved oxygen content of the water) objectives on the river, the Delaware will be just as cloudy as it ever was; it will be just as difficult to obtain access to the river; boating will be neither better nor worse than it was; the drinking water will taste the same as it always did. Perhaps good fishing will be a few minutes closer, and during some years more shat will "survive" their journey up and down the river. Is this what all the talk about improving "the quality of life" amounts to? The question will be asked not only in the Delaware Valley but in every major industrialized area in the nation. For Congress, as we shall see, has adopted the equivalent of the DRBC's

---

[177] Ackerman 1974, p. 5

objective to serve as national policy for the coming decade.[178]

The following quotations from the 1976 Report on the Council of Environmental Quality, the President's advisors for environment, give a good indication of how accurate these gloomy predictions might be (please remember that this is only for water quality control, although similar circumstances seem to be emerging in the other domains of environment):

> The United States is undertaking its fourth year of effect towards meeting the goals of the 1972 amendments to the Federal Water Pollution Control Act. This period has been one of high expectation and significant frustration. Water quality has not improved as rapidly as we had hoped, and there are still substantial delays in fully implementing many sections of the act.[179]

Continuing with this analysis, the CEQ (Council on Environmental Quality) notes that,

> In many cases, the substantial costs involved in going from the 1977 to the 1983 standards may not noticeable improve water quality because of the small amount of pollutant loadings from natural sources compared with pollutant loadings from natural sources, unregulated agricultural activities, urban stormwater runoff, and other nonpoint sources…
>
> According to a study conducted by Enviro Control for CEQ, from 40 to 80 percent of the total degradable material entering city surface waters comes from

---

[178] Ibid., p. 142
[179] Environmental Quality 1976, p. 11

sources other than treatment plants; this strongly implicates urban stormwater.[180]

A considerable amount of additional evidence exists to illustrate that this trend in dealing with the environmental deterioration situation in the U.S. is continuing. From the evidence presented previously, Sweden appears to be doing much better, although there are some similar problems there. A thesis appears to be emerging that we in the western industrialized nations have followed too narrow of an interpretation of the reality we interact with.

Bateson, an anthropologist, further supports this thesis. He points out the dilemma which man finds himself in when relying solely on "unaided consciousness" for decision-making.

> The point, however, which I am trying to make in this paper is not an attack on medical science but a demonstration of an inevitable fact: that mere purposive rationality unaided by such phenomena as art, religion, dream and the like, is necessarily pathogenic and destructive of life; and that its virulence springs specifically from the circumstances that life depends upon interlocking circuits of contingency, while consciousness can see only short arcs of such circuits as human purpose may direct.[181]

Bateson further claims that reliance on the "short arcs provided by rationality," is, "a monstrous denial of the integration of the whole" (which forms a total mind). To do this poses unnecessary dilemmas for mankind, in that,

> Unaided consciousness must always tend toward hate: not only because it is good common sense to exterminate the other fellow, but for the more profound reason that, seeing only arcs of circuits,

---

[180] Ibid., p. 24
[181] Bateson 1973, p. 119

> the individual is continually surprised and necessarily angered when his hardheaded policies return to plague the inventor.[182]

Reliance on a narrow form of rationality for decision-making, and the dilemmas introduced thereby, is illustrated by the U.S. system of environmental regulation described in Chapters 2, 3 and 4. The Legalist's mode of general regulation described in Chapter 6 outlines other characteristics of approach social regulation through rationalism.

On the other hand, as many difficulties await those who rely on experience and observation (empiricism) for knowledge for social regulation. A major difficulty is that experience tends to be too slow of a means to knowledge under conditions generated by complex industrial-based societies where the social structure is interconnected to technological change-rates. This poses a problem in that,

> Increases in the rate of change of technology have decreased the effectiveness of experience as a teacher. It is too slow. Trial and error require more time than is currently available between changes that require response. The lag between stimulus and response brought about by reliance on experience permits crises to develop to a point at which we are forced to respond to them with little relevant knowledge.[183]

Under the conditions of continual situation change it is difficult for humans to gain the needed understanding of a situation before it changes. The chances for desirable stimulus-response behavior becomes greatly reduced. As there become more "reality" for man to manage, the chances of adequate management are reduced if only reason, or only experience, are relied on. The critical importance of reality management for social systems as we currently know them was pointed out in Chapter 5. The price of failure is the loss of the potentials of social action offered by the regulation of social systems

---

[182] Ibid., p. 119
[183] Ackoff 1974, p. 5

(which could have regulated man's relations to natural systems in a way which is beneficial to both). Or, as Vickers (1970) stated the situation, "Passing from a man-made order of human life, to a more biological order." A traditional means to try overcoming the limitations of either rationalism or empiricism has been to attempt synthesis of what is believed to be the desirable characteristics of both. Each time a synthesis is attempted, it is believed that it offers a more adequate interpretation of reality. This appears to be in the interest of the objective posed here – requiring multiple interpretations for a mode of social regulation. That it might not be is seen by following the route of historically isolated viewpoints becoming dogmas, then being joined through synthesis, and the synthesis then becoming dogmatic.

That the American School of Pragmatism's synthesis of reason and experience might not be appropriate for the requirements of the appreciative mode of regulation was presented previously. The ex post facto type knowledge gained by pragmatism is difficult to use in real time. In situations like environmental deterioration, reason tends to give stable information about dynamic situations; and experience must wait for the situation to occur. The objective of appreciate regulation is to actively "design" future situations, with what knowledge can be gained from both reasons and experiences, in terms of ideals of what ought to be.

Interpretations of reality may not be the reality, but they do lend themselves to utilization in the design of future realities by posing an "ideal," an allowing action to then achieve it. Many of the concepts which mankind presently relies on to guide behavior are indications of this potential of designing reality through interpretation. Active adaptation, planning, or even self-fulfilling prophecies are modes of inventing a reality through an interpretation. A difference between these concepts and ideals is that each of them deals with means to achieve a projected reality, while an ideal is the projected reality. The importance of this distinction was seen in Chapter 5 where it was illustrated that active adaptive behavior could be blamed for a great deal of the environmental deterioration situation, in that the adaptation was carried out without much sense of a desirable end-state, except to be active.

In the appreciative mode of regulation there is an ideal (or end-state) of stability for the purpose of integration of life systems, and not the end-state o stability for its own sake, as is demonstrated by the legalistic mode. The importance of ideals, beyond the means to achieve them, is seen through reference to the historic reliance on ideals. For example, Plato used ideals to direct the "actual." As Cornford states it,

> Challenged to show that the ideal state can exist, Socrates first claims that an ideal is not the worse for not being realizable on earth. The assertion that theory comes closer than practice to truth or reality is characteristically Platonic…
>
> An ideal as an indispensable value for practice, in that thought thereby gives to action tis right aim. So, instead of proving that the ideal state or man can exist here, it is enough to discover the least change, within the bounds of possibility, that would bring the actual state nearest to the idea.[184]

The concept of the ideal allows one of the clearest senses of the informal approach to regulation attempted in this dissertation and illustrates the power of its potential for social regulation of societal problems, like environmental deterioration (or as the problem was renamed in Chapter 5, environmental disintegration.

It is important to note that reliance on ideals, in line with the anarchist's characteristics, is anti-utopian in character. Combining this note with Ackoff's version of interactive planners we see a basis for action which corresponds with the characteristics of the appreciative mode of social regulation.

---

[184] Cornford 1941, p. 176

Interactivists plan to do better in the future than the best that presently appears to be possible. They pursue ideals that they know can never be attained but that can be continuously approached. Thus, to them formulation of ideals and the design of idealized futures are not empty exercises in utopianism, but necessary steps in setting long-range directions for continuous development.

They treat ideals as relative absolutes: ultimate objectives whose formulation depends on our current knowledge and understanding of ourselves and our environment. Therefore, they require continuous reformation in light of what we learn from approaching them.[185]

An important element of negotiation, within the appreciative mode of regulation, is values, where a requirement for negotiation to be successful is the movement of values. Concentration on ideals during negotiation appears to be an effective method of enhancing the conditions for appreciative regulation. Although it appears as a contradiction, ideals also provide an effective way to aid in bringing the regulation process into real time, another requirement of the appreciative mode. Relating ideals to values lessons this apparent contradiction.

Normally, values are considered "of the present circumstances," and not stated with respect to a time frame. They are brought into an action time frame through the delineation of goals and objectives which are to enhance the chances of satisfying the values. Although values are intimately connected to goals and objectives, there is a qualitative difference. Valuing automobiles, or the movement capability offered by automobiles, is different than the objective of acquisition of an automobile.

---

[185] Ackoff 1974, pp. 26, 27

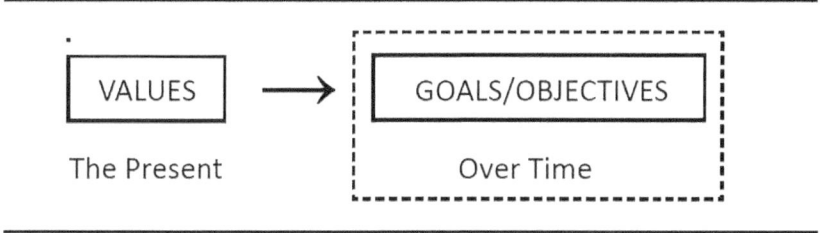

FIGURE 9.1: GOALS/OBJECTIVES FORMED FROM VALUES

Adding ideals to the figure again takes us outside, or beyond, time. As such, it provides a closer connection between values and ideals.

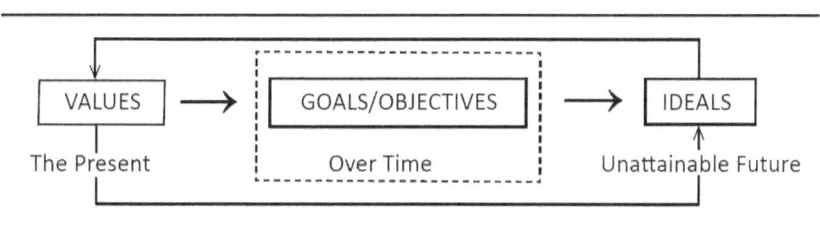

FIGURE 9.2: IDEAS FROM VALUES VALUES/GOALS/OBJECTIVES

The difference between the class of things called values and the class of things which goals, objectives and ideals belong to it that values identify difference in an existing situation, which the second class is directed towards achievement of difference over time, called change. There is a subtle difference here which is quite difficult to get to, but nonetheless it is important to the regulation mode called appreciation. Almost all aspects of the modes of regulating environmental deterioration investigated (this includes those of the U.S., Great Britain, France, The Netherlands. Belgium, Sweden, the Common Market, and the U.N.) concentrated on goals and objectives, with little reference to values of ideals. Another way of stating this is that they relied on time to resolve the situation. The appreciative mode lies outside time through concentration on values and ideals for resolution of the problem. Values are of the present, while ideals lie outside future achievement but can shape values and thereby control action in the present.

To better illustrate the significance of ideals shaping values within negotiation processes of appreciative regulation, the ideal of integration, as presented in Chapter 5, is considered with the current mode of legalistic regulation for environmental protection. This reliance on ideals for social regulation is probably not that different from Aristotle's notation of social regulation, described in Chapter 1, through "Sovereignty resting with the non-written law," or Langer's (1942) concept of the "virtual image" allowing the illusion of infinite potentiality for human actions while offering a structure to the acts.

9.5 Summary – Appreciative or Legalistic Mode

The flow chart that follows summarizes the main elements discussed in the first part of this chapter.

FIGURE 9.3: NEGOTIATING FOR THE INTEGRATION OF LIFE

The appreciative mode of social regulation is based on values – their formulation, reformulation and flow to approximate the ideal of reality – where "reality is an inexhaustible composition of complementary views" (Vickers, 1970, p. 92). Values are treated as the basic regulator of society, where they are "The tissue of self and mutual expectations." This collective expectation "sets the standard of what ought to be, and by which deviance is defined: and it is itself constantly on the move under the influence of the process which it mediates" (Ibid., p. 82).

On the other hand, the legalistic mode of social regulation avoids many of the ambiguous concepts of appreciation. Legalism begins with the hard facts and acts to further explicate them. Figure 9.4 illustrates such.

CRISIS	Stimulus for Activity
INVESTIGATION	Determining the Facts of the Case
GOAL SETTING	To Alleviate the Crisis
MAJORITY BUILDING	To Sanction the Legitimacy of the Law
LAW FORMULATION	To Organize the Facts for Goal Achievement
ADMINISTRATION	To Force the Law on those not Sanctioning It
LEGAL ORDER	To Stabilize the Situation for Administrating

<u>TABLE 9.4: A CRISIS IN LEGAL ORDER</u>

Appreciation relies on values. Legalism relies on legislation. Lawyers are taught to exclude values while judges must declare they have no room for values in their search for "due process." This has become a major reason for failure for legalese to capture the public's attention or judgement as credible in important areas. The only explicit value in "the law" is the law, except for when monetary value is seen to be the basis for judgments, which seems rather often in modern decision-making process based on money as status. There are many variations in how to express what the law is but most come down to the law itself as the value. Although the range is wide, it tends to be in one general direction with time, and not open to flexibility. The law can be seen as:

i. The formal expression of conventional morality, which with time be immorality, or what the state should enforce; or
ii. A system of rules held to be "binding," even "obligatory;" or
iii. A system of rules held to be aimed at realizing justice; or
iv. A system of rules discoverable by reason; or
v. The commands of the sovereign; or
vi. What judges decide in the courts; or
vii. A system of rules backed by coercive sanctions[186]

And many similar things.

Although this begins to bring together the significance of the distinction between appreciative and legalistic regulation, it is still rather complex. Another way to distinguish between the two is in terms of the dominant element which each relies on. Some indications were suggested previously, where the legalistic mode was primarily stimulus-response activity, and the appreciative mode attempted response-prior-to-stimulus (i.e., planning). There still must be an element which is central to each type of activity which will aid in our understanding of the activity.

Langer gives us an indication through her distinction between signs and symbols and the quite different role each plays in human activity, even though the same environmental object may be used in both cases.

The fundamental difference between signs and symbols is this difference of association, and consequently of their use by a third party to the meaning function, the subject; signs announce their objects to him, whereas symbols lead him to conceive their objects. The fact that the same item – say, the little mouthy noise we call a "word" – may serve in either capacity, does not obliterate the cardinal distinction between the two functions it may assume.[187]

Or put in another way, "The sign is something to act upon, or a means to command action; the symbol is an instrument of thought" (Ibid., p. 63). The considerable importance of being able

---

[186] Benn and Peters 1958, p. 65
[187] Langer 1942, p. 61

to conceptualize the situation which we as humans are part of was pointed out in Chapter 1. The U.S. approach to regulation primarily relies on signs, not symbols. To continue with this, Langer connects concept to ideals.

> The power of conception – of "having ideals" – is man's peculiar asset, and awareness of this power is an exciting sense of human strength. Nothing is more thrilling than the dawn of a new conception. The symbols that embody basic ideas of life and death, of man and the world, are naturally sacred.[188]

The discussion, as presented in Chapter 1, on the "symbolic environment" illustrated the considerable importance of symbols and their manipulation for control of the physical environment. This led to the assumption, discussed in Chapter 2 that control over man-nature relations would require "control" over man-to-man and man-to-self relations; where both of the last two areas are steeped in manipulation of the symbolic environment.

Looking closely at the central elements involved in legalism and appreciation we see that the crucial distinction is: <u>although each mode of regulation may be looking at the same element, each looks at it in different terms</u>. A man (or a group of men) views an object; if he, or they, are relying on the legalistic mode of regulation, he treats the <u>object as a symbol which leads towards the conception of an object;</u> if he relies on appreciation, he treats the <u>object as a symbol which leads towards the conception of an object</u> (Langer, Ibid.). In the first instance the object serves as a "factual stimulus" for some type of response, where the facts become filtered and reduced to approximate a cause-effect situation. In the second instance the object joins with a larger set of facts and values in order to approximate a more holistic appreciation of the situation. The purpose of this is to lead toward a more informed response, prior to projected stimuli.

For example, if a production facility manager (as an object) is observed dumping dangerous chemicals into a river, the legalistic

---
[188] Ibid., p. 151

mode of regulation would take this fact as a sign that an immediate and definite response was required to the pouring stimulus. After a lengthy procedure of drawing up legislation, a stature is instituted to "announce" that such behavior will not be tolerated (e.g.., see the U.S. Water Quality Amendments of 1972). When the dumping is observed under the appreciate mode of regulation, it is added to a collection of other facts and values which serve to symbolize an existing interpretation of reality and the purposes it serves. The assortment of facts and values are identified, discussed, and reorganized through a process of interactive negotiation between the major principles involved in the situation (e.g., The Swedish environmental regulation system attempts to do this.)

Legislation relies on signs to become a static sign of social regulation. Negotiation relies on symbols to become an ongoing symbol of social regulation. Even where legislation openly desires to become a symbol, it remains at best a sign. The U.S. National Environmental Policy Act of 1969 illustrated an implicit attempt for a law to become a symbol of a new conceptualization of man-nature relations. That it has served only as an announcement that a new conceptualization was necessary can be seen from the activities of the U.S. during the past ten years.

To better describe the nature of the ideal of integration, it is important to examine the countertendency of present society: the quest for <u>pure fact</u>. The notion of fact also lies at the dividing line between signs and symbols.

> The same items that are <u>signs</u> to our animal reflexes are the contents for certain <u>symbols</u> of this conceptual system. If we have a literal conception of a house, we cannot merely think of a house, but <u>no one when we see it</u>; for a sensory sign stimulated practical action also answers to the image with which we think.
>
> This dual operation of a datum as sign and symbol together is the key to realistic thinking: the envisagement of <u>fact</u>. Here, in practical vision, which

> makes symbols for thought out of signs for behavior, we have the roots of <u>practical</u> intelligence. It is more than specialized reaction and more than free imagination; it is conception anchored.[189]

Although a fact is a member of the class called "intellectually formulated events," it has a more specific purpose than that, in that it serves to "recognize the link between symbolic process and significant response, between imagination and sensory experience" (Ibid., p. 269). Facts now appear to lie at the center of human interpretation of reality, or at least form the emphasis of intellectual ambition.

> The desire to construct a world-picture out of facts superseded the older ambition to weave a fabric of "values," in which things and events were interpreted as manifestations of good and evil, related to powers, wills, minds, but not essentially to each other.[190]

Langer claims that the great scientists never lost sight of what they were after and always valued the integrated interrelations between facts, but that most scientists were not great and turned the quest for facts into an obsession where the facts in themselves became the value. This is another way of describing the founding conditions for environmental disintegration. Within the appreciative mode of social regulation, the connecting tissue between facts is assumed to be values (Vickers 1970). Both facts and values are crucial for adequate interpretations of the reality to be regulated, thus values then assume a new role in the intellectual system and counteract some of the tyranny of facts, especially facts held in isolation. Where "science is an intellectual scheme for handling facts,"[191] it serves as a human means to either aid in understanding a situation, or further obscure it, but it is neither good nor bad. One indication of its misuse is when it is used to discern "pure fact" as the ideal of truth. Historians who disregard

---

[189] Langer 1942, p. 267
[190] Ibid., p. 272
[191] Ibid., p. 275

Collingwood's (1956) definition of history as "an interpretation of past events for present purposes" and look in archives for truth are symptomatic of the search for pure fact.

> Hoping to find something without looking for it, expecting to obtain final answers to life's riddle by resolutely refusing to ask questions – it was surely the most romantic species of realism yet invented, the oldest attempt ever made to get something for nothing.[192]

The legalistic mode of regulating environmental deterioration is covered with examples of the "perpetual-motion-machine-mentality" towards reality. Repeated reference to "pollution less production facilities," "absolutely clean water," and disappearance of solid waste residues are all violations of thermodynamic laws; yet are based on reference to legal and scientific pure fact. Langer connects this tendency of modern man to the logical manifestations which we have now arrived at – the continual reliance on facts from worst-case examples to set the mode of regulation. Becker's indictment is not complementary, and neither is Langer's."

> But it does sum up the attitude of that mighty and rather terrible person, the Modern Man, toward the world: the complete submission to what he conceives as "hard, cold fact." To exchange fictions, faiths, and "constructed systems" for facts is his supreme value; hence his periodic outbursts of "debunking" traditions, religious or legendary; his satisfaction with stark realism in literature, his suspicion and impatience of poetry; and perhaps, on the naïve uncritical level of the average mentality, the passion for <u>news</u> – news of any sort, if only it purports to be <u>so</u>; which paradoxically enough, makes us peculiarly easy victims to propaganda. Where a former age would

---

[192] Becker, 1932, pp. 221-236, in Langer 1942, p. 275

have judged persuasive oratory largely on its origins in God or Devil, i.e., in the right or the wrong camp, we profess to judge it on the merit of alleged <u>facts</u>, and fall to the party that can muster the most spectacular "cases."[193]

Thus, we see the basic mechanism involved in the majority building approach to social regulation used in the U.S., where the interpretation of the reality to be regulated is dependent on "the most spectacular cases."

Mankind's relations to nature can be described as a process of moving from communication with nature, through symbolism and values, to the facts contained in signs. We appear to have paid a price for so doing, in that we have lost touch with ideas involved in natural order and total life systems; i.e., we have lost our sense of integration of the objects we find placed in our perceptual and conceptual environments. If not viewed as an enemy, we think of nature as raw material, where the ideal if for man to "create" new artificial raw materials with properties which surpass those of nature. For example, the plastic trees used along the freeway in California (Chapter 1) have more desirable properties than nature's trees, at least if evaluated in terms of signs, and disregard for symbols (although it is a symbol of homocentric man).

> Nature, as man has always known it, he knows no more. Since he has learned to esteem signs above symbols, to suppress his emotional reactions in favor of practical ones and make use of nature instead of holding so much of it sacred, he has altered the face, if not the heart of reality. His parks are "landscaped," and fitted into his world of pavements and walls; his pleasure resorts are "developments" in which a wild field looks unformed, unreal; even his animals (dogs and cats are all he knows as creatures, horses are parts of milk-wagons) are fantastic "breeds" made by his tampering.

---

[193] Langer 1942, p. 276

No wonder, then, that he thinks of human power as the highest power, and of nature as so much "raw material"! But human power is knowledge of natural facts and the scientific laws of their transformation.

With his new outlook on the world, of course the old symbolism of human values has collapsed.[194]

Legalism appears as the natural manifestations of this course of events. That the legalistic mode of social regulation has increasing difficulties being an adequate regulator of reality has been pointed out repeatedly in this dissertation. Many other researchers are beginning to add evidence to this indictment. A recent study at the Wharton School of the University of Pennsylvania on "The Impact of OSHA" (Occupational Health and Safety Administration and act) supports the thesis in this dissertation. Another study (into energy conservation guidelines) just completed by Charles Masterson of the Architectural Research Corporation of Washington, D.C. for HUD also supports the concern behind the thesis. Masterson's study concluded that prescriptive standards for energy conservation were counter-productive to energy conservation, in that they added to costs without noticeable energy savings. Both studies suggested "guidelines" as the most viable alternative. The thesis of this dissertation goes further and argues that the use of guidelines was found throughout the environmental protection area and the results were not improved. What is needed is a reexamination of the man-to-man guidelines we call social regulation, and the establishment of a mode of social regulation which leads to an appreciation of the wider environment which man is only a component of.

9.6 Conclusions

1. The experiential base provided a relatively clear indication of current properties and direction of efforts to regulate

---

[194] Ibid., p. 279

environmental deterioration. The theoretical basis comes from Emery and Trist (1973) in their thesis that "leading systems" provide an effective means to understand total societal systems, and the direction in which they are headed. Twenty production facilities were found to be representative of the values and activities of the ten industrial production companies engaged in pollution activities, and the industry. All refined raw materials from nature were refined for later use in manufacturing and direct consumption. The ten companies account for one-hundred billion 1976 dollars in annual sales.

2. The social regulation systems of the U.S. and of Sweden provided a clear comparative basis to test the two alternative modes of social regulation in the dissertation. The majority-building approach of the U.S. proved to be a basis for the <u>legalistic mode of legislation</u>. On the other hand, the negotiated compromises encouraged in the Swedish system encouraged a more fluid, <u>appreciative mode of regulating change</u>. The Swedish approach illustrated the fundamental importance of building relations as environmental control. This includes relations to the natural, to the artificial, to others, and perhaps most important, to one's self. In relating to self, integrity is fundamental to process and success.

3. That under conditions of systemic operations in social affairs (see Chapter 2), the legalistic mode of regulation and its analytic basis does not allow for adequate interpretation of the system requiring regulation. Legalism depends on the rigid clarity allowed in hierarchical organization.

4. That the negotiation aspect of appreciative regulation has an inherent advantage of flexibility for regulating systemic complexity and thereby counteracts the regulator's dilemma. The conditions under which negotiation are most necessary, are the same conditions which enhance its chances for success; ambiguity. It works best from the networked form of organization, not the traditional Catholic Hierarchical form. Moves towards distributive

authority become essential to distributive responsibility for problem-solving.

5. The appreciative system ideal remains ambiguous, in that the dialectical concept of integration, which forms the centerpiece of the ideal, must deal with individuation and involvement (process and behavior) at the same time. This is to the advantage of the appreciative mode of regulation in that each community, region, or nation is required to institute its own "negotiation" process of arriving at a definition of integration. The only requirement for the process is that the integration relates to living systems beyond mankind.

6. That various strategies for societies to work towards the achievement of the ideal must be delineated; a task which lies outside this dissertation. Early indications in the research suggested humans will need to become non-strategic in so doing. Advances in such planning efforts are being made towards such. An example of this is the planning method which incorporates fluid planning with innovative organizational design and non-static institution building, as advocated by Ozbekhan and Ackoff. The characteristics of this approach are consistent the appreciative mode of regulation. They are both adaptive, participative, and continuous.

7. That the chances for success of a decision coming out of a mode of social regulation are proportional to the diversity of the array of viewpoints present in and represented by the mode of regulation. As humans begin to confront the continually integrating consequences of actions bringing deterioration to nature, humans will require better responses. Much change, including business as unusual via more distributed knowing and acting, with be required. If the threats come from climate change, as articulated in the Exxon science studies; then very much change will be required of humans. The danger is that as deterioration increases and interacts more will be required than what humans are capable of.

References

- Abbott, Edwin A., Flatland, London: Seeley & Co., 1884
- Ackerman, B., and Ackerman, A., The Uncertain Search for Environmental Quality, The Free Press: New York, 1974.
- Ackoff, Russell, A Concept of Corporate Planning, Wiley—Interscience: New York, 1970.
- Ackoff, Russell, Redesigning the Future, Wiley—Interscience: New York, 1974.
- Ackoff, R. L. "Toward a System of Systems Concepts," Management Science, 1971.
- Angyal, Andras, Foundations for a Science of Personality, The Viking Press: New York, 1941.
- Ashby, Ross, Design for a Brain, Chapman and Hall: London, 1960.
- Bateson, Gregory, Steps to an Ecology of Mind, Paladin: Herts, England, 1973.
- Becker, Ernst, Denial of Death, 1974,
- Benn, S. I., and Peters, R.S. , The Principles of Political Thought, The Free Press: New York, 1959.
- Bertalanffy, "The theory of open systems in physics and biology," Science, Vol. III (1950), pp. 23-29.
- Brezlna, D. and Overmyer, A., Congress in Action, The Free Press: New York, 1974.
- Burns, T. and Stalker, G., The management of innovation, Tavistock Publications: London, 1961.
- Collingwood, R.G., The Idea of History, Oxford University Press: London, 1956.
- Cornford, ed., The Republic of Plato, 1941.
- Churchman, W., and Ackoff, R. L., Methods of Inquiry, Educational Publishers: Ste Louis, 1950.

- Dubos, Rene, <u>A God Within</u>, Charles Scriber's Sons: New York, 1972.
- Ekelof, Gunnar, <u>Selected Poems</u>, Penguin Books: Middlesex, England, 1971.
- Emery and Trist, <u>Towards a Social Ecology</u>, Plenum Press: London, 1973.
- Emery, F. E., <u>Systems Thinking</u>, Penguin Books: Middlesex, England, 1969.
- <u>Environmental Quality</u>, Council on Environmental Quality, Washington, D.C., 1975.
- <u>Encyclopedic Dictionary of the Environment</u>, The New York Times: New York, Ed. Paul Sarnoff, Avon Books: New York, 1971.
- Etzioni, Amita, <u>A Comparative Analysis of Complex Organizations</u>, The Free Press: New York, 1961.
- Georgescu—Roegen, N. <u>The Entropy Law and the Economic Process</u>, Harvard University Press: Cambridge, Mass., 1971.
- Goffman, Ervin, <u>Frame Analysis</u>, Harper & Row: New York, 1974.
- Goldman, Marshall, <u>Environmental Pollution in the Soviet Union</u>, The MIT Press: Cambridge, Mass., 1972.
- Hawk, D. L., and Miller, T., "Ar de amerikanska 'miljoeffektbeskrivningarna' nagonting for Sverige?" (Are American Environmental Impact Statements something for Sweden?), *Plan*, Oslo, Norway: Plan International Publications. No. 5—6, Nov. 1976.
- Hawk, D. L., "Environmental Protection: Analytical Solutions in Search of Synthetic Problems," Institute of International Business: Stockholm, Sweden, Sept. 1977.
- Hedlund and Julander, "The Role of Life Styles In Sweden," Institute of International Business Series, Stockholm School of Economics, Stockholm, Sweden, 1977.
- Interstate Commerce Commission Report, Washington, D.C., "Ex Parte Number 281 at 314," September 27, 1972.
- Interstate and Foreign Commerce Committee of the House report on "Federal Regulation and Regulatory Reform," Oct. 1976, Washington, D.C
- Jung, C. G., <u>Man and his Symbols</u>, Doubleday & Co.: Garden City, N.Y., 1964.

- Kent, George, The Effects of Threats, Ohio State University Press: Ohio, 1967.
- Kneese, A., Economics and the Environment, Penguin Books: Middlesex, England, 1977.
- Langer, Susanne, Philosophy in a New Key, Harvard University Press: Cambridge, Mass., 1942.
- Langer, Susanne, Mind: An Essay on Human Feeling, The Johns Hopkins University Press: Baltimore, 1967 (Volume I).
- Langer, Susanne, Mind: An Essay on Human Feeling, The Johns Hopkins University Press: Baltimore, 1972 (Volume II).
- Lewin, Kurt, Field Theory in Social Science, University of Chicago Press: Chicago, 1951 (reprinted, 1976).
- Los Angeles Times, Feb. 8, 1972.
- Lundqvist, Lennart, "Environmental Policies in Canada, Sweden, and the United States: A Comparative Overview," published in Administrative and Policy Studies Series, George Frederickson, Ed., Indiana University, 1974.
- Management Science, R. L. Ackoff's article, "Towards a System of Systems Concepts," 1971.
- Newsweek, August, 15, 1977.
- Nyberg, Alf, "On the Transport of Sulfur Over the North Atlantic," Swedish Meteorological Institution: Norrkoping, Sweden, 1976.
- Ozbekhan, Hasan, "Thoughts on the Emerging Methodology of Planning", University of Pennsylvania: Philadelphia, 1974.
- Perlmutter, Howard, Towards the Theory and Practice of Social Architecture, Tavistook Pub.: London, 1965.
- Public Law: "National Environmental Policy Act," Washington, D.C., 1969.
- Public Law: "National Environmental Policy Act," Washington, D.C., 1969.
- Public Law: "Water Quality Amendments of 1972," Washington, D.C., 1972.
- Rapoport, Anatol, Conflict in Man—Made Environment, Penguin Books: Middlesex, England, 1974.
- Rapoport, Anatol, Two—Person Game Theory, Michigan University Press: Ann Arbor, Michigan, 1966.

- Russell, Bertrand, The ABC of Relativity, Mentor Book: New York, 1958.
- Ryle, Gilbert, Dilemmas, Cambridge Press: Cambridge, England, 1953.
- Schon, Donald, Beyond the Stable State, Random House: New York, 1971.
- Science, 1973, Vol. 179, p. 446.
- Sommerhoff, G., "The Abstract Characteristics of Living Systems", published in Systems Thinking, F. E. Emery, (bd.) Penguin Books: Middlesex, England, 1969.
- Strauss, A, et al. "The hospital and its negotiated order," in Friedson, E. (ed.). The hospital in modern society, The Free Press: New York, 1962.
- Taylor, F. W., The Principles of Scientific Management, Harper & Row: New York, 1911.
- The Republic of Plato, Francis Cornford translation, Oxford University Press: London, 1945.
- Tomasson, Richard, Sweden: Prototype of Modern Society, Random House: New York, 1970.
- Toronto Globe and Mail, Toronto, Canada, May 25, 1971.
- Vickers, Geoffrey, Freedom in a Rocking Boat, Penguin Books: Middlesex, England, 1970.
- Vickers, Geoffrey, Value Systems and Social Process, Penguin Books: Middlesex, England, 1968,
- Westerlund, Staffan, "Miljofarlig Verksamhet," Norstedt: Stockholm, Sweden, 1975.
- Whitehead, A.N., and Russell, B., Principia Mathematica, 3 Vols, 2nd ed., Cambridge University Press: Cambridge, England, 1910 – 1913.
- Yale Law Journal, Vol. 83, pp. 1315—1348, also in the Environmental Law Review, 1975, pp. 717—751.
- Zartman, William, The 50% Solution, Anchor Press: Garden City, N.Y., 1976.

www.ingramcontent.com/pod-product-compliance
Lightning Source LLC
Chambersburg PA
CBHW060350080526
44583CB00012B/250